ORIGAMI

Menagerie

21 CHALLENGING MODELS

Manuel Sirgo Álvarez

DOVER PUBLICATIONS, INC., MINEOLA, NEW YORK

To Nelly, my wife.

Bibliographical Note

This Dover edition, first published in 2008, is a new English translation of *Imaginando en papel,* originally published in Spanish by Editorial Miguel A. Salvatella, S.A., Barcelona, Spain, 2006, and includes all of the original diagrams, illustrations, and photos. This Dover edition is published by special arrangement with Editorial Miguel A. Salvatella, S.A., Calle Santo Domingo 5, 08012 Barcelona, Spain

Library of Congress Cataloging-in-Publication Data

Sirgo Álvarez, Manuel, 1960–
    [Imaginando en papel. English]
    Origami menagerie : 21 challenging models / Manuel Sirgo Álvarez.
        p. cm.
    ISBN-13: 978-0-486-46593-7
    ISBN-10: 0-486-46593-4
    1. Origami. I. Title.

TT870.S52313 2008
736'.982—dc22

2008006619

Manufactured in the United States of America
Dover Publications, Inc., 31 East 2nd Street, Mineola, N.Y. 11501

Foreword

I've known Manuel for some time now and, as in any good friendship, we have shared many different experiences.

We first met over the phone. He called me to ask for a copy of the newsletter in which his first figure, the orb-weaver spider, had been published. Later, we met in Zamora at the AEP convention. The following year, we met again in Santiago, and then in Zaragoza, and the last time we saw each other was at a convention in Barcelona.

After his first origami model was published in *Pajarita,* he created many other models. They were published in several origami newsletters all over the world, but it was his first book that began to open doors for him.

The book and the expositions he organized at each convention allowed people from other countries to see his incredible, ever-increasing collection of original origami creations. In Santiago, he caught the attention of Kamiya; in Seville, that of Hojyo Takashi. Both talked about Manuel while in Japan, writing articles about him for *Origami Tanteidan,* and selecting some of his works for publication in the annual newsletters. Soon after, he received the best accolade of all; he was invited to what is, in my opinion, the best international convention in the world—Italy.

Manuel is an innovator and a real fighter. The word "fear" doesn't exist in his vocabulary. In less than a year, he created 80 figures, making notes about their design in sketches of the figures; these same sketches helped Aníbal Voyer create the drawings for his first book. In Zamora, I was fortunate enough to be able to admire this incredible work and see the selection of figures included in the book. I also saw how Manuel enjoyed collaborating with members of the association. When he agreed to be the newsletter's editor, he didn't know anything about computer design or how to make publication mock-ups, but he knew one thing: "It's all a book." Soon after, the next edition of the *Pajarita* newsletter came out and nobody even noticed the change in editor.

Some years later, I invited Manuel to come to a gathering of friends in Zaragoza. I was surprised when he accepted. I was able to see another side of him: a happy, dynamic, and talkative person. I also noticed some great improvements in the design of his models; more detailed figures, perfect paper selection, the use of diverse techniques, and improved presentation format. He presented more than 100 designs and there was only one word to describe them: INCREDIBLE! He left everybody at that gathering speechless after seeing the variety of animal origami laid before them: birds, mammals, mythological creatures, and—above all—INSECTS.

Since then, we have kept in close contact and he always tells me about his new creations. He shows me pictures of his models, talks about how he creates the appropriate type of paper for each design, and how he analyzes each square of paper before making his creations. I know he achieved this level of maturity after reading *Origami Design Secrets* by Robert Lang.

After Italy, he promised me he would stop making insect origami and dedicate himself to other types of models; a promise he only partially kept. Manuel became more thoughtful and studious regarding his figures, techniques, and finishing touches. In this book, you'll have the opportunity to see how his design and folding techniques have evolved. Manuel surprises us with 21 superior-level figures—not only of insects, which predominate in the book, but also other figures meant for thicker paper, including some that you can fold using thick wet paper. These include the dugong, narwhal, sea lion, and crocodile with some incredible finishing touches.

This book is a compilation of the results of an intense study of design and folding methodology. You will notice improvements in these two aspects right off, starting with the first figure. Your results will be what we all hope for—INCREDIBLE.

What surprises me the most about Manuel is that even though he has a wife and kids, in addition to his classes, he still has time to design and even sketch out his models. By the way, I love his sketches. Manuel is inconspicuous and introverted. Many times I have seen him walking alone, paper in hand, in his own world. However, when you truly get to know him, you find that he is a warmhearted, sensitive person.

After having been in the origami world for so many years, I have learned that you can tell how sensitive a person is by watching him or her fold paper. You only need a moment with Manuel to see how sensitive he is and how good he is at what he does.

Thank you, Manuel, for everything you have taught me.

Felipe Moreno

Contents

Introduction

Imaginando en Papel [the original Spanish version of *Origami Menagerie*] is my second book of origami figures. As with any book, this book has several objectives. I don't want to be pretentious; I just want to explain how to fold some of my origami figures, without the commitment of a regular publication. I want to draw my figures at my own pace, and at the same time satisfy my origami-folding friends' request made after the publication of my first book *Papiroinsectos,* to continue publishing my figures.

You will also find explanations about folding techniques, finishing touches, and how to prepare the paper for the figures in this book. Every figure you see majestically presented here was folded by Pere Olivella, an expert origami-folder, who made all the figures for this book.

I still don't feel qualified to write about origami design (everything in due time). People often ask me what method I follow to design my models. I usually answer that I can explain how I started, but not how I do it now. When I first started, I used classic bases, paying attention to their points, length, and other aspects, to see what models could come out of them. I would just start with the base and fold and fold until, for better or worse, I had made the figure I set out to make. So, from the "waterbomb" base, I made a turtle, a bear, or an orangutan, each with something in common: four long points and a short point. I remember that, around that time, I asked Anibal Voyer what he thought about this way of starting to learn how to create models. He told me it seemed like a fantastic method, which really motivated me.

Little by little, I started to change my method. First, I would think of a model, then I would work on the base most similar to what I wanted to create. I would modify the base, and from this modified base, would stretch it, double and triple the number of points, etc., and fold the model. To this day, this is the method I use most often, because I'm a little lazy when it comes to creating new bases. I only create one when I have a model that I'm putting a lot of effort into and I don't really have a suitable modifiable base for it. To tell you the truth, what I like the most is the process that goes from the base until the finished model. I let my fingers play with the paper, trying to make the folds the paper itself shows me, in the direction toward which I think it is pointing me. I don't think that the base is insignificant; it just doesn't motivate me that much. I actually use several methods.

This means that, quite often, my use of paper is not optimized—a very trendy technique in modern origami. I'm sorry, but I don't follow mathematical optimization methods. I have designed some models following this technique, which I deeply value when applied by other origami creators, but which I find rather boring when I use it for my own models. Had I focused on applying those design techniques, I'm sure that instead of the more than 200 models I have designed in the last five years, I would have, at most, about one-fifth of that number done by now.

This book features easy, intermediate, advanced, and very advanced models. These categories are very subjective and arbitrary. "Very easy" (Level 1) models are those I believe to be suitable for teaching children. There are none of these in this book. Level 2 is the lowest difficulty level in this book. They are "easy," but require you to know how to fold the following simple bases: kite, fish, bird, frog, and its variants. There are five Level 2 models in this book. There are another five Level 3, or "intermediate," models, for which you must be very familiar with the blintz base, open/closed sink, and color change techniques. There are five models that fall into the "advanced" (Level 4) category. You must be an expert folder, familiar with every kind of base, and able to use every folding technique, no matter how complex it is (unsink, folding an open model, etc.). In Level 5, "Very Advanced," there are six models. The same Level 4 skills are required here, but you will demand more of the paper. For quality folding, you will need special paper and model-finishing techniques.

Some models use the same base and have similar folding sequences. In order not to be repetitive, I have chosen to include one main model and a variation.

I also wish to sincerely thank those who, in one way or another, helped me and motivated me to finish the book. Starting with:

My wife Nelly and my kids, Marta and Victor, who I have spent many hours away from while drawing, but being the origami enthusiasts that they are, have always kept me motivated.

To Pere Olivella Coll, the exceptional origami-folder I mentioned earlier, and winner of several folding contests, who has not only folded all the models in this book, but who also contributed many suggestions for improving the folding sequences and found mistakes in the drawings. His efforts saved me many hours of work and, without his help, this book would have taken a lot longer to finish and see the light of day. Thanks, Pere!

I would also like to thank Felipe Moreno, former AEP president and a magnificent origami folder, who also detected flaws in my models and was there for me when I needed him.

To Alfredo Pérez Jiménez and Juan Pedro Rubio Peña: I thank you both for your suggestions, support, and advice on the "CPs."

To Nicola Bandoni and Román Díaz, two wonderful designers who have always supported and motivated me.

To Anibal Voyer, for his technical help with model drawing and for all our talks (it is so nice to be able to talk to a genius whenever I want).

To Nicolas Terry, a "magical" creator. In his hands, paper is magically transformed. For his extraordinary efforts over the past four years to selflessly promote my work on his website.

I cannot end these acknowledgements without mentioning Vicente Palacios, to whom I owe so much, both regarding my hobby and my renown in the world of origami. Of course, I would also like to thank Editorial Salvatella, for their patience with deadlines and great publishing work.

I hope you all enjoy this book.

Manuel Sirgo Álvarez, León, March 21, 2006

Folding the Models

It is extremely important to choose the appropriate paper before folding a model. Sandwich paper can be used for most models. "Sandwich paper" is the common name for aluminum foil (like the kind you use in the kitchen), to which tissue paper has been glued on both sides. You may use a glue stick, diluted white glue, diluted latex, adhesive spray, etc. There are several detailed articles on the Internet about this process. You can make the sandwich paper in whatever color you need, or with two colors, and decide how thick the sheet should be by gluing tissue paper to one side only, depending on how flexible you need it to be. I suggest that you get the sandwich paper ready by gluing tissue paper on both sides, so that the foil is not visible when the paper is folded. Besides, it makes the paper less flexible and easier to fold. Folding origami figures with sandwich paper is a very delicate task, but once you get some experience, this is the best kind of paper because it allows you to shape the whole figure in the final steps. When folding sandwich paper, one of the fundamental steps is to smooth out each fold, as if you were trying to erase it.

Another suitable type of paper is foil paper. It is thicker than sandwich paper, but it is still thin enough to allow for easy shaping of the finished model. There are several resources for getting foil paper in the color you want. This paper is sold in rolls and one side is a metallic, available in various colors, and the other is white. You can glue tissue paper to foil paper, as with sandwich paper, which will make it thicker and a little less flexible. Another option, which I frequently use, is to paint the white side with a tempera-based paint mixed with latex and diluted with water. The latex gives it a satin-like texture and ensures that the tempera does not crumble during folding. The amount of water used will depend on how thick you want the paint to be. The less water there is, the more solid and thick the color will be. The more water you use, the more diluted the color will be, and the easier it will be to spread on the paper and without increasing the paper's final thickness much. There is a product called AQUALUX, made by Titán, which is a mix of tempera and latex, which I apply directly to the paper using a small paint roller so that the result is more uniform.

Foil paper that is prepared this way does not tear as easily as the untreated kind. Just like with sandwich paper, you must smooth out each fold. In both cases, I use my fingernail to mark all folds, since the stronger the mark, the easier it is to fold. To make sink folds easier, the best method is to mark the valley fold, smooth it out, make the mountain fold, and smooth it out. This way, the sink fold will be easier.

Several models in this book can be folded perfectly well with the wet technique. To do this, you must use paper that contains glue. When wet, this kind of paper becomes soft and can be easily folded. You'll need to use tweezers or other tools to submerge the paper so that it keeps the desired shape. Once the paper is dry, the model will be perfectly rigid and keep the desired shape. The most suitable kinds of paper are Canson Miteintes (160 g) and Ingres (100 g). There are several detailed articles available on the Internet about this technique.

Craft paper is another possibility. There are a great variety of textures, thicknesses, and colors, although the color options are a lot more limited than those for tissue paper. These are hard to find; they are only available in some stores and the variety is limited. Another option is to buy paper online, even though it is expensive and distributors often require a minimum amount per order that is more than most people need.

There are several advantages to using craft paper: it has a more pleasant and realistic texture, it creates long-lasting models that will stand the test of time, and it is easier to use to make complex folds, such as sinks, which can be done without any preparation. There are some downfalls as well, because it is hard to make craft paper bi-colored. Maybe the easiest way is using adhesive spray and gluing tissue paper or another craft paper to it—the latter may make the paper extremely thick and unfit for more complex models. Another inconvenience is that they are hard to mold and don't hold their shape. In most cases, folds open easily, so you'll need to use a finish like methylcellulose after the wet-paper technique.

Among the craft paper types I have tried, the one made of banana fiber yields the best results. It holds folds well, without the aid of any product, although the finished results are better if you do use one. Lokta paper varies from very thin to fairly thick. In both cases, methylcellulose will be needed for the final touches.

Methylcellulose is the glue used to hang wallpaper. It is sold in powder form and must be diluted according to the manufacturer's instructions. I like using a thicker, almost gelatin-like mix, because it does not saturate the paper as much or deform the treated area, and it dries faster. Depending on the model I am folding, I apply methylcellulose during the folding process, or use it exclusively at the end. It is important to apply it in one or a few places and let it dry before applying it in other areas. For that area to have the exact shape we want, we will need to use clothespins or other tools to hold the model. If I apply methylcellulose to an insect model, for example, I will first shape it and then harden the exoskeleton, followed by the head, antennas, and, finally, the legs. If I were to start with the legs, upon shaping the exoskeleton, the orientation of the legs might no longer be correct, and I would have to redo them.

The advantage of using methylcellulose is that it hardens the paper without gluing it, so if the result is not what you had in mind, you can moisten it a bit and change the shape. It is a slow process that requires several days to complete. Another advantage is that it makes the paper thinner, which helps you make thin, but hard legs.

Methylcellulose helps with putting the finishes touches on a model, but it does not make miracles. You must fold a model well and make precise folds to get a good result. In this book, you'll also learn about other kinds of paper you can use.

Here are some small tips, hints, and guidelines for folding the models shown in this book:

Level 2 models are fairly accessible to beginners. By Level 3, the figures are harder and will demand more attention to folding precision. This doesn't mean that easier models allow for a lack of precision, it is just that they are more forgiving.

Foil paper, even 5.9 x 5.9 inches (15 x 15 cm) pieces, is perfectly suitable for Level 3 models. However, the models will be easier to fold using sandwich paper. The Crocodile allows—almost demands—thicker paper. If you are making a large version of the model, you can use Canson paper. This thicker paper should be craft-style paper, like thick Lokta or even Batik (although the latter requires a great amount of effort due to volume of the layers), and calls for the use of methylcellulose and moistening of the areas that require shaping.

For Levels 4 and 5, folding precision is crucial. Sandwich paper or thinner craft paper, like thin Lokta, banana fiber paper, treated tissue paper, etc., are the most suitable kinds.

The Macaw can be folded with any kind of paper, in any size up to 5.9 x 5.9 inches (15 x 15 cm). It is a great model to hold on your finger, like a pet.

The swimming Swan needs more flexible paper, such as foil or sandwich paper, which allows you to give it a nice shape and greater elegance.

For better results and a satin-like finish, I cover the white side of a sheet of foil paper with diluted latex, even though it is not necessary. On the foil side, I glue some black tissue paper. The Sea Lion, Dugong, and Narwhal must be folded with flexible foil paper, or thicker paper following the wet technique, so you can give them more volume and a better appearance. Sandwich paper is not recommended, because the finished model would be too flimsy. These models are not difficult and are very rewarding.

I used foil paper for the Narwhal, gluing dark tissue paper on the foil side and leaving the white side untreated to easily get the right color and shape of the horn. I use thick Lokta paper with methylcellulose finishing for the Sea Lion and Dugong, shaping the neck and face with the help of tweezers, so that these areas would dry correctly.

The Black Widow and Harvestman *(Phalangium)* have the same base, but have different final steps. Sandwich and foil paper, which allow for easy final shaping, are perfectly suitable for these models.

The Crocodile and the "Eagle ray" or Stingray can be folded using a great variety of paper, including some thick ones. I have folded both models using Lokta paper. The Crocodile would have been better with a more rigid paper, such as Ingres, to make step 114 easier.

I don't have many tips for Levels 4 and 5. As I said before, paper selection is crucial for these models and folding precision makes a large difference between just finishing the model and getting a great final result.

The Walking Stick and Black Ant will turn out perfectly if you follow the folding process. As for the Walking Stick, the best effect is achieved by carefully following step 86, when you make the model completely round and force the legs a little bit to put them in the right place. The Leaf Mantis requires careful final shaping to achieve the best effect. I suggest that you look at pictures of Manuel Sirgo's finished model.

On your first attempt at folding the Crayfish, you must use a large piece of paper—larger than 11.8 x 11.8 inches (30 x 30 cm), at least 19.7 x 19.7 inches (50 x 50 cm). This model, along with the Pseudoscorpion and Scorpion *(Buthus),* requires some final shaping to get a good finished result.

The European Stag Beetle *(Lucanus cervus)* and Stag Beetle *(Cyclommatus imperator)* models require steps that easily lead you to the finished result; only a little shaping of the abdomen is needed.

The flying Rhinoceros Beetle *(Dynastes neptunus)* is the most complex model in the book. You must pay special attention to step 75, carefully follow all the instructions, and complete intermediate steps 76 and 77 to obtain an error-free model.

Pere Olivella

Folding Instructions

- - - - - -   *Valley Fold*

—·—··—··—   *Mountain Fold*

················   *X-ray View*

—————   *Mark*

Fold Forward

Fold Backward

Fold Inward

Repeat

Fold and Unfold

Accordion Fold

Accordion Sink

Open up

Sink, Flatten

Turn the Model Over

90°   *Rotate the Model*

Enlarged View

Reduced View

Hold By

Stretch

Color Facing Down

Color Facing Up

Same Color on Both Sides

Meaning of the Symbols

Next, a few of the symbol meanings will be explained for the beginners.

Valley fold

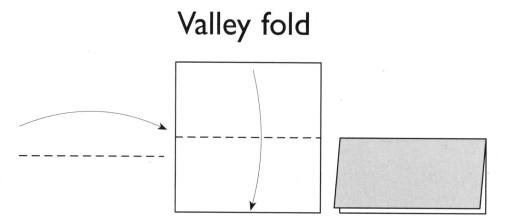

A valley fold is represented by a dashed line and an arrow with a symmetrical head, which indicate the direction the paper should be folded. In this example, the paper is folded in half; the top half is folded so that it rests on the bottom half.

Mountain fold

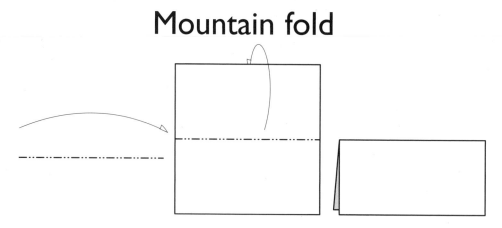

A dashed and dotted line and an arrow with an asymmetrical head indicate the direction in which the paper should be folded. Usually, when this type of arrow is used, the paper should be folded away from you, exactly the opposite of a valley fold.

Fold and unfold

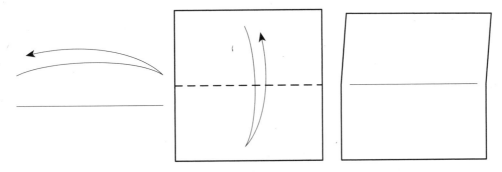

This symbol indicates that we should make a valley fold and then unfold it, going back to the original position. The only change will be a mark where the paper was folded.

Accordian fold

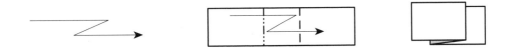

This fold consists of a valley fold followed by a mountain fold. The arrow, as usual, indicates the direction in which the paper should be folded and the zigzag line shows what the end result will look like when viewed from the side.

Fold over and over

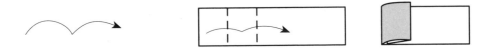

This process involves making two or more consecutive folds on the same side. They can be either valley or mountain folds; the process is the same.

Sink

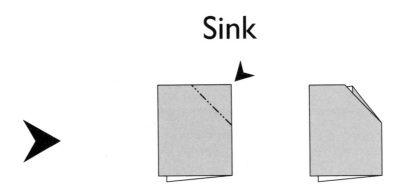

This fold is achieved by pushing a point inward to "sink" it. The model should still be flat after this fold is completed.

Rotate

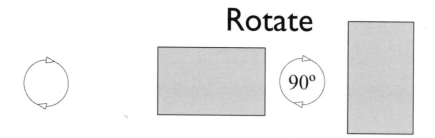

This process involves rotating the model in the direction indicated by the arrows. The rotation angle is written inside the symbol.

Turn over

The symbol is composed of an arrow with a loop in the tail, which indicates that we should turn the paper over, putting the side that was facing up, down on the table.

Enlarged view

This indicates that the next step has been drawn on a larger scale, so that it can be more easily understood.

Reduced view

This arrow if often used after showing an enlarged detailed view. After folding this area, we redraw the model on a smaller scale.

Repeat

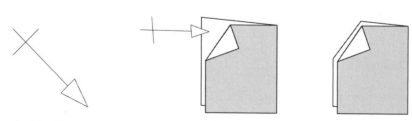

This symbol indicates where and how many times you should repeat the previous steps (as many times as the number of dashes on the arrow.)

Model Difficulty

The difficulty levels are as follows:

Level 1: Beginners who have mastered the following: kite and fish bases, mountain folds, valley folds, hood folds, and preliminary and waterbomb bases.

Level 2: Beginners who have mastered the following bases: kite, fish, bird, and frog. Basic folds, with the exception of unsink.

Level 3: Intermediate folders who have mastered all the bases, including the blintz frog, and every type of fold.

Level 4: Advanced folders who have mastered models that have many steps and some open models.

Level 5: Advanced folders who have mastered models that require particularly thin paper or have a large number of steps.

LEVEL 2

Swan swimming
Macaw
Dugong
Narwhal
Sea Lion

LEVEL 3

Black Widow
Harvestman
Stingray
Crocodile
Star

LEVEL 4

Swan
Walking Stick
Stick Insect
Leaf Mantis
Black Ant

LEVEL 5

Crayfish
Pseudoscorpion
Scorpion
Stag Beetle
European Stag Beetle
Rhinoceros Beetle flying

Swan swimming

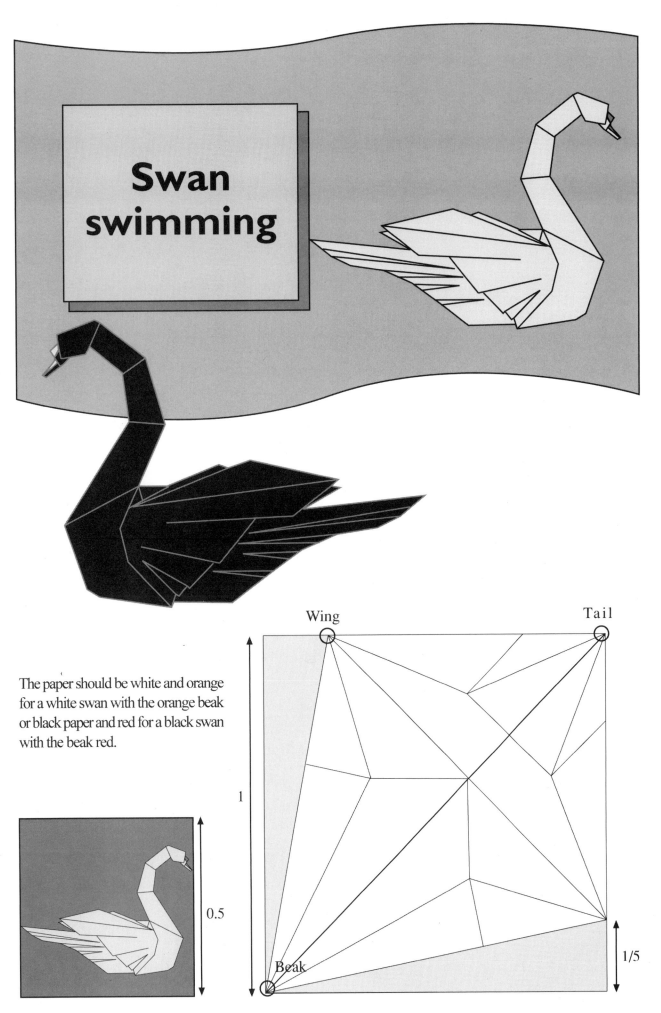

The paper should be white and orange for a white swan with the orange beak or black paper and red for a black swan with the beak red.

Wing

Tail

1

0.5

Beak

1/5

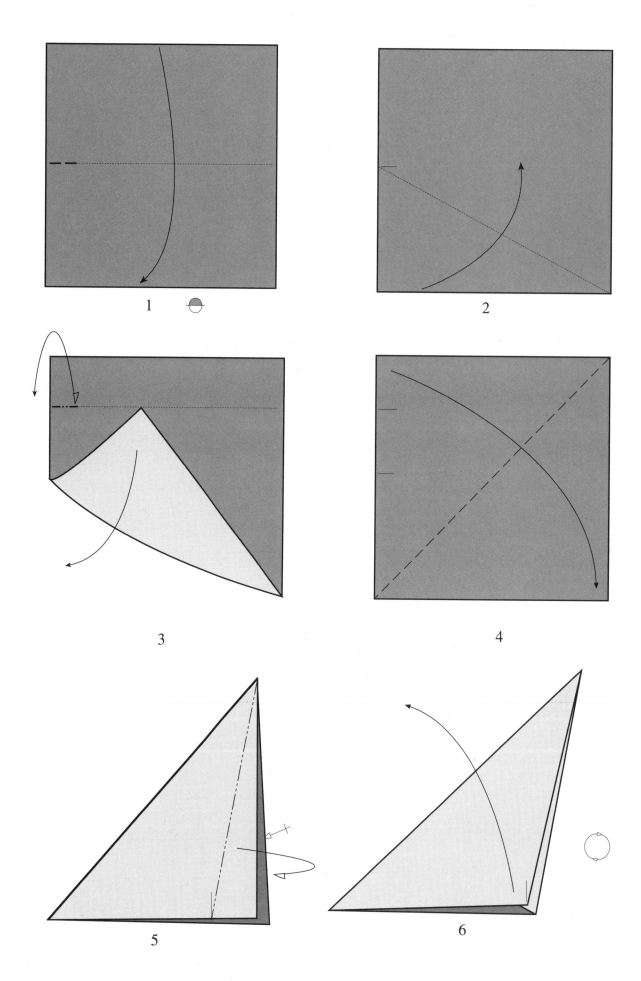

1

2

3

4

5

6

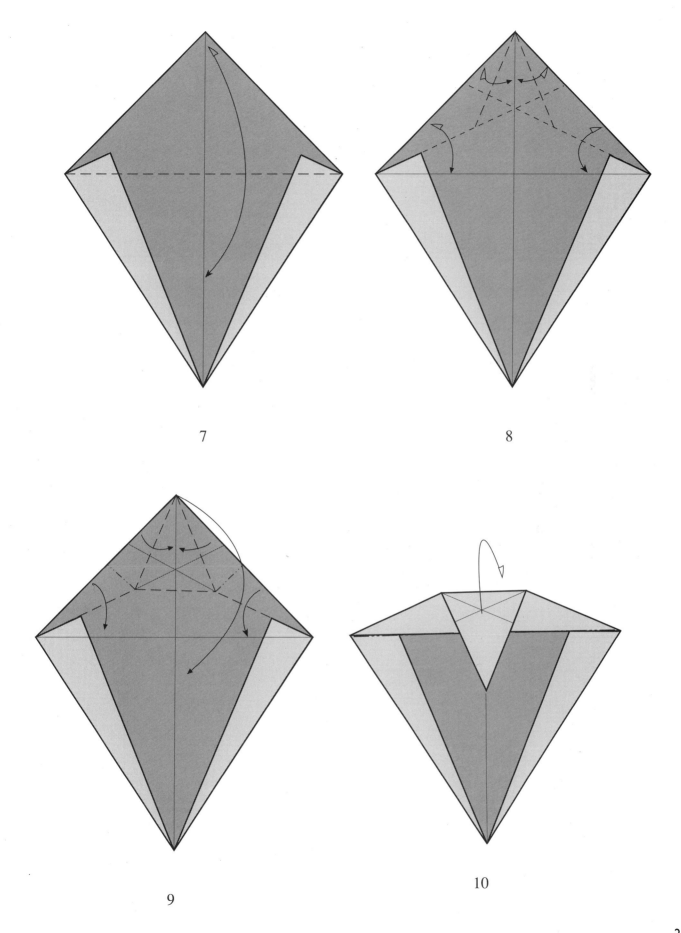

7

8

9

10

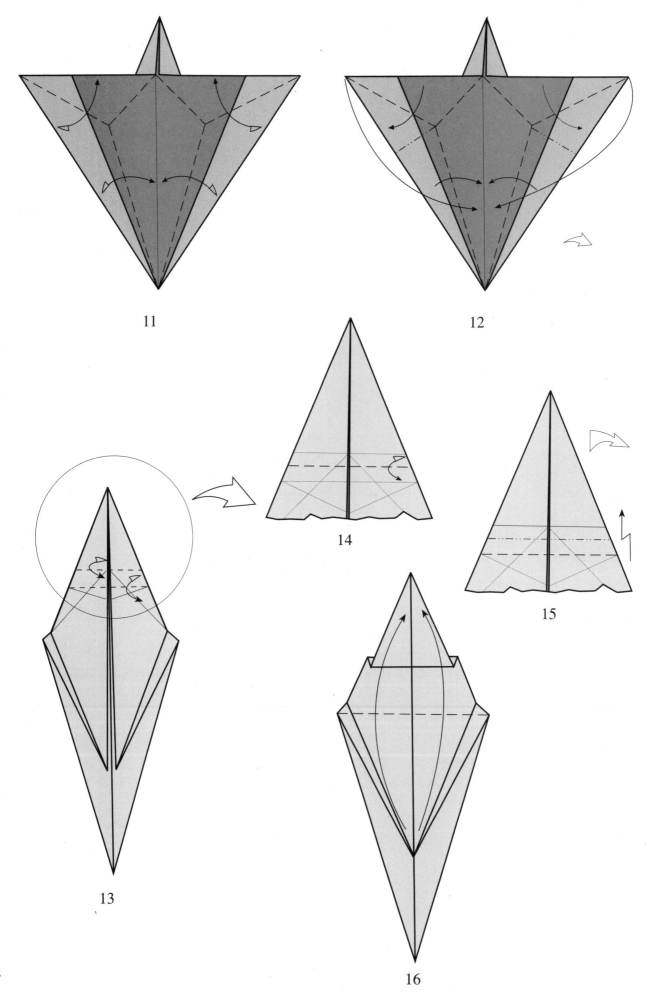

11

12

13

14

15

16

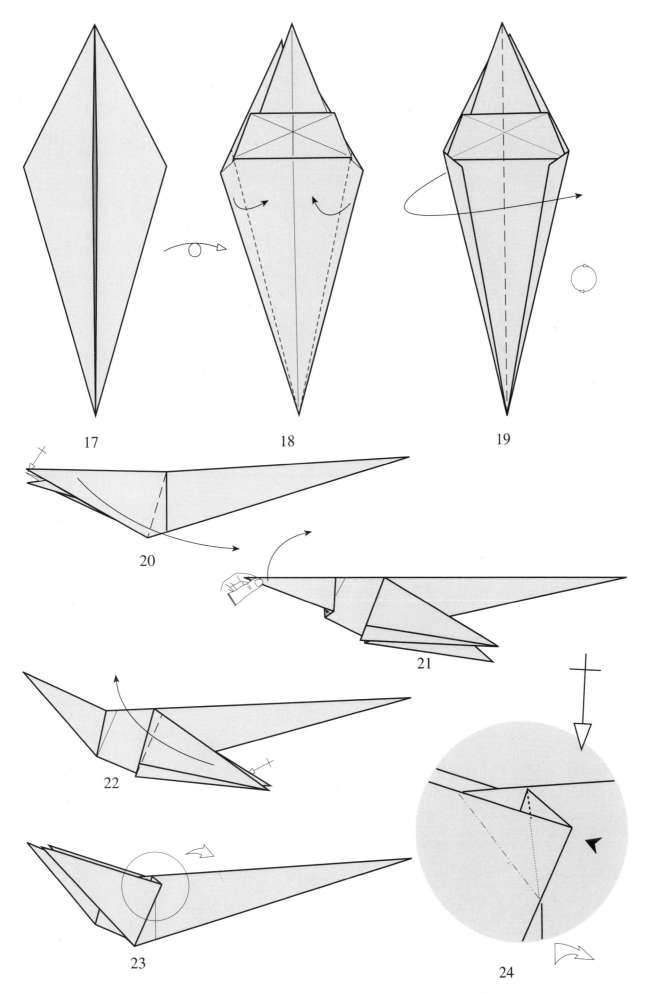

17

18

19

20

21

22

23

24

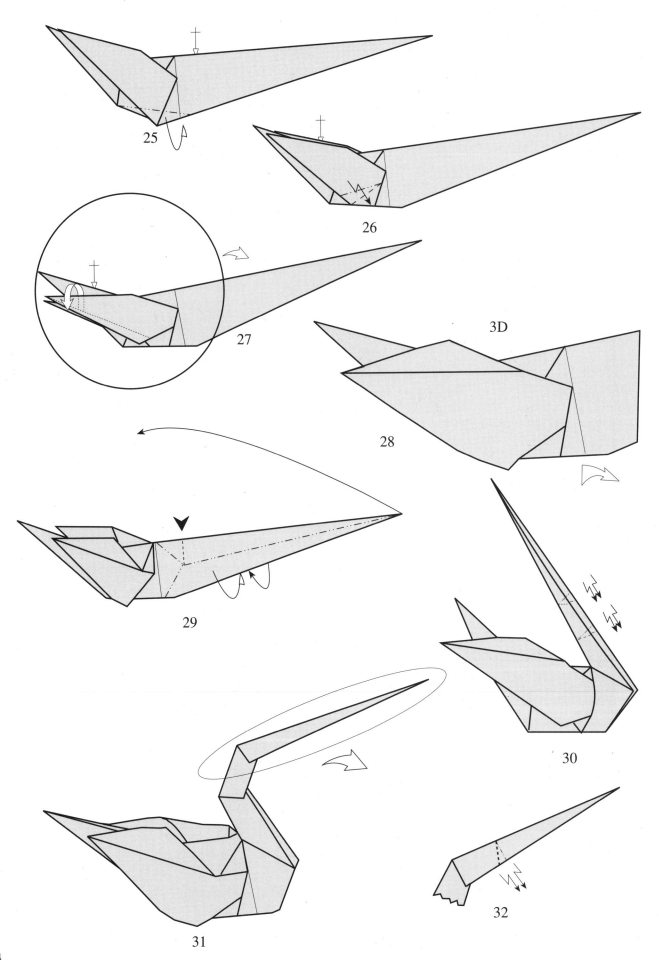

25

26

27

3D

28

29

30

31

32

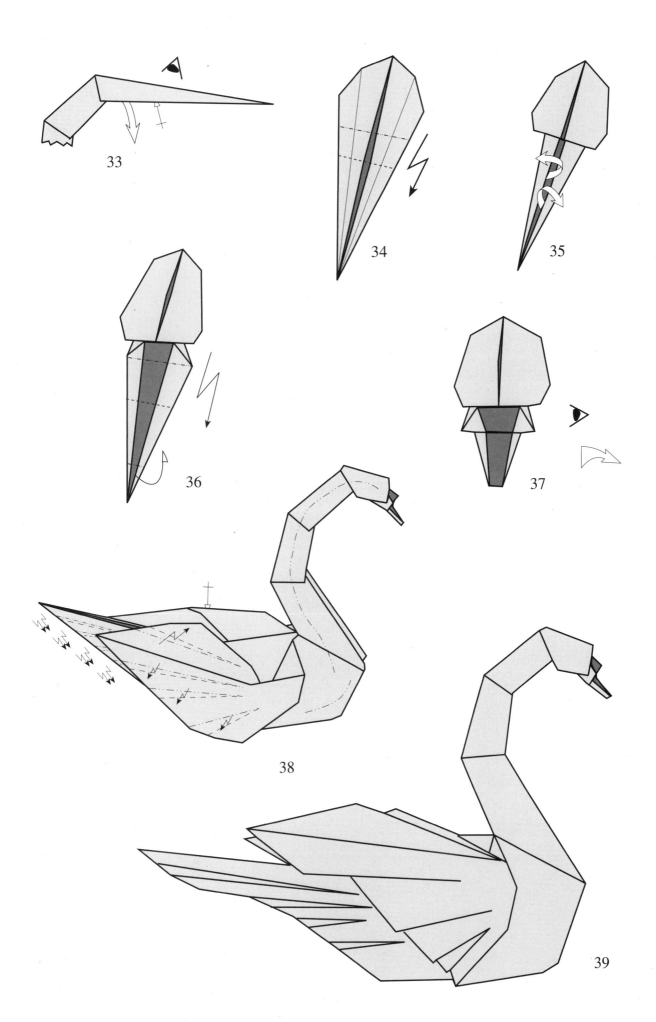

33

34

35

36

37

38

39

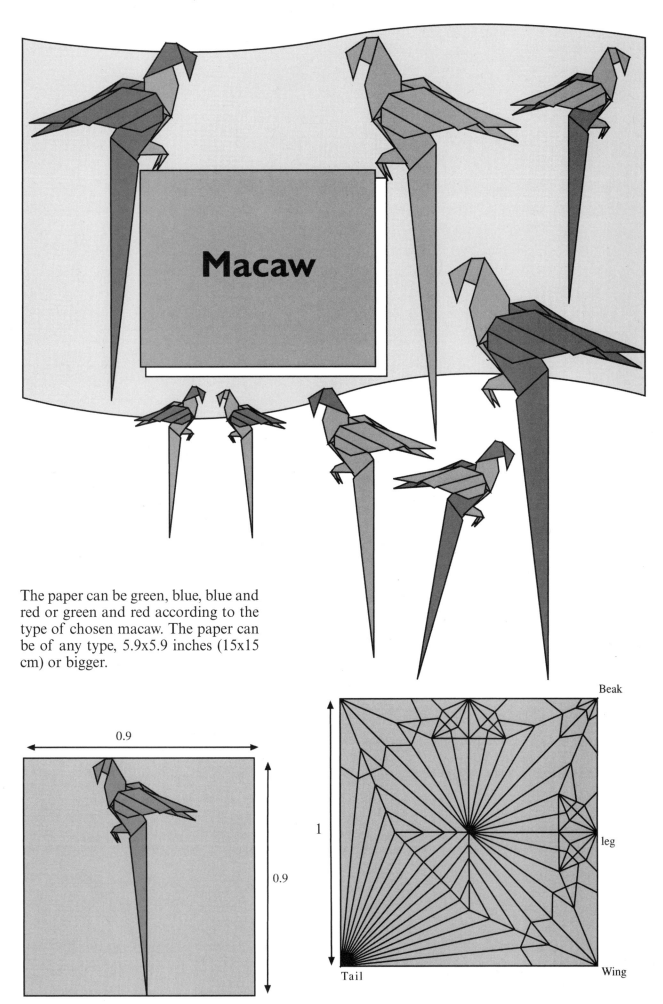

Macaw

The paper can be green, blue, blue and red or green and red according to the type of chosen macaw. The paper can be of any type, 5.9x5.9 inches (15x15 cm) or bigger.

0.9

0.9

0.9

Beak

1

leg

Tail

Wing

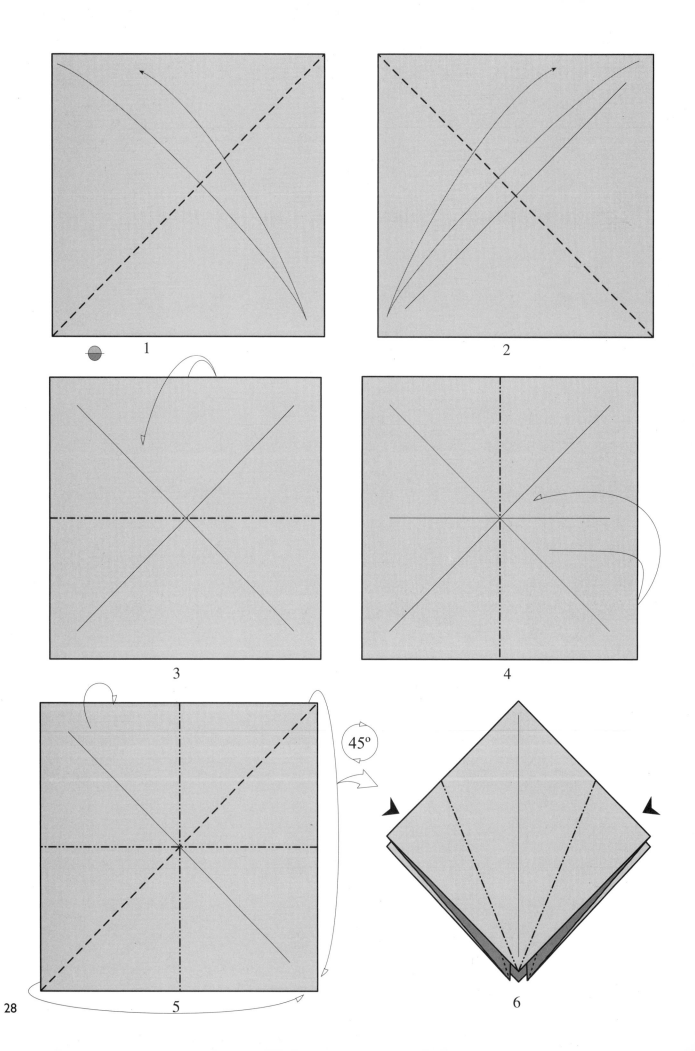

1

2

3

4

45°

5

6

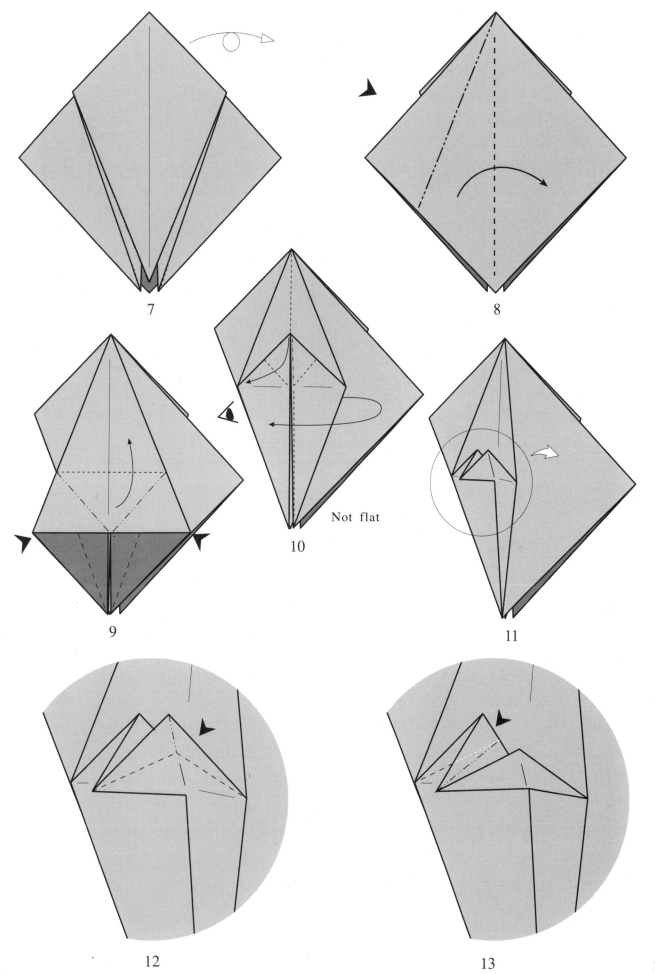

7

8

9

10

Not flat

11

12

13

29

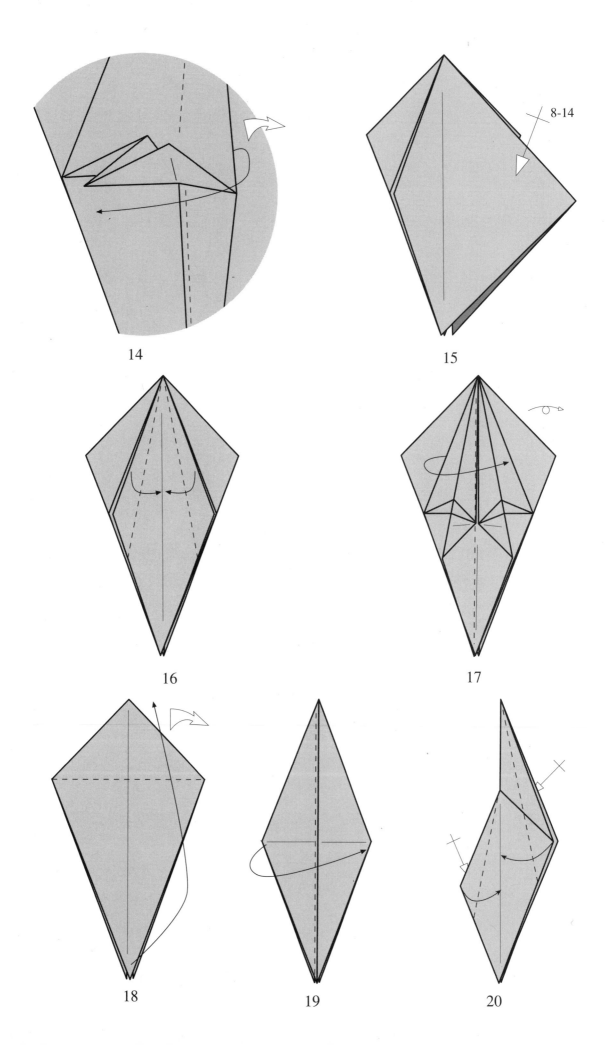

14

15

8-14

16

17

18

19

20

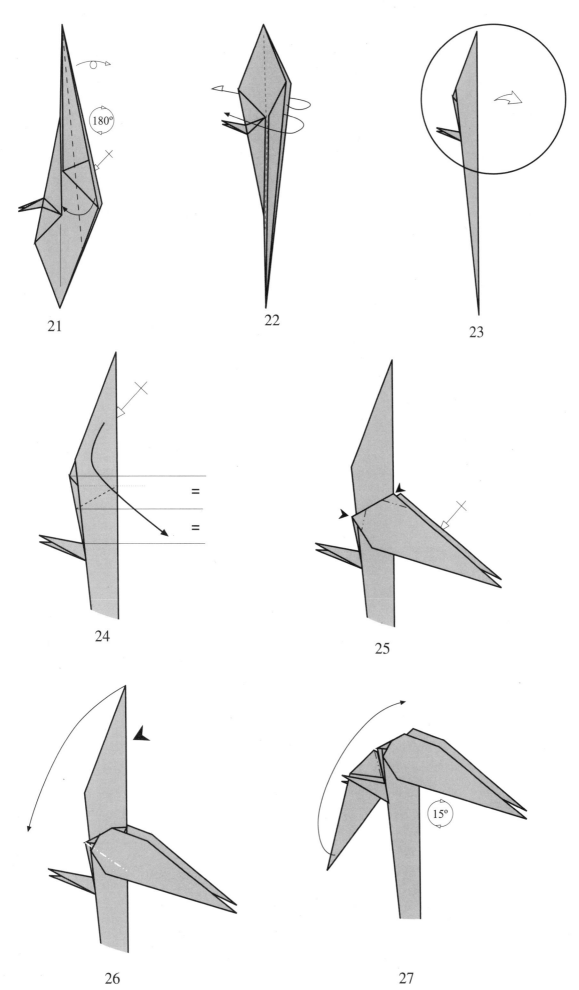

21

22

23

24

25

26

27

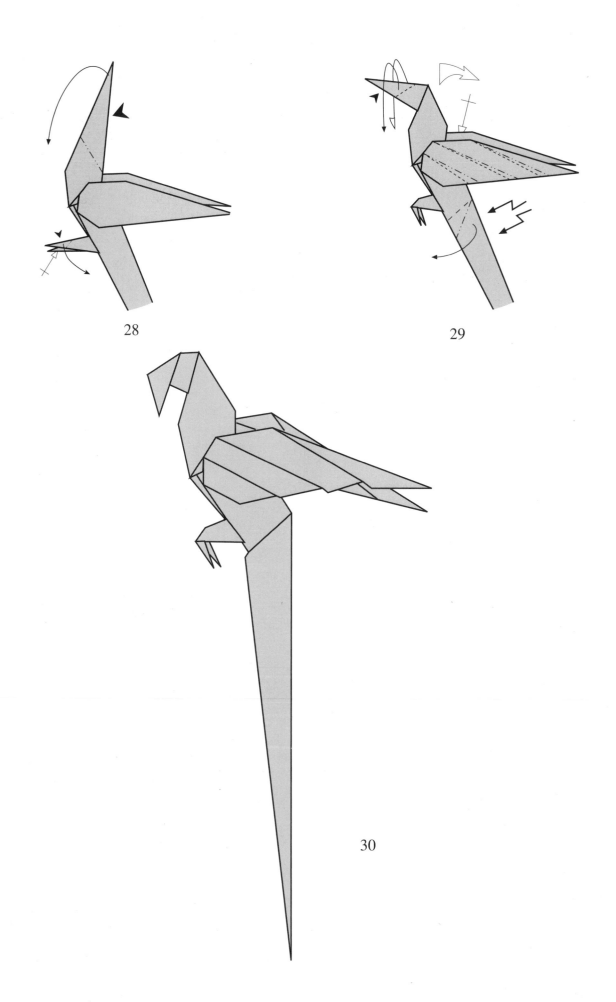

28

29

30

Bicolor macaws
Diverse variants

J. C. Borrego and M. Sirgo

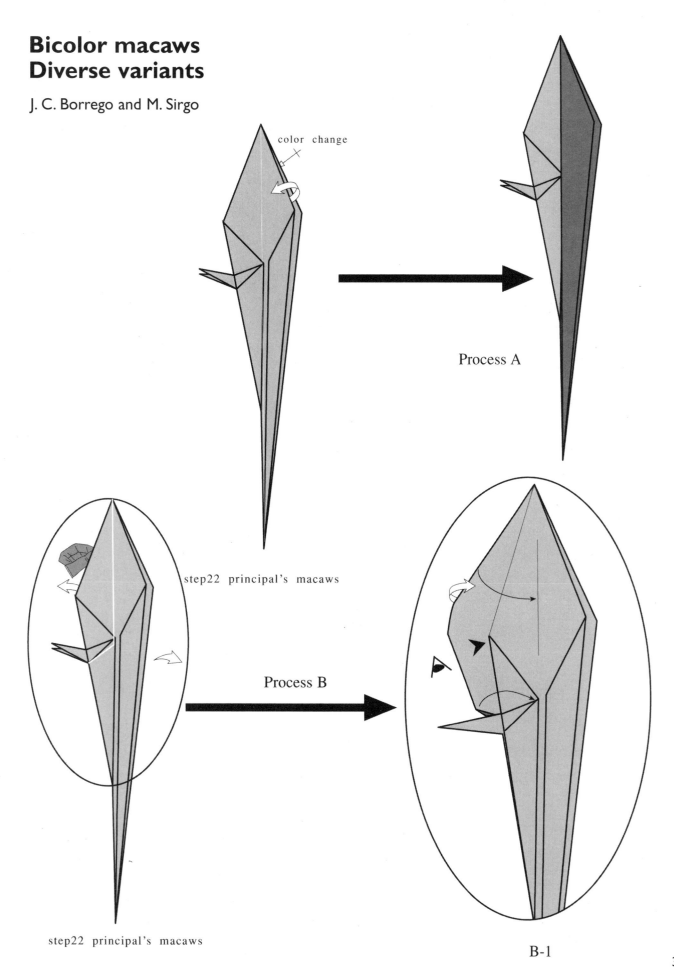

color change

Process A

step22 principal's macaws

Process B

step22 principal's macaws

B-1

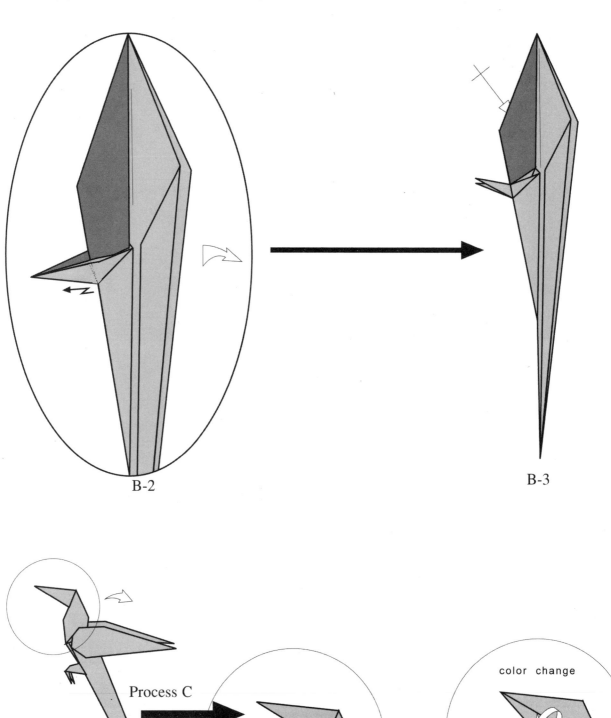

B-2

B-3

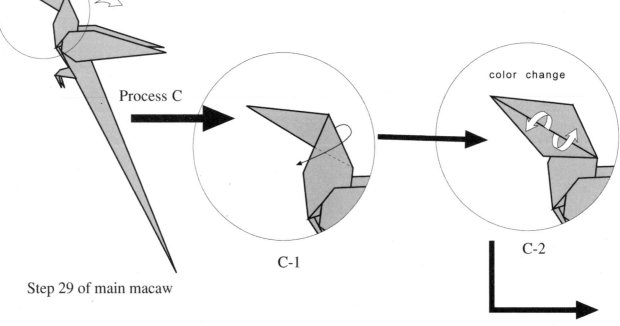

Step 29 of main macaw

Process C

C-1

color change

C-2

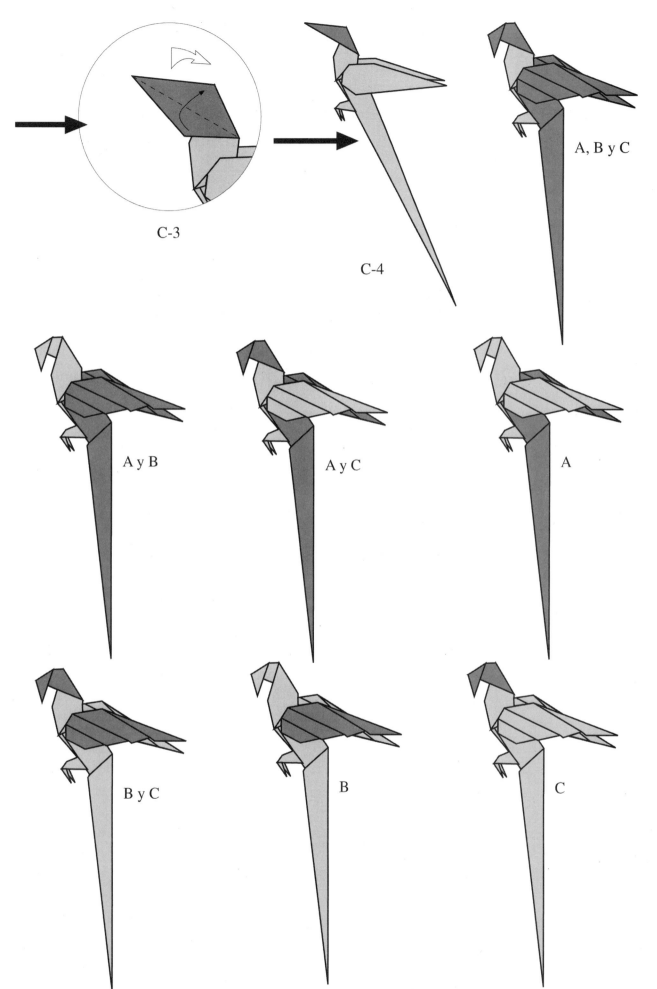

C-3

C-4

A, B y C

A y B

A y C

A

B y C

B

C

35

Dugong

The paper should be gray. Any paper type can be used, 120 grams, using the technique of humidified paper.

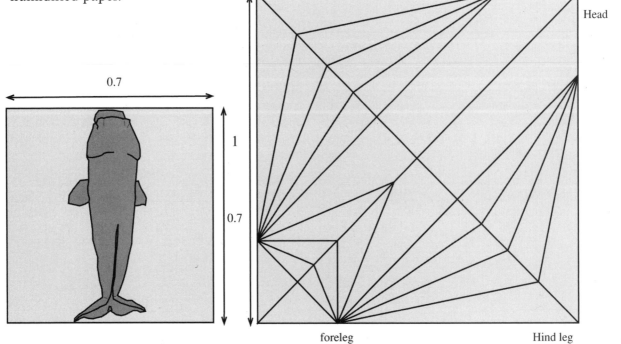

0.7

1

0.7

Head

foreleg

Hind leg

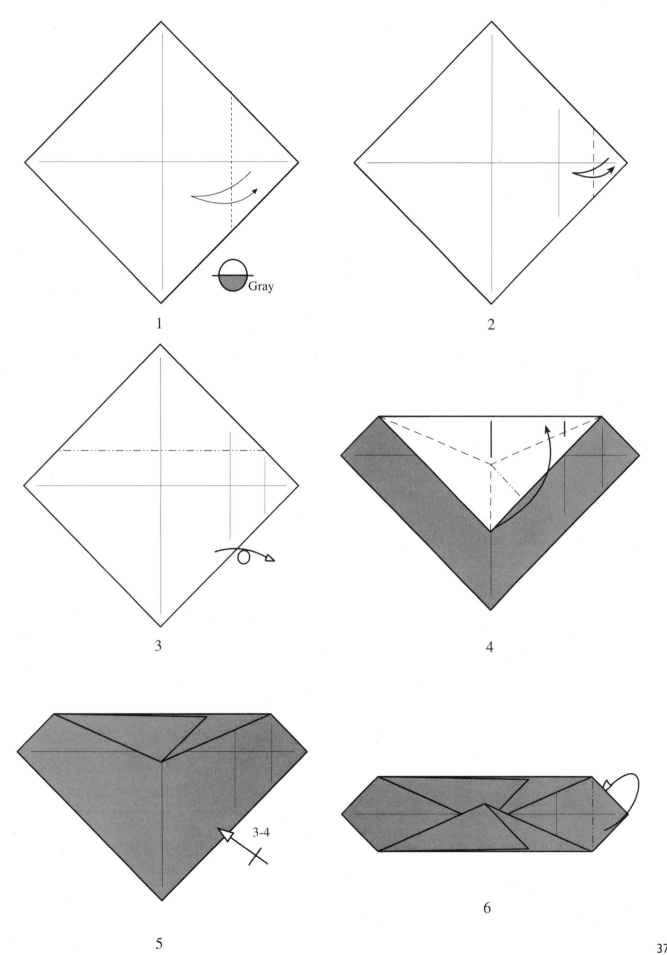

1

2

Gray

3

4

5

3-4

6

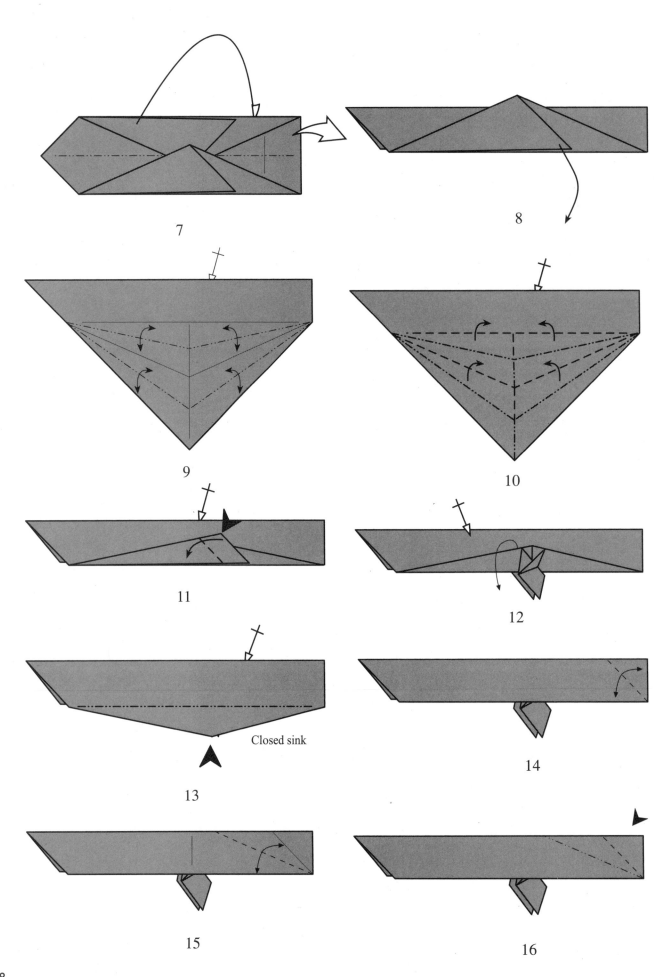

7

8

9

10

11

12

Closed sink

13

14

15

16

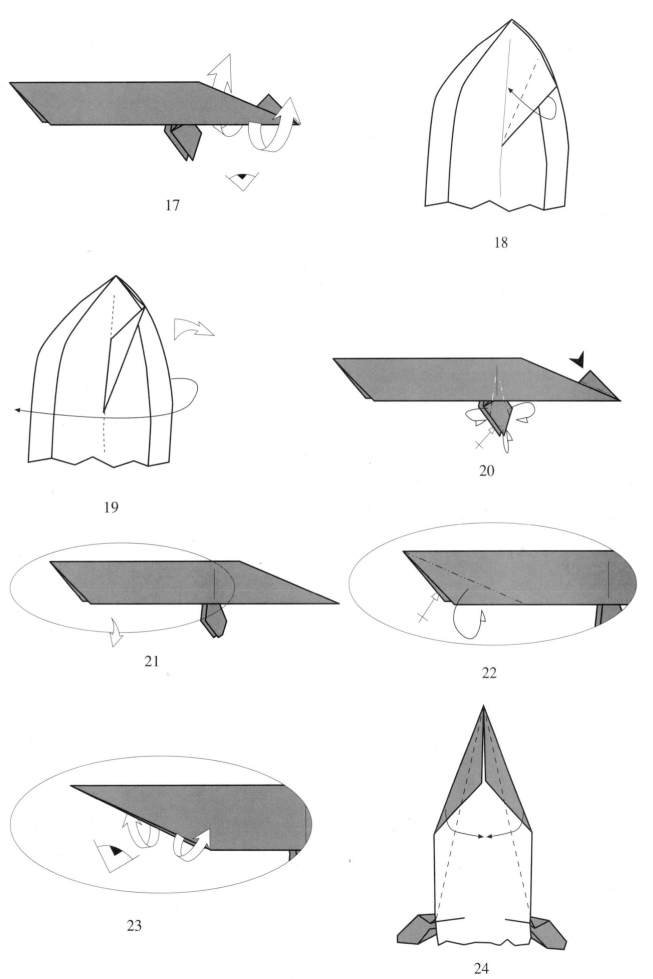

17

18

19

20

21

22

23

24

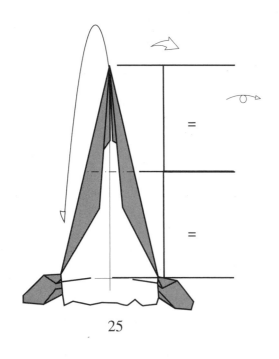

25

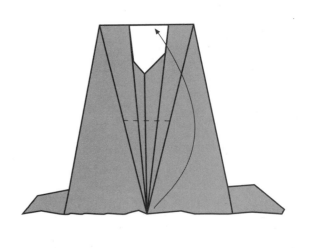

26

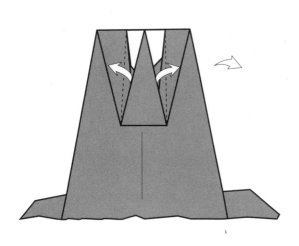

27

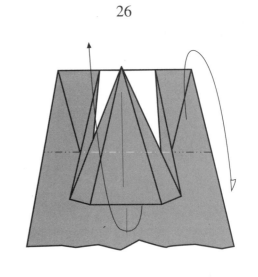

28

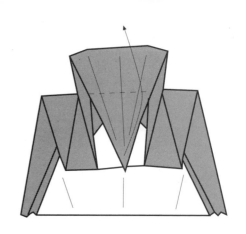

29

30

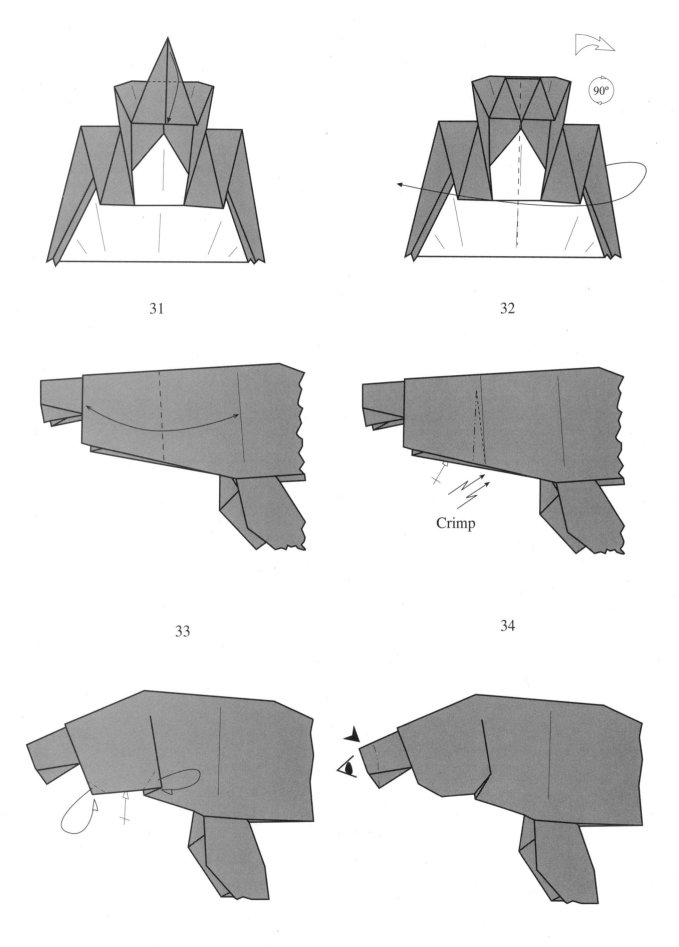

31

32

33

34

Crimp

35

36

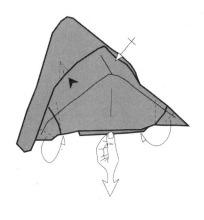

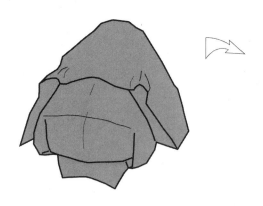

37

38

3D effects

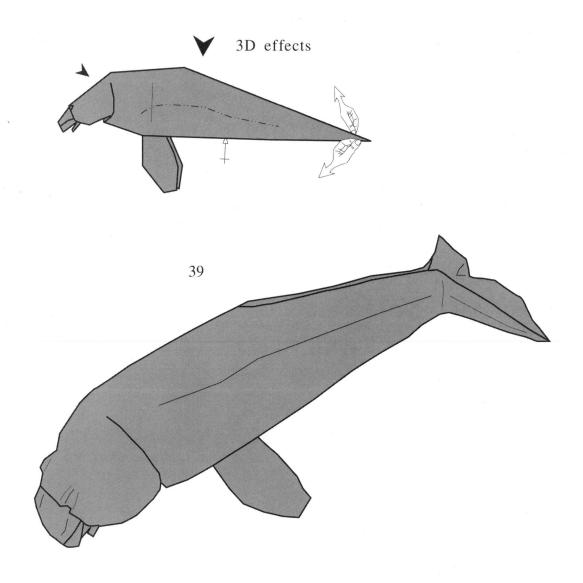

39

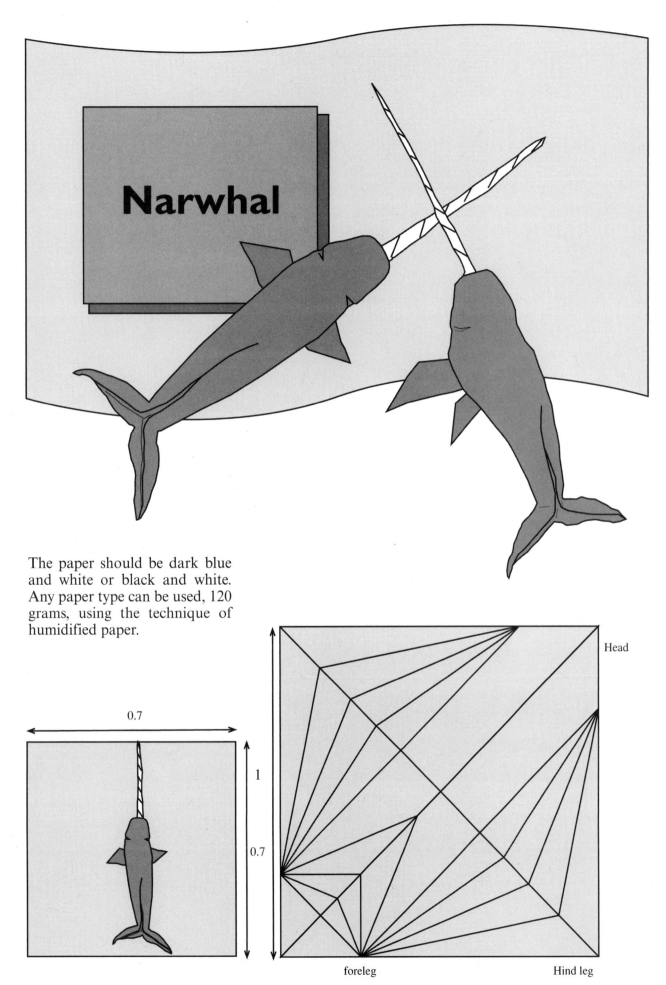

Narwhal

The paper should be dark blue and white or black and white. Any paper type can be used, 120 grams, using the technique of humidified paper.

0.7

1

0.7

Head

foreleg

Hind leg

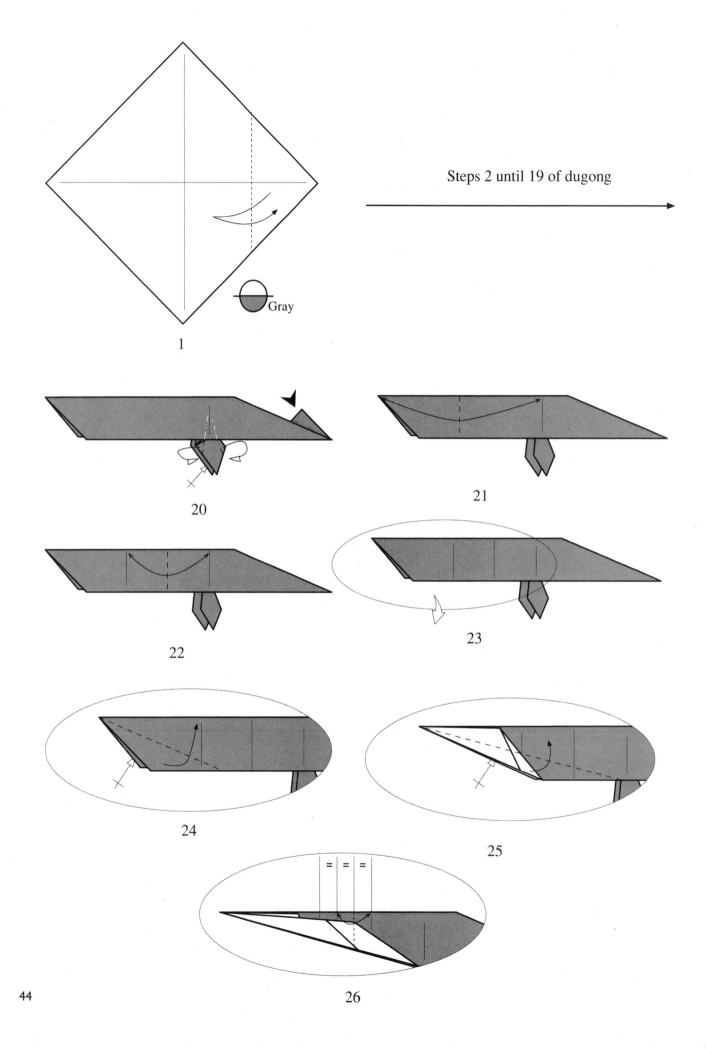

Steps 2 until 19 of dugong

Gray

1

20

21

22

23

24

25

26

44

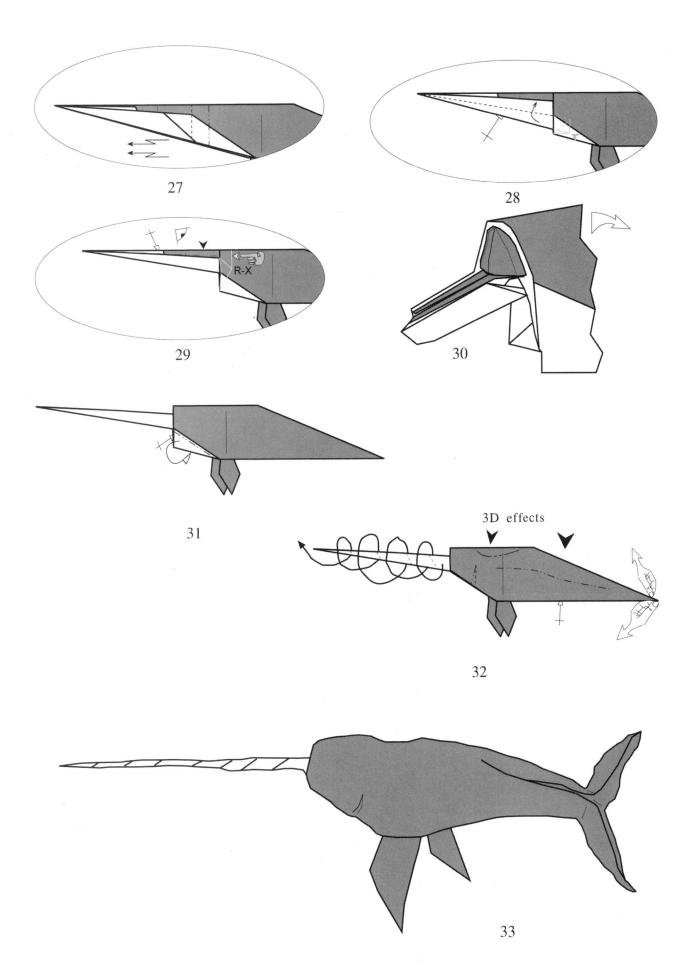

27

28

29

30

31

3D effects

32

33

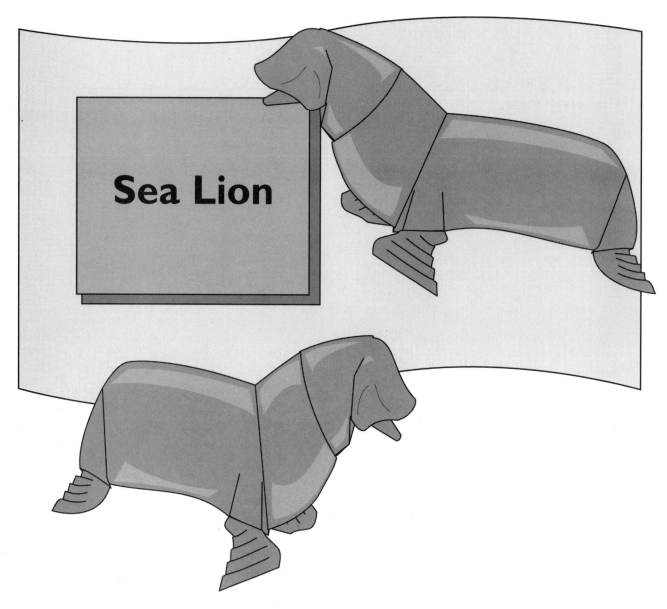

Sea Lion

The paper should be brown. Any paper type can be used, 120 grams, using the technique of humidified paper.

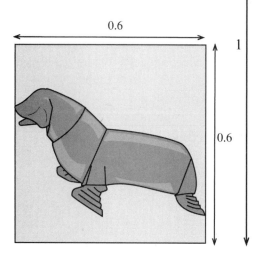

0.6

0.6

1

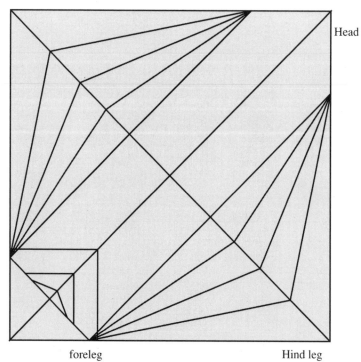

Head

foreleg

Hind leg

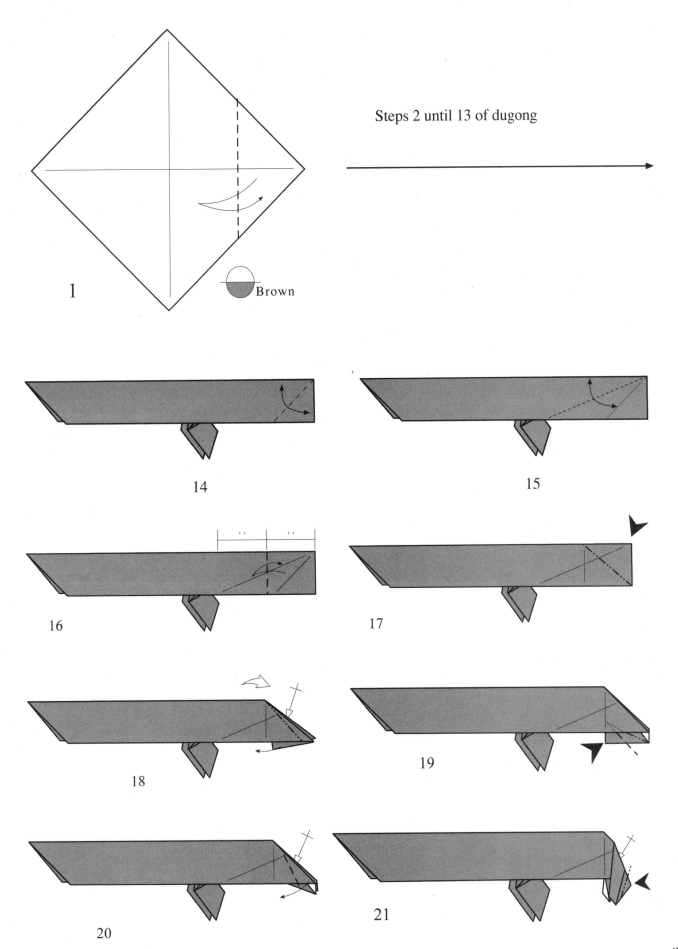

Steps 2 until 13 of dugong

1

Brown

14

15

16

17

18

19

20

21

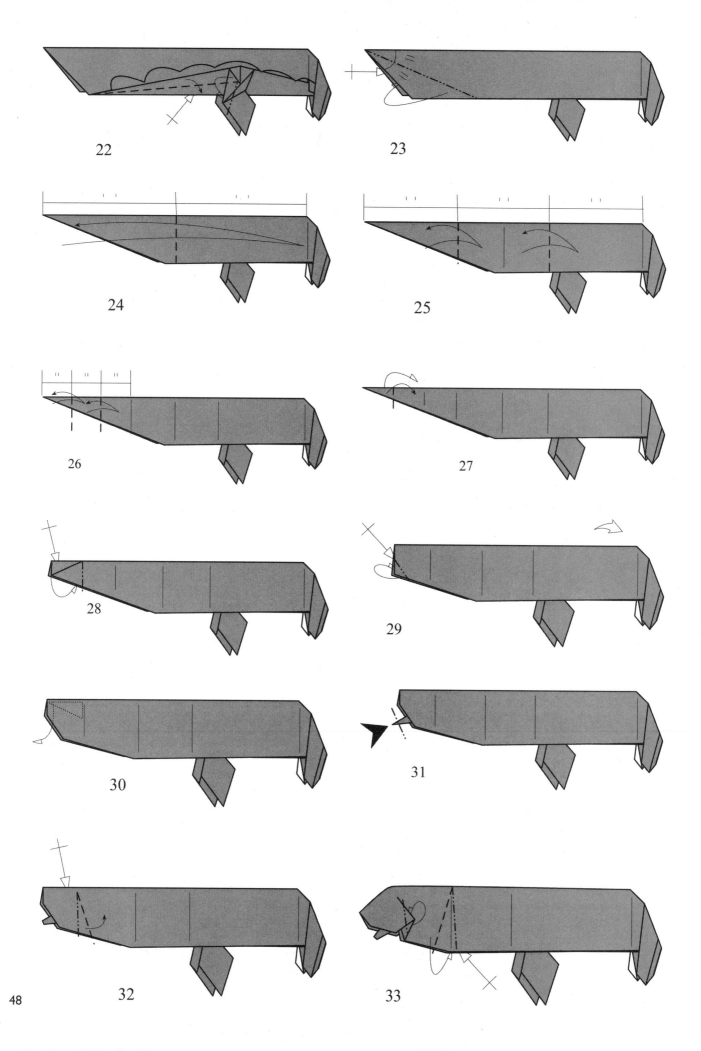

22

23

24

25

26

27

28

29

30

31

32

33

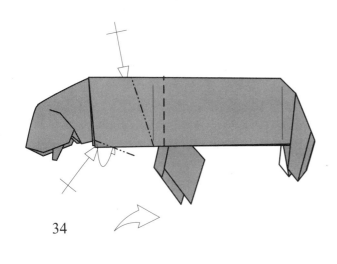

34

35

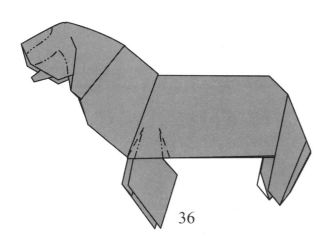

36

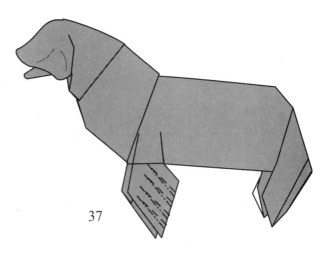

37

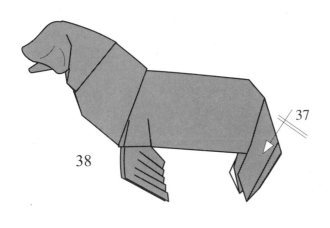

38

37

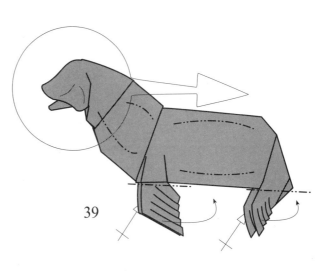

39

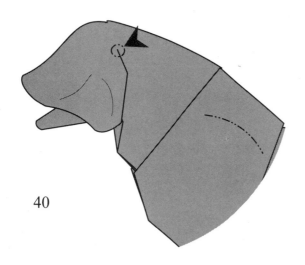

40

41

Black Widow

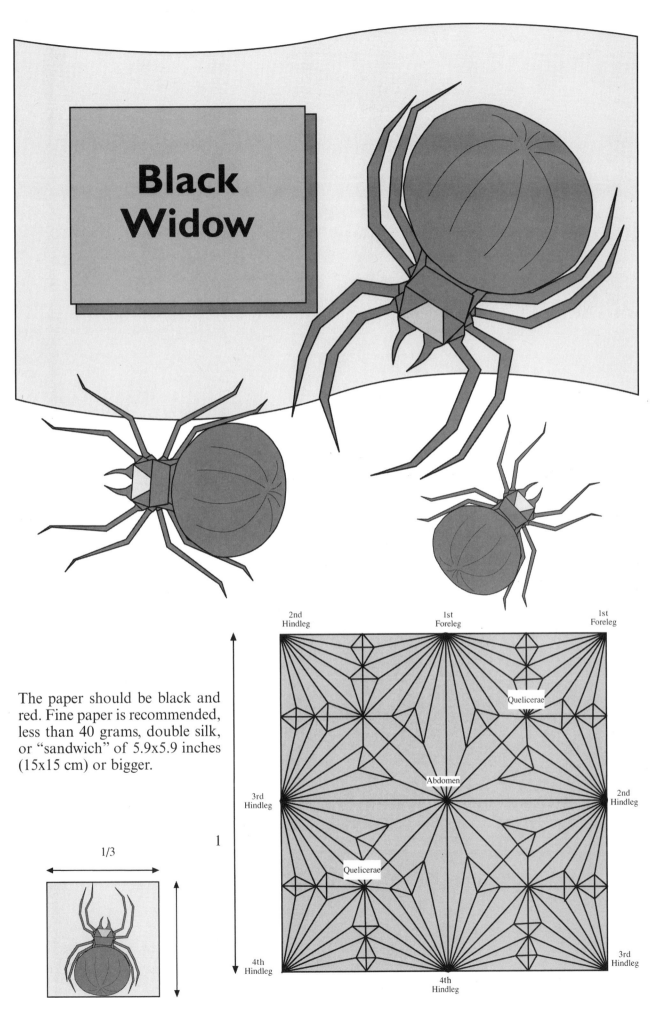

The paper should be black and red. Fine paper is recommended, less than 40 grams, double silk, or "sandwich" of 5.9x5.9 inches (15x15 cm) or bigger.

1/3

1

2nd Hindleg

1st Foreleg

1st Foreleg

Quelicerae

Abdomen

3rd Hindleg

2nd Hindleg

Quelicerae

4th Hindleg

3rd Hindleg

4th Hindleg

51

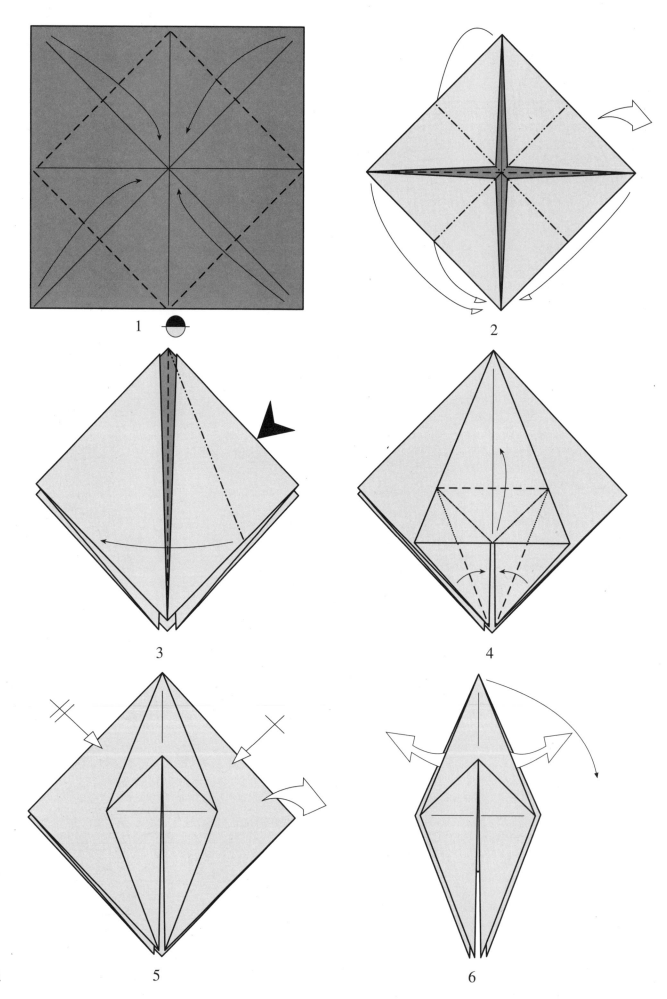

1

2

3

4

5

6

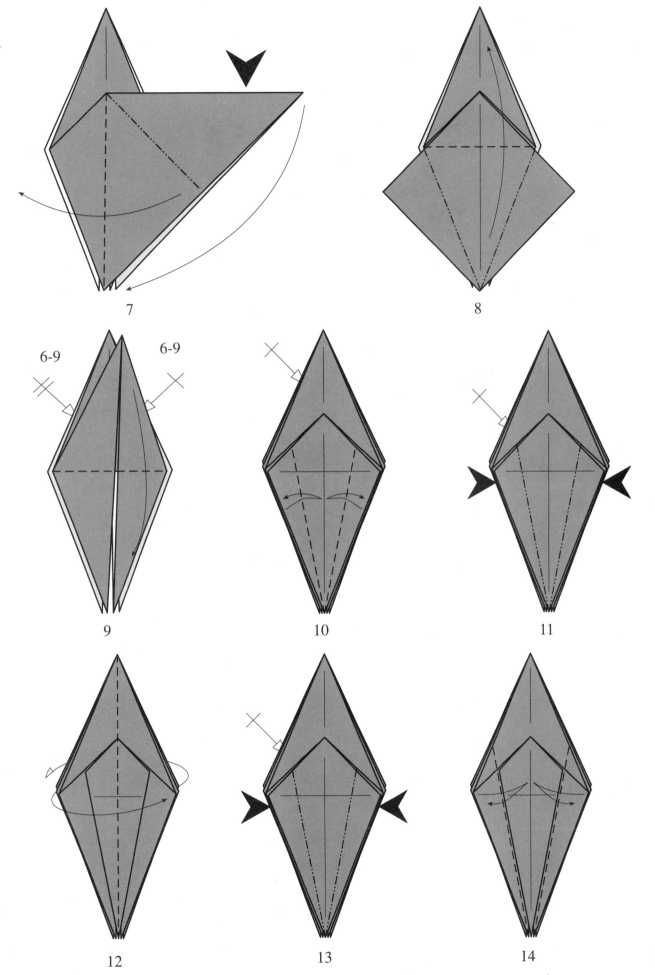

7

8

6-9   6-9

9

10

11

12

13

14

53

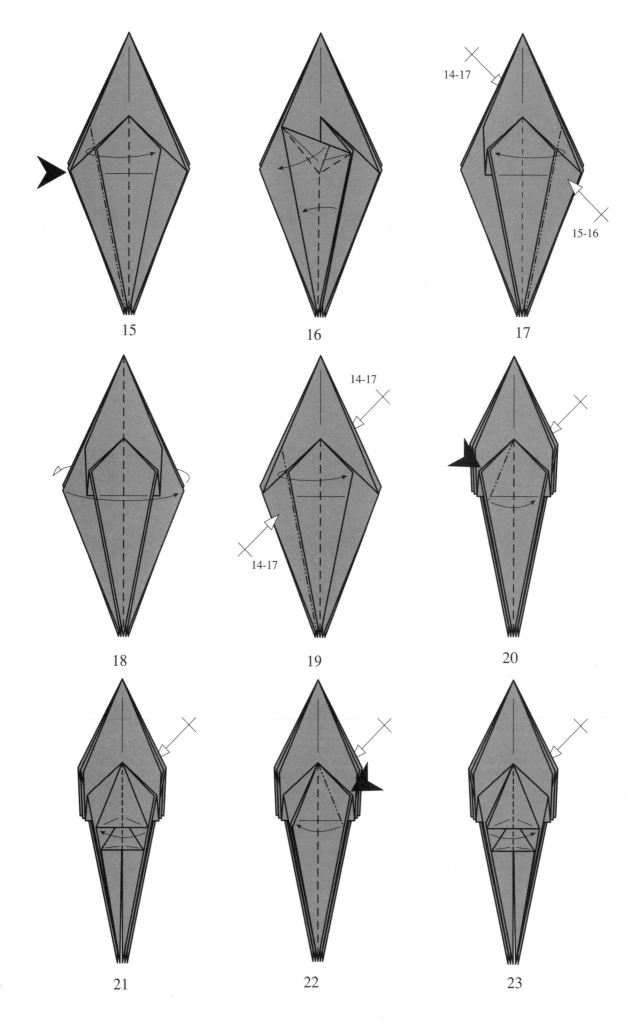

15

16

17

18

19

20

21

22

23

54

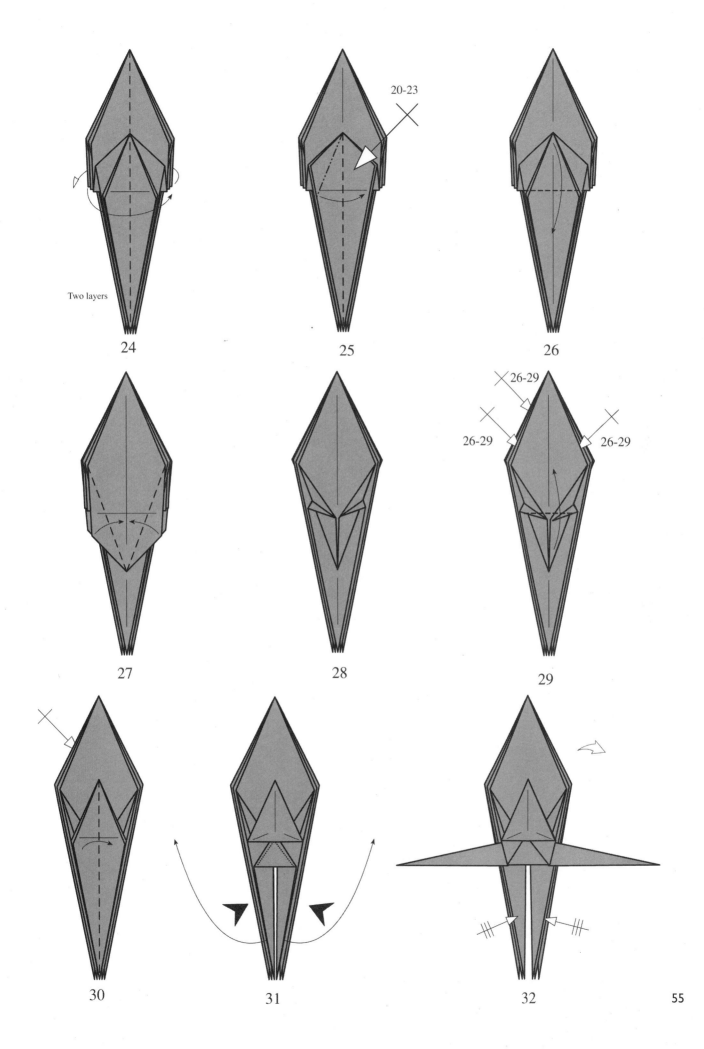

24

Two layers

25

20-23

26

27

28

29

26-29
26-29
26-29

30

31

32

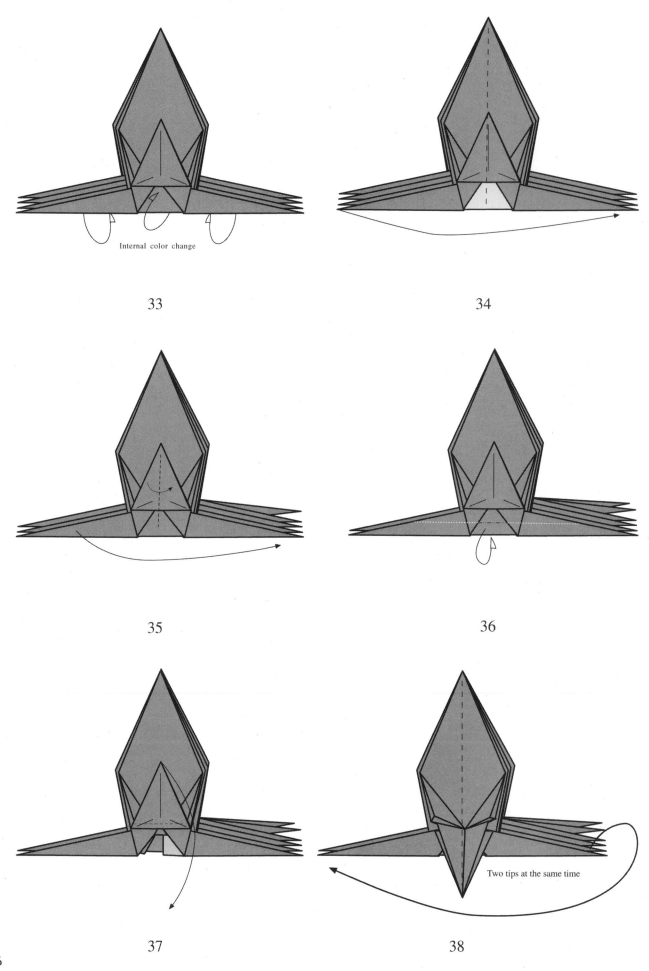

33

34

Internal color change

35

36

37

38

Two tips at the same time

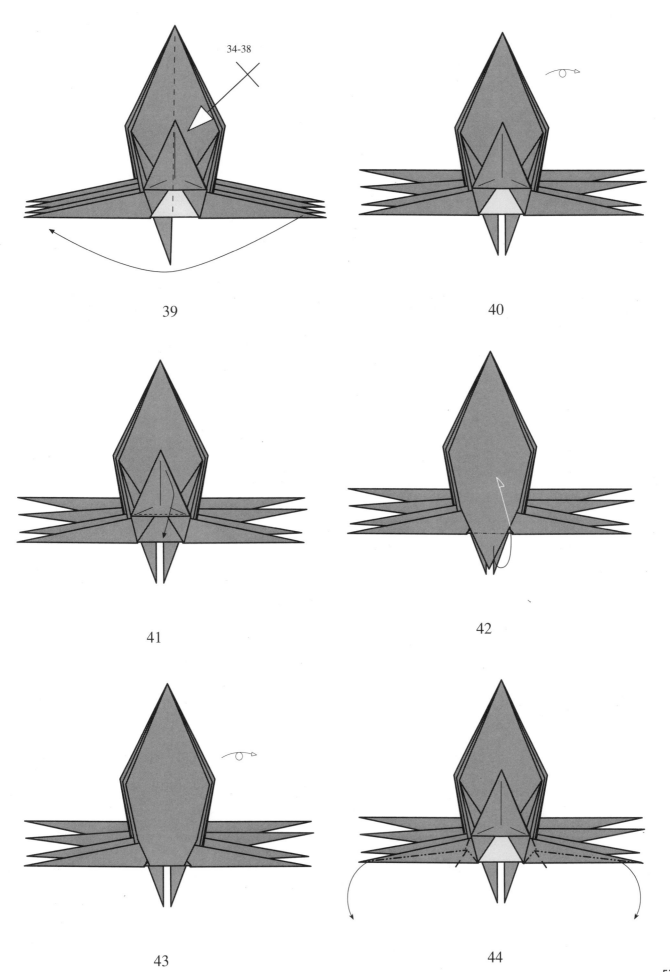

34-38

39

40

41

42

43

44

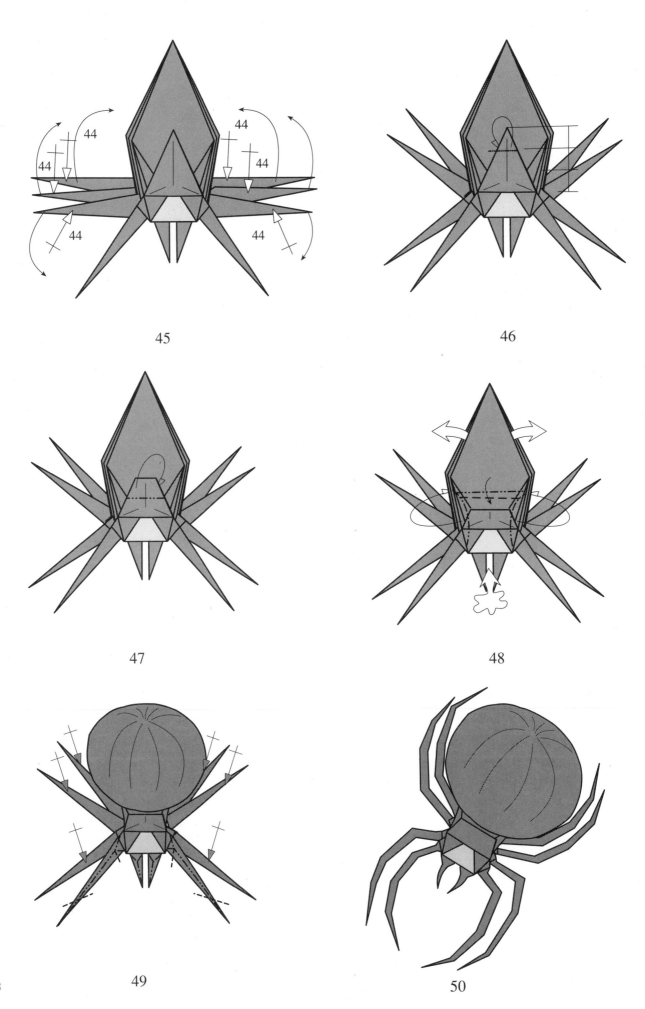

45

46

47

48

49

50

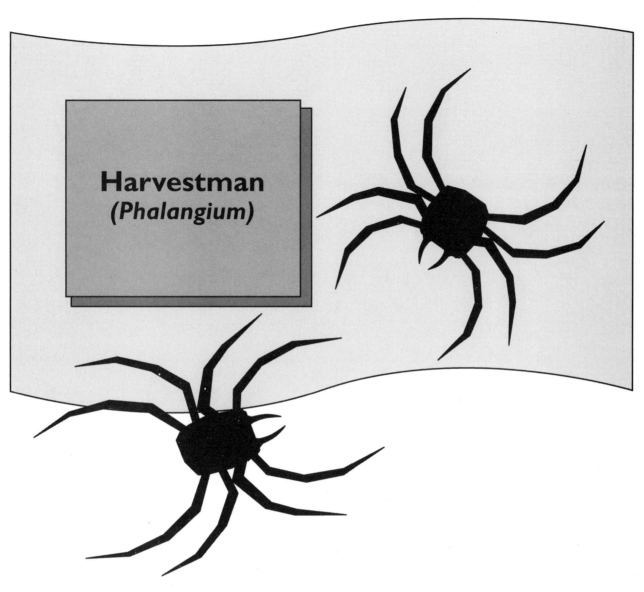

Harvestman
(Phalangium)

The paper should be black. Fine paper is recommended, less than 30 grams, double silk, or "sandwich" of 7.9x7.9 inches (20x20 cm) or bigger.

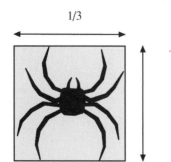

1/3

1

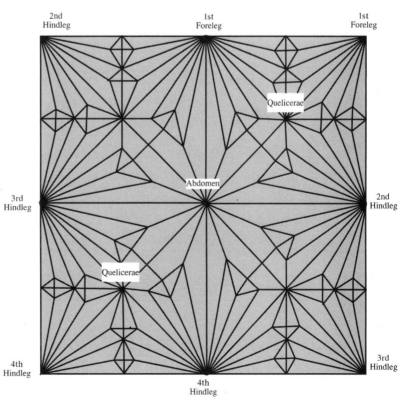

2nd Hindleg   1st Foreleg   1st Foreleg

Quelicerae

Abdomen   2nd Hindleg

3rd Hindleg

Quelicerae

4th Hindleg   3rd Hindleg

4th Hindleg

59

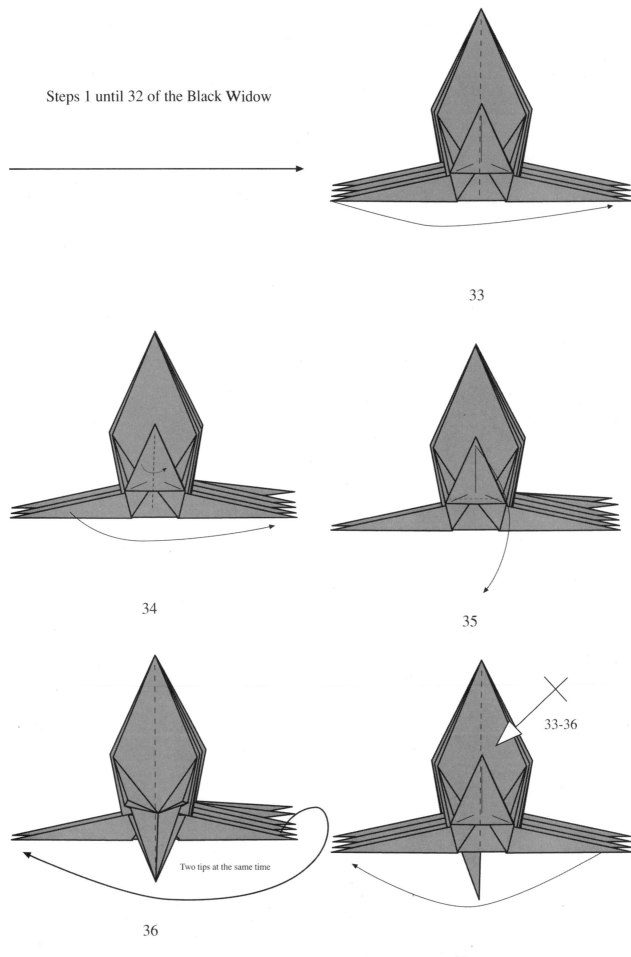

Steps 1 until 32 of the Black Widow

33

34

35

36

Two tips at the same time

33-36

37

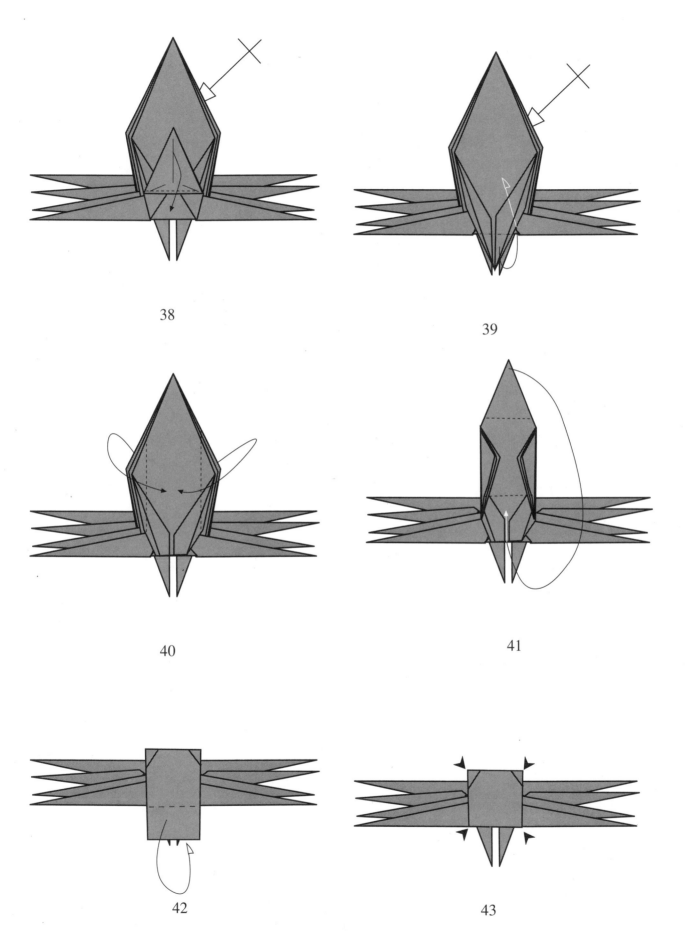

38

39

40

41

42

43

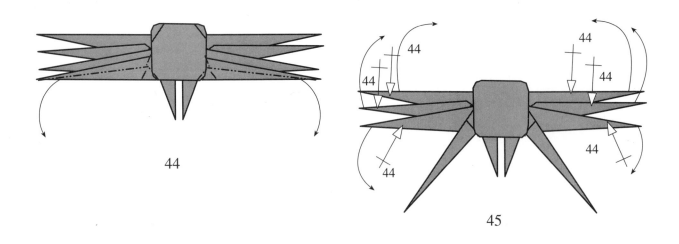

44

45

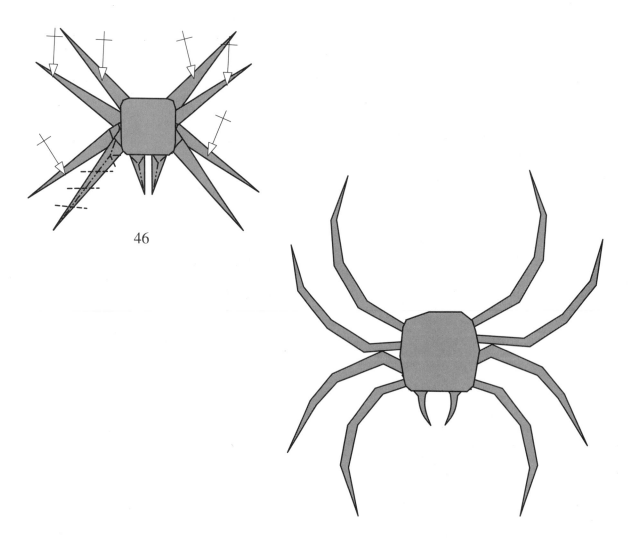

46

47

Stingray (Eagle ray)

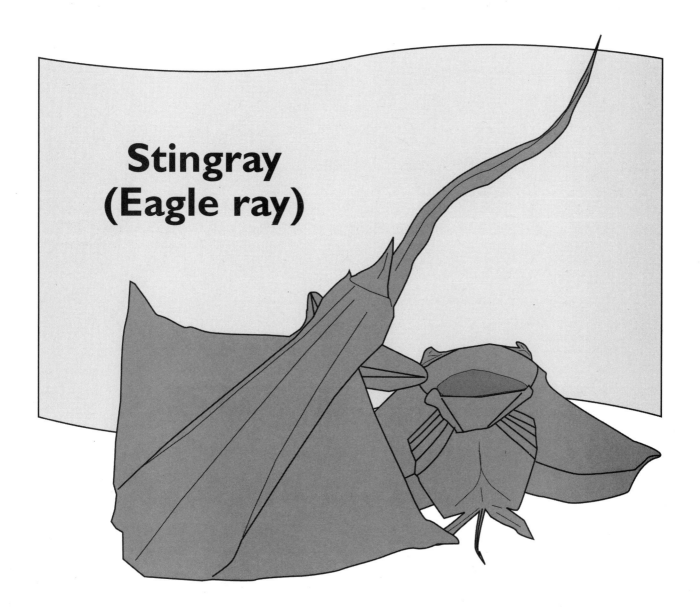

The paper can being of varied color. It is recommended 7.9x7.9 inches (20x20 cm) or bigger.

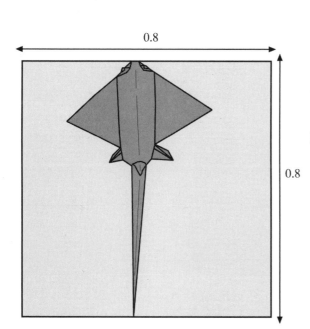

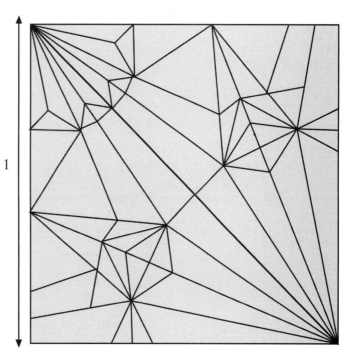

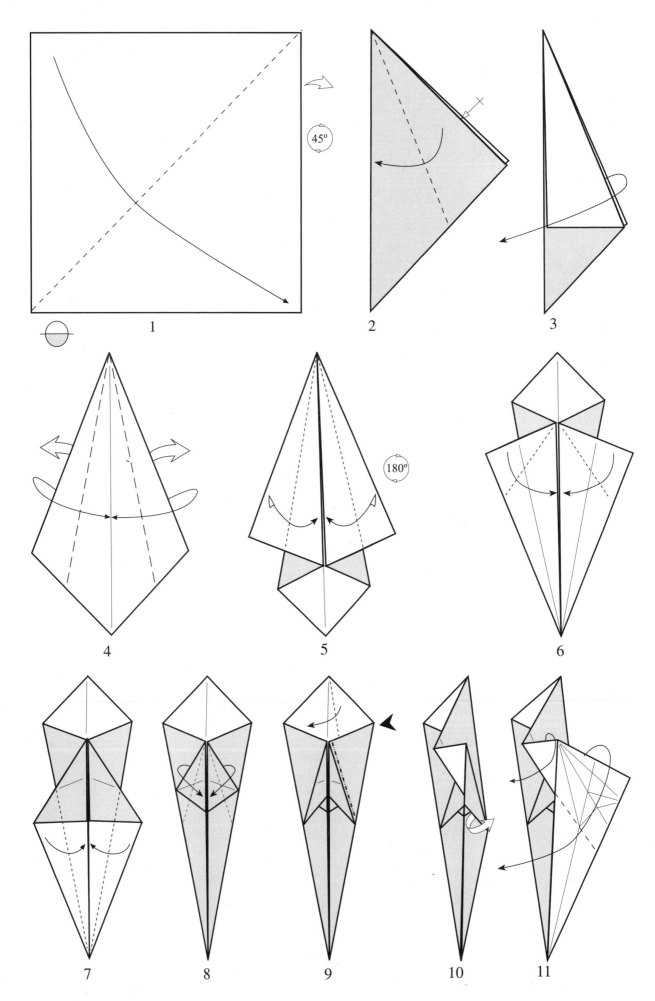

1

2

3

4

5

6

7

8

9

10

11

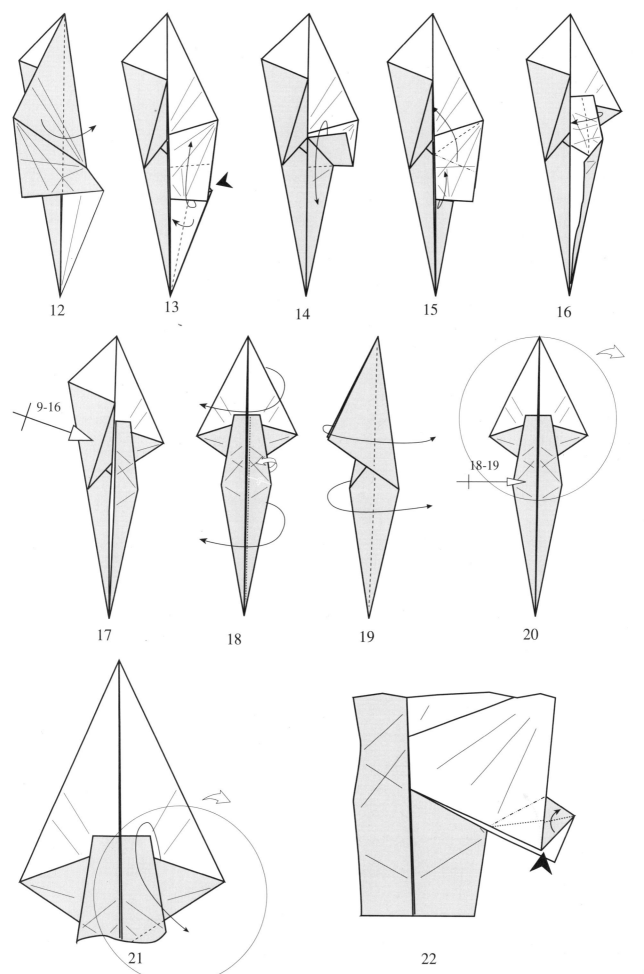

12

13

14

15

16

9-16

17

18

19

18-19

20

21

22

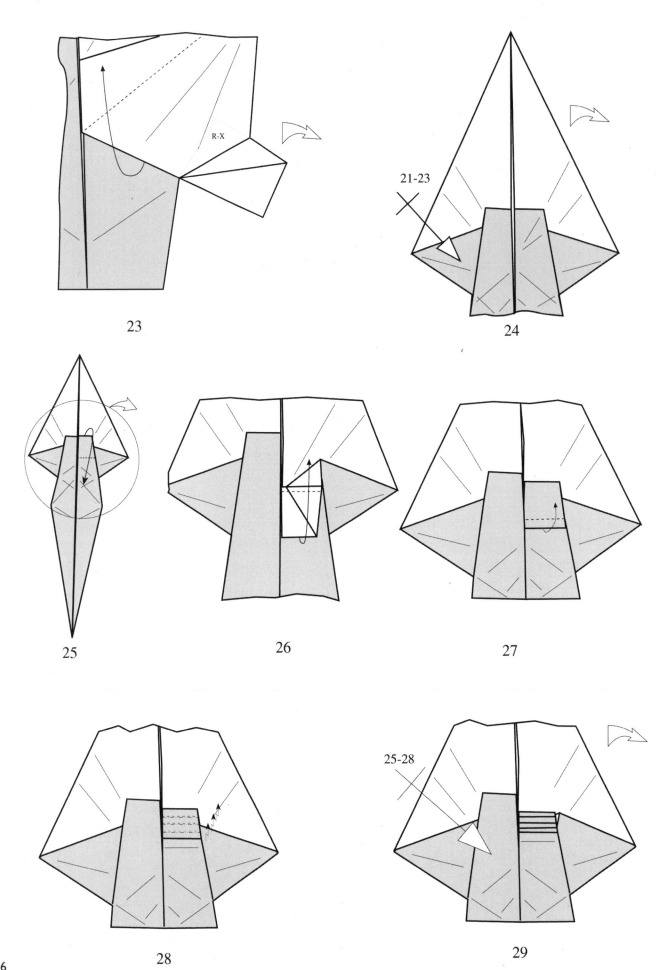

23

24

25

26

27

28

29

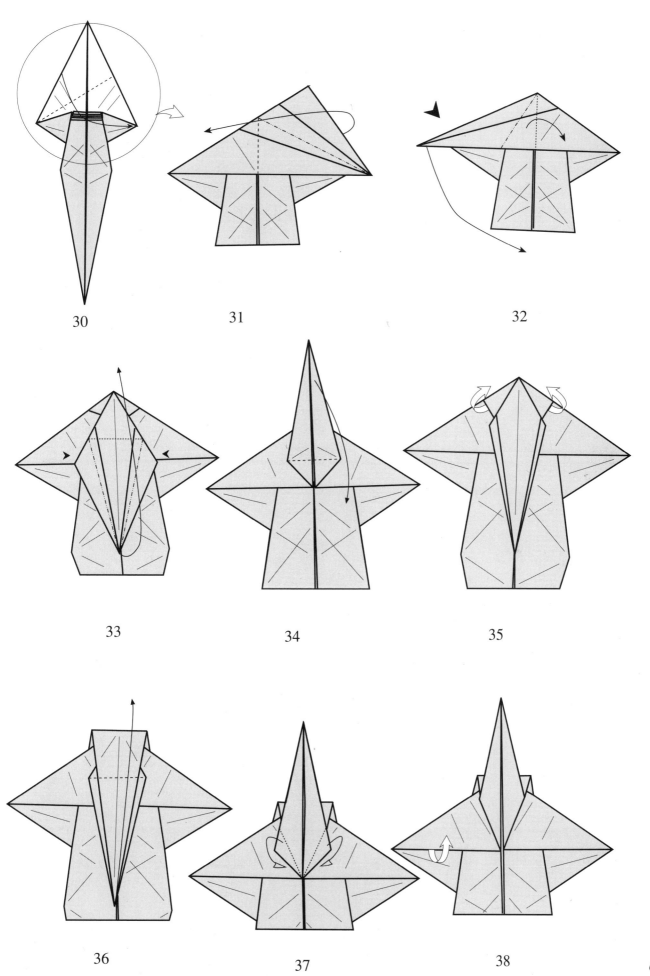

30

31

32

33

34

35

36

37

38

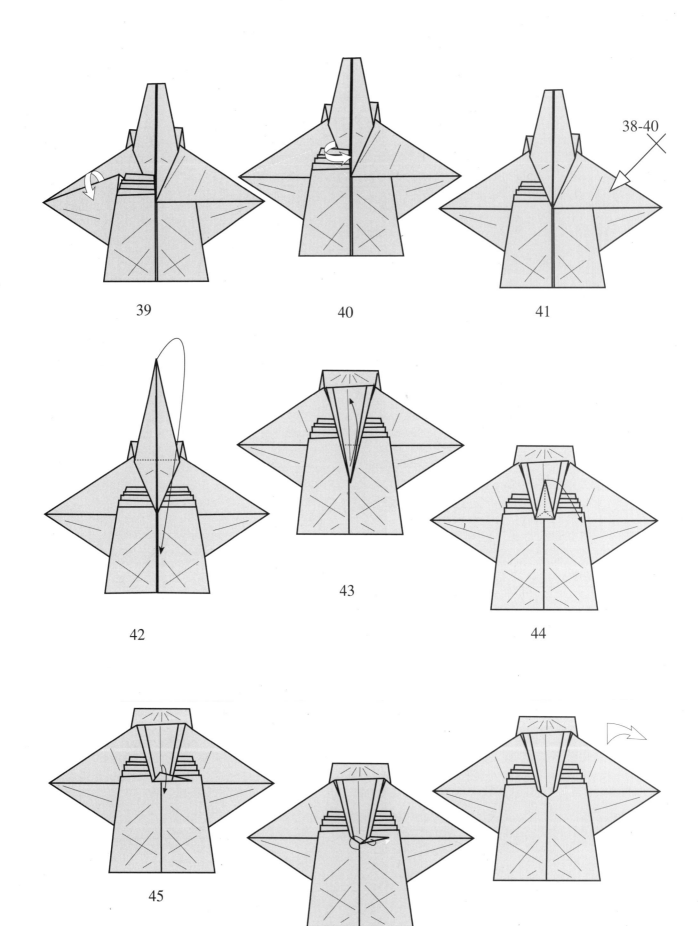

39

40

41

38-40

42

43

44

45

46

47

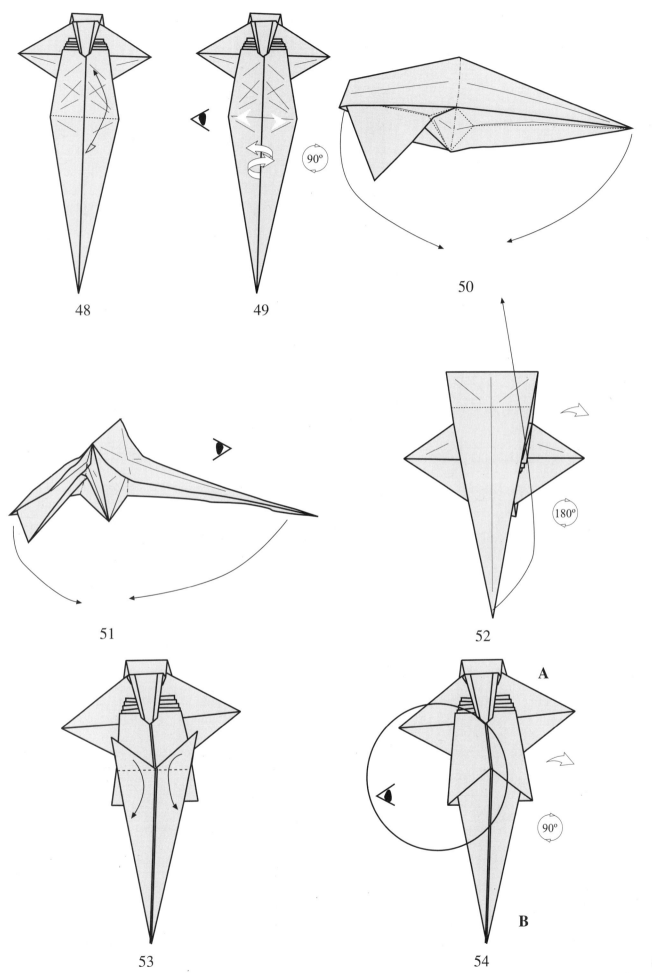

48

49

90°

50

51

52

180°

53

54

A

B

90°

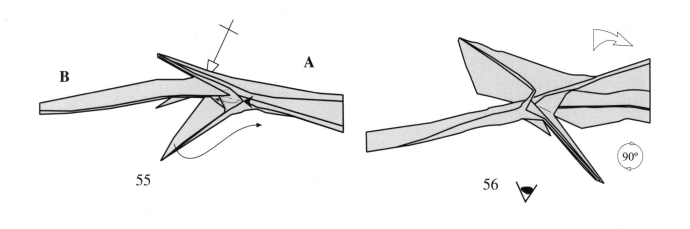

B   A

55

56   90°

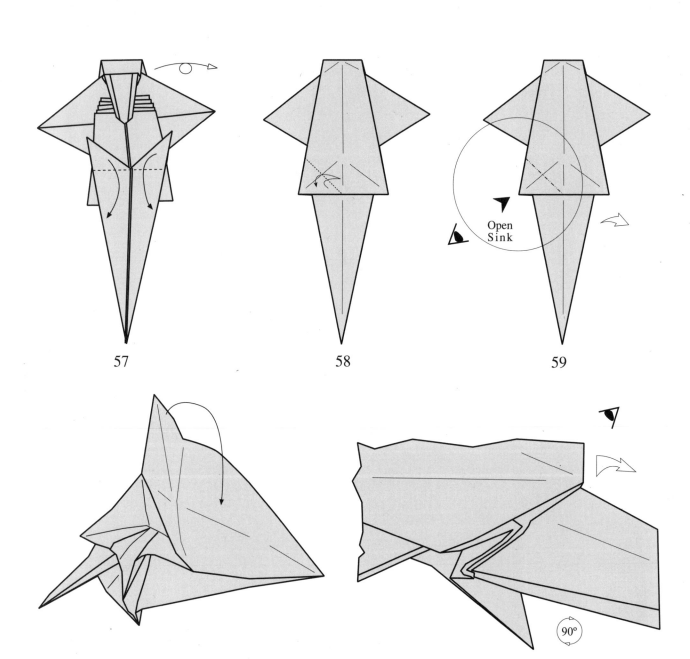

57

58

Open
Sink

59

60

61   90°

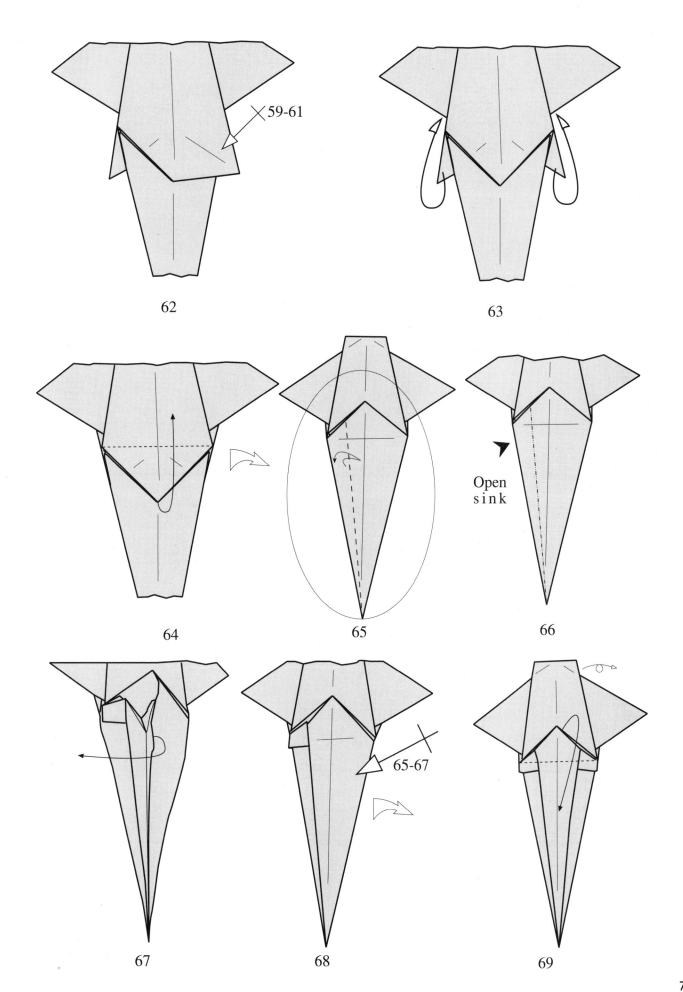

62

63

64

65

66

Open
sink

67

68

65-67

69

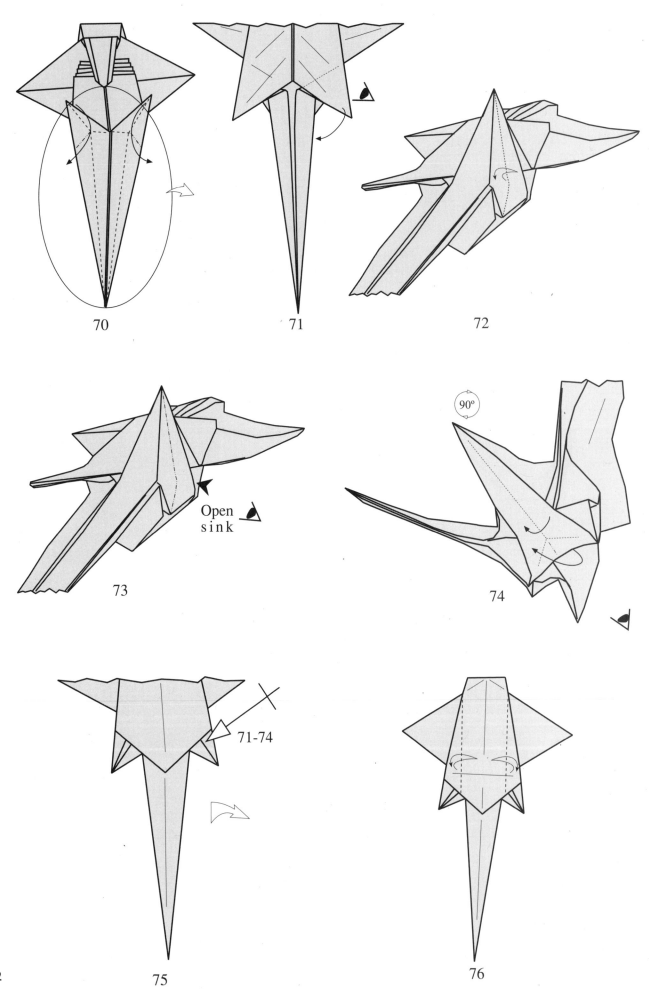

70

71

72

73

Open
sink

90°

74

71-74

75

76

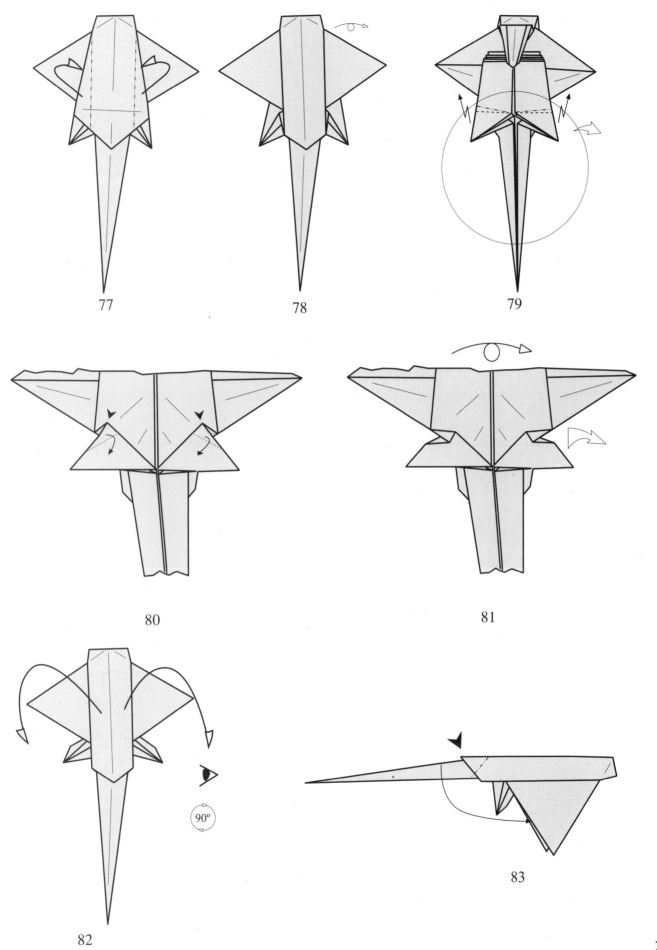

77

78

79

80

81

82

90°

83

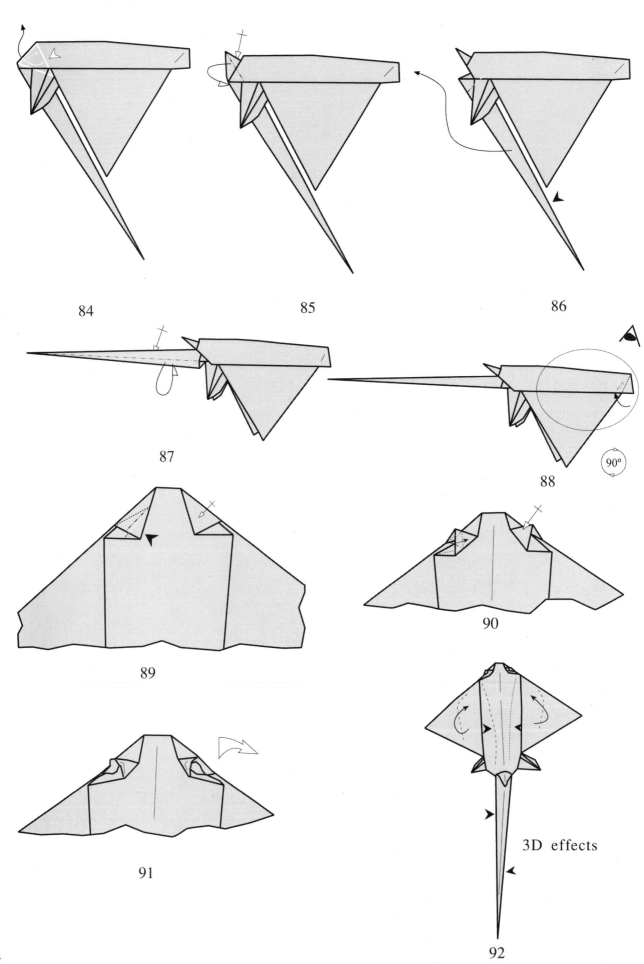

84

85

86

87

88

90°

89

90

91

92

3D effects

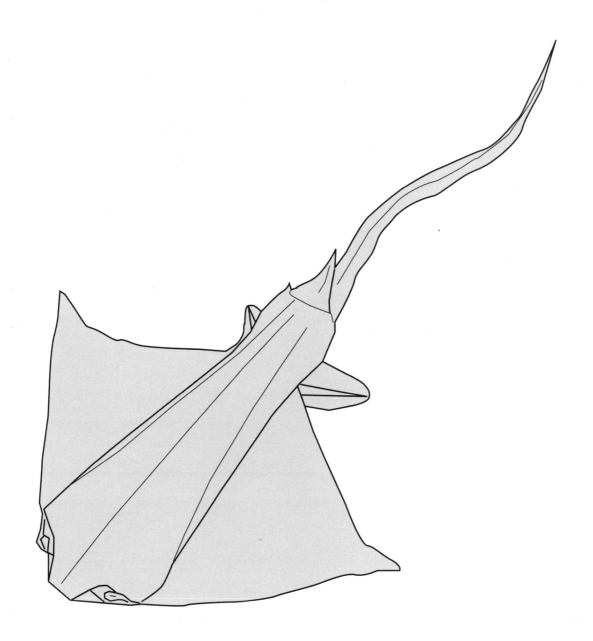

93

Nile Crocodile

The paper should be gray or dark green.

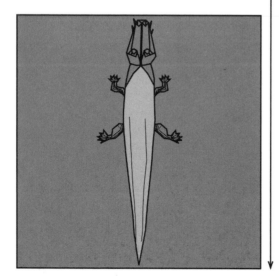

0.7

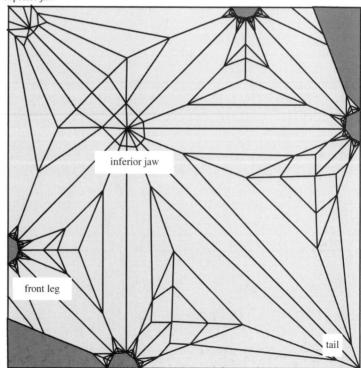

superior jaw

1

inferior jaw

front leg

tail

back leg

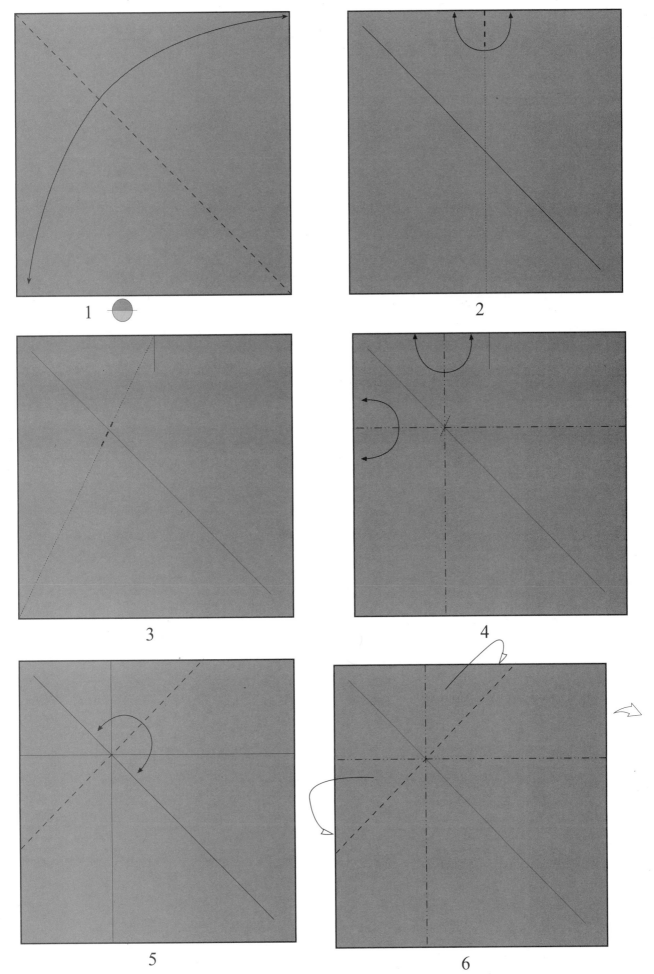

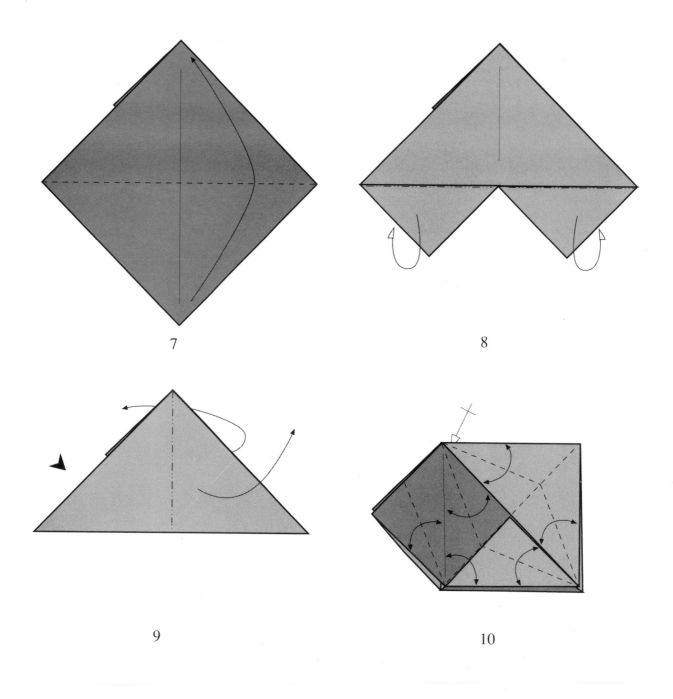

7

8

9

10

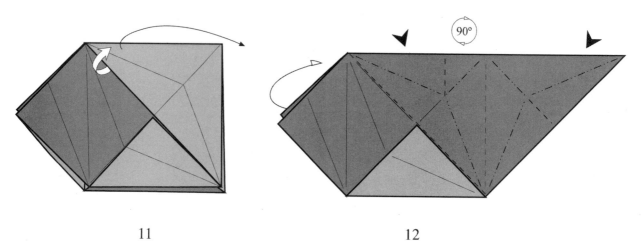

11

12

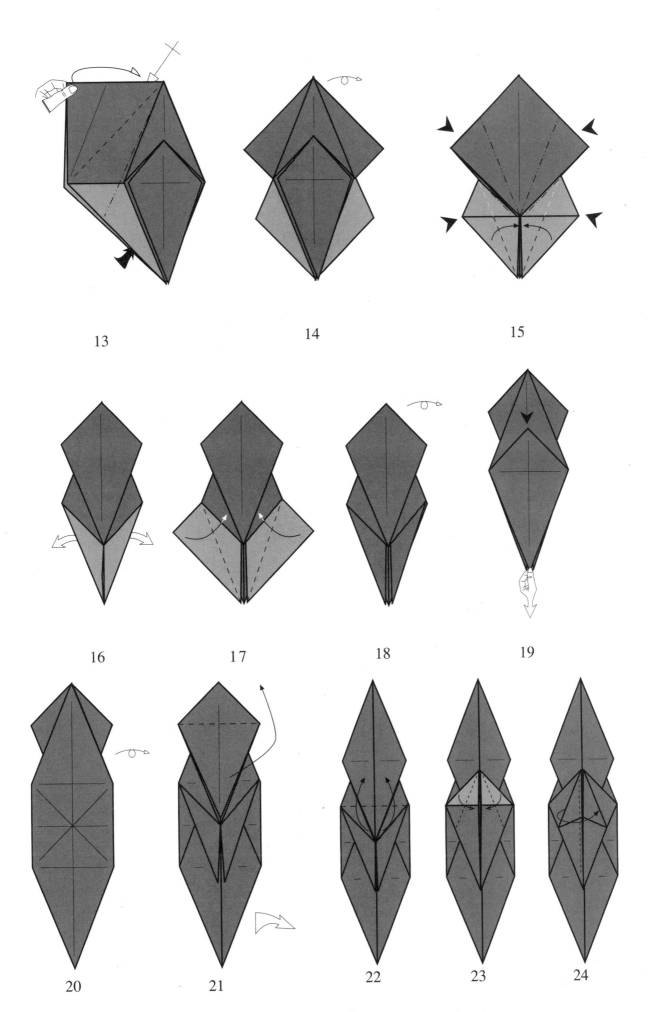

13

14

15

16

17

18

19

20

21

22

23

24

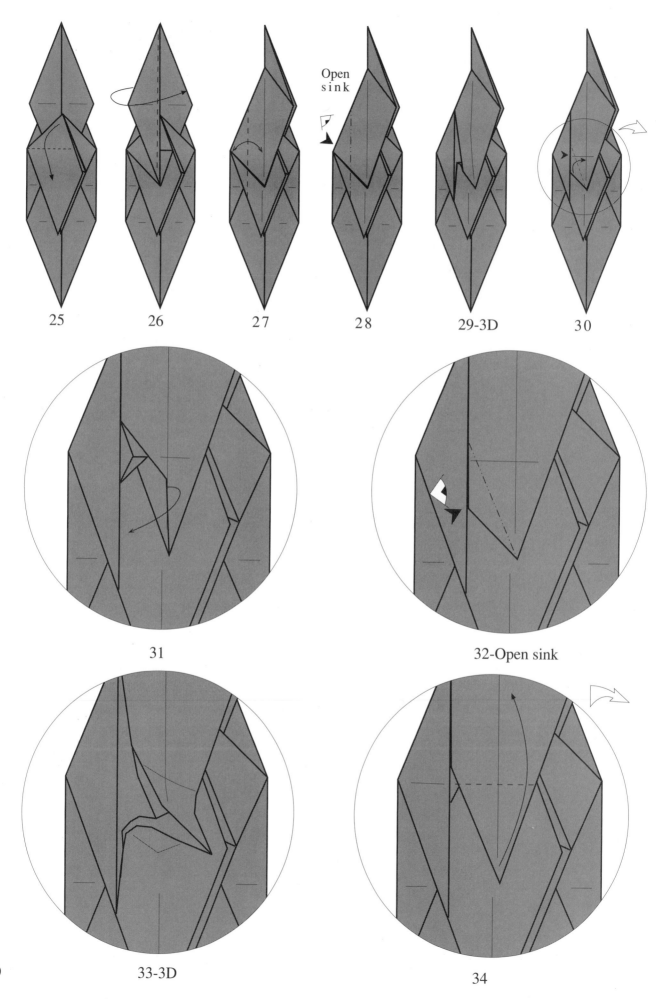

Open
sink

25   26   27   28   29-3D   30

31   32-Open sink

33-3D   34

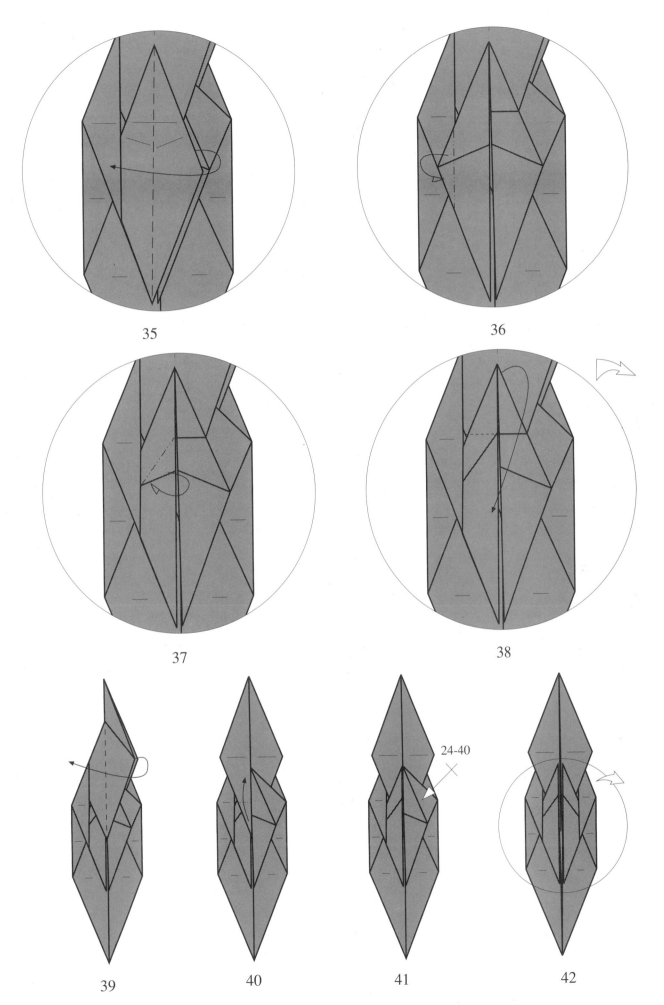

35

36

37

38

24-40

39

40

41

42

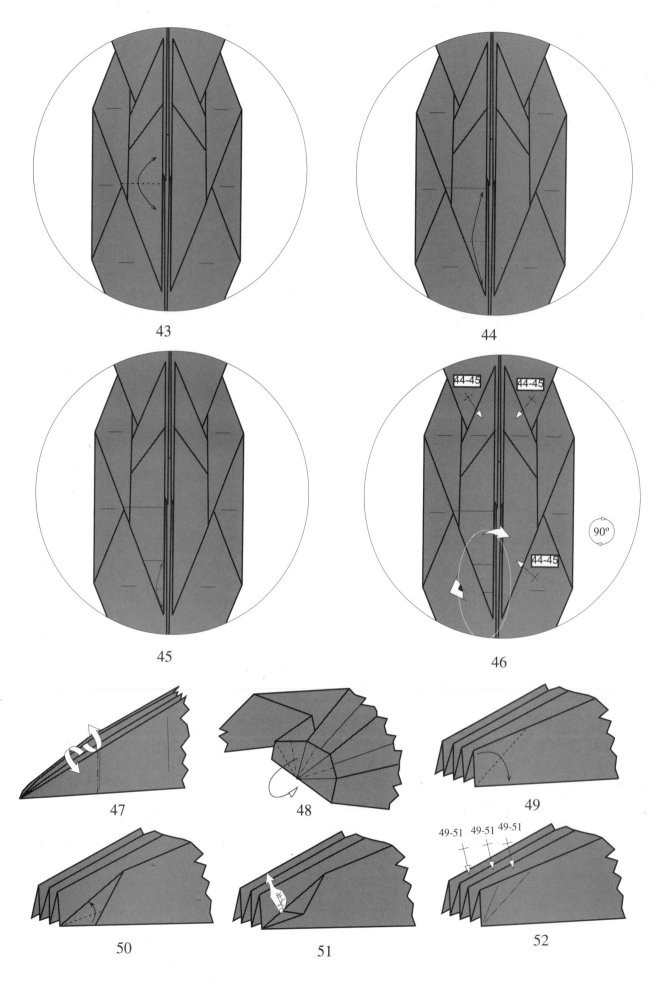

43

44

45

46

90°

44-45

44-45

44-45

47

48

49

50

51

52

49-51 49-51 49-51

82

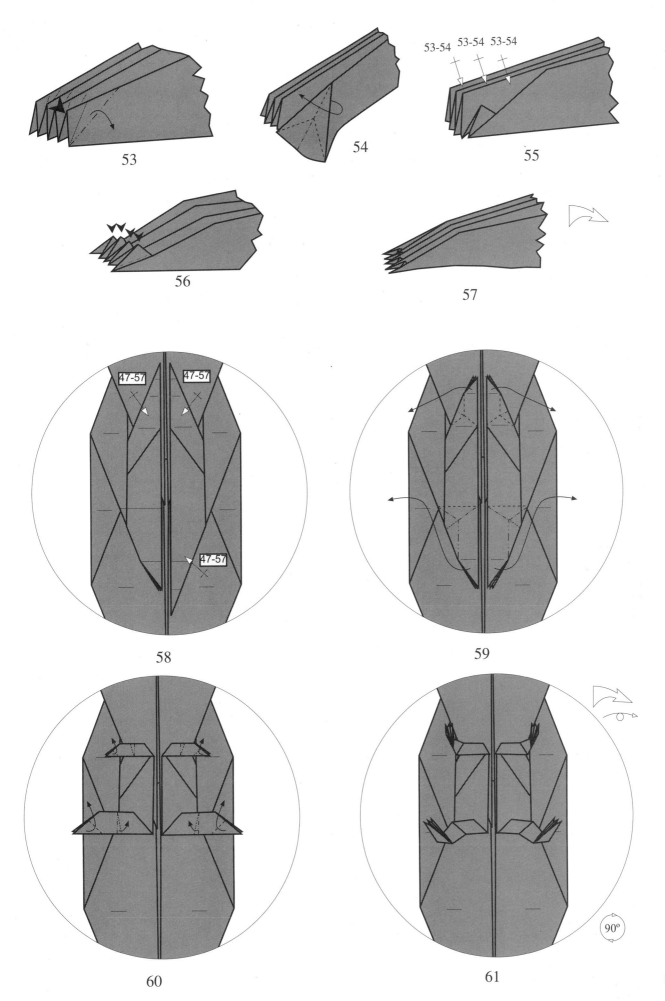

53

54

55
53-54 53-54 53-54

56

57

47-57 47-57

47-57

58

59

60

61

90°

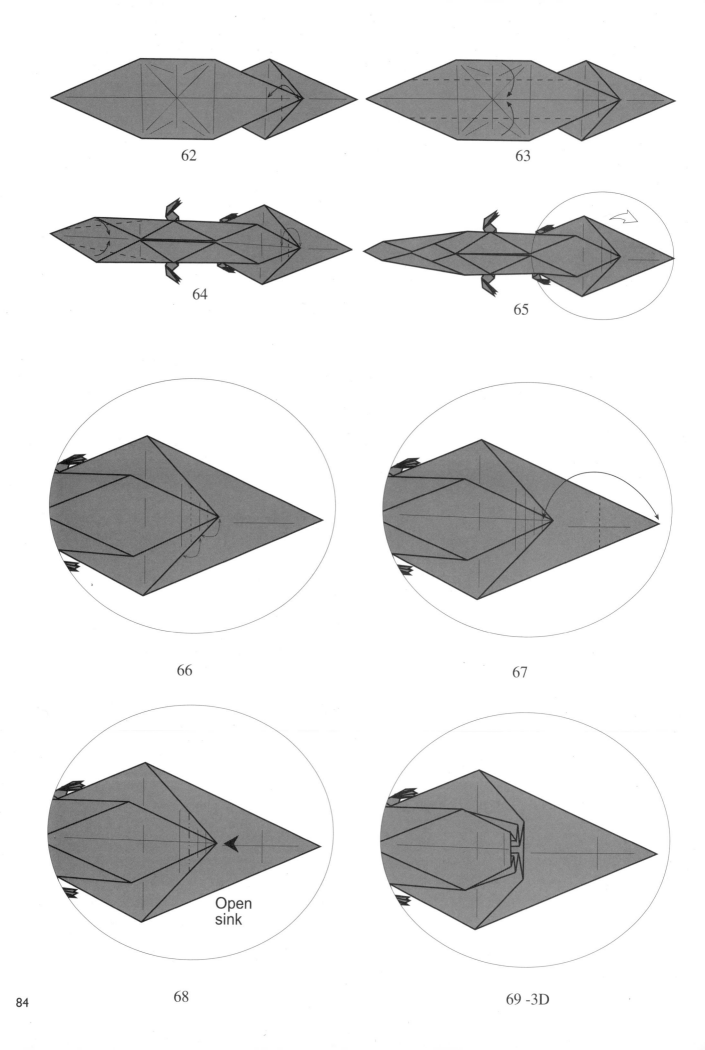

62

63

64

65

66

67

Open
sink

68

69 -3D

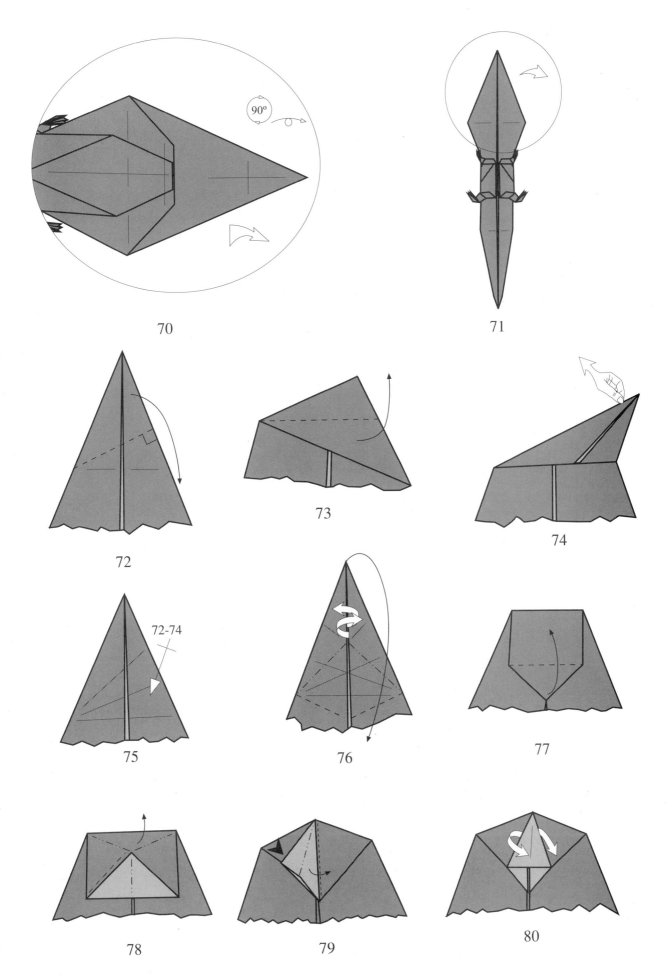

70

71

72

73

74

75

72-74

76

77

78

79

80

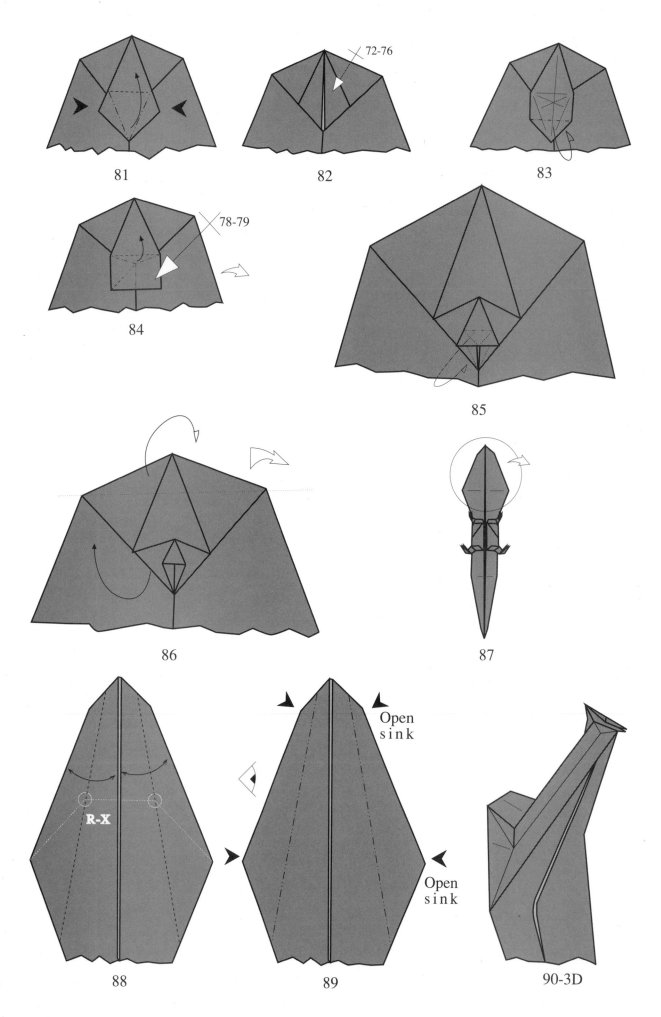

81

82

72-76

83

84

78-79

85

86

87

88

R-X

89

Open
sink

Open
sink

90-3D

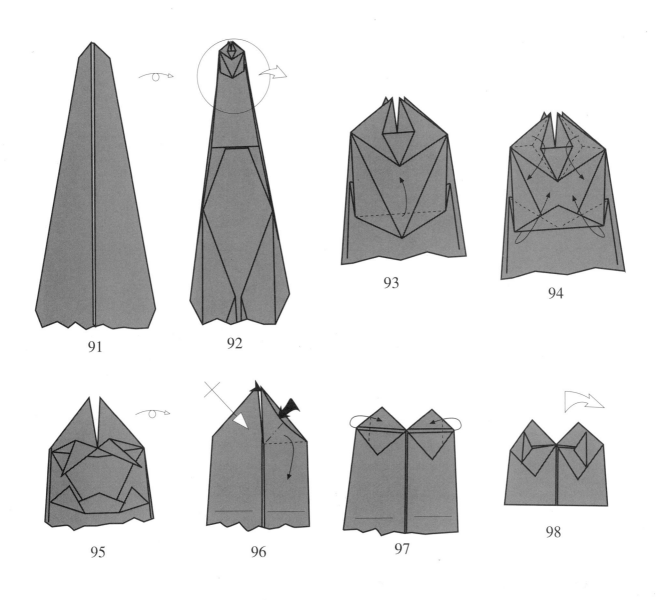

91 92 93 94

95 96 97 98

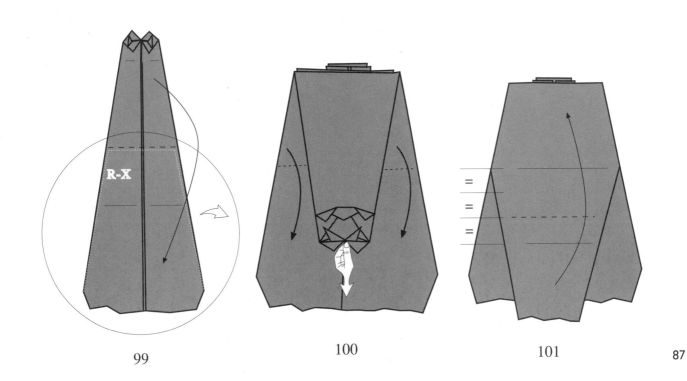

99 100 101

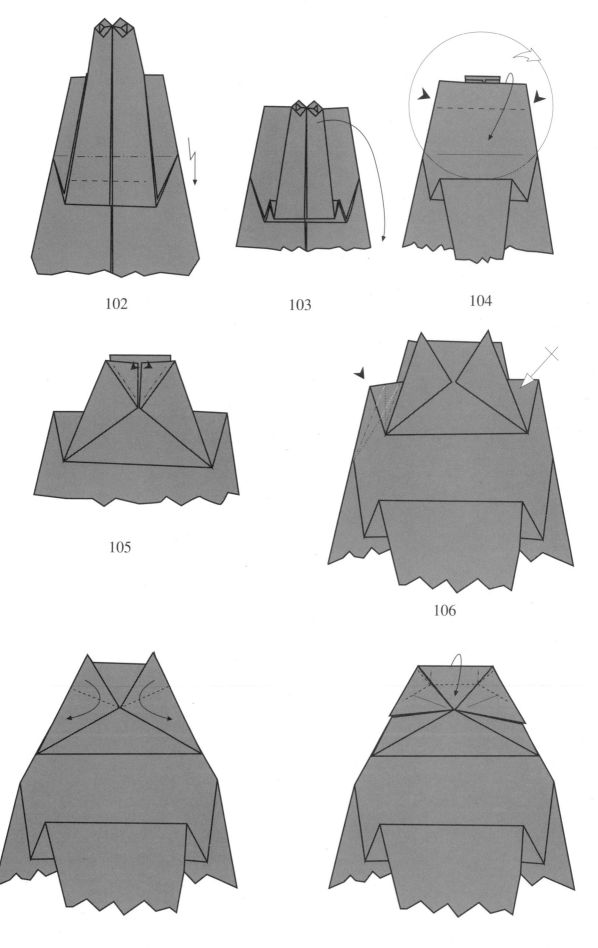

102

103

104

105

106

107

108

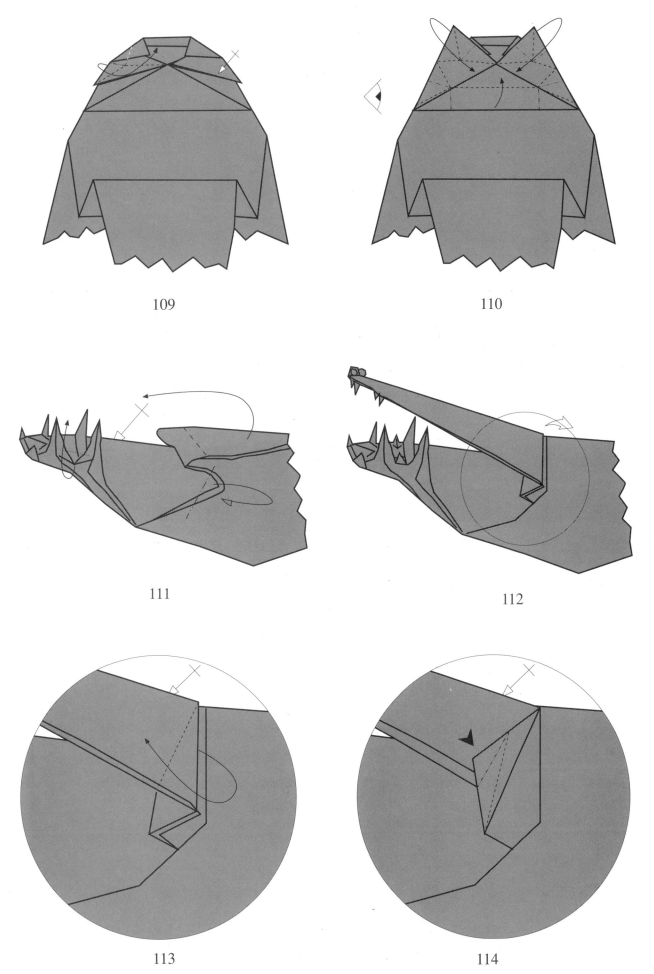

109

110

111

112

113

114

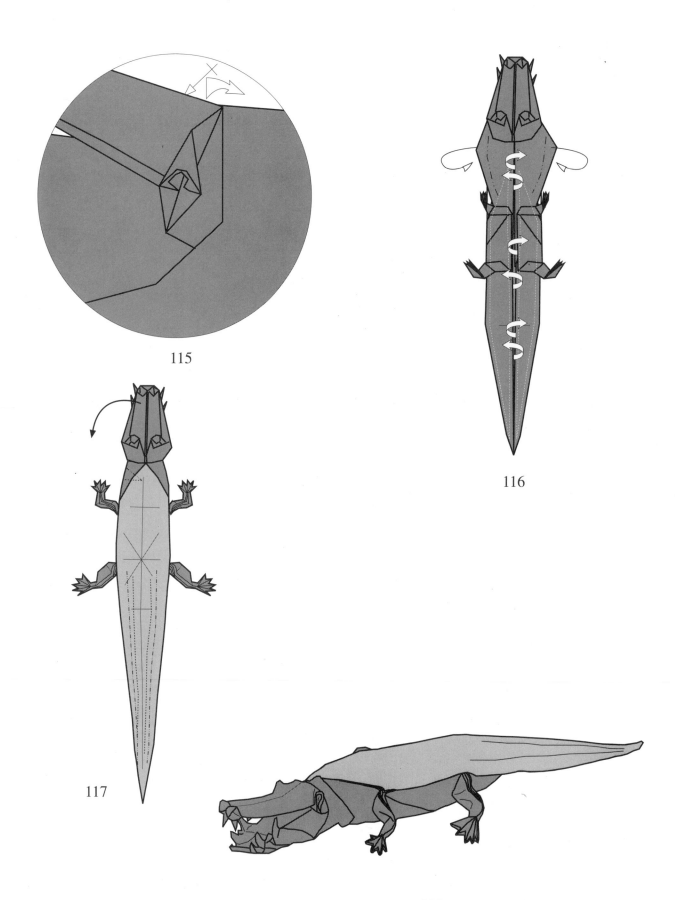

115

116

117

118

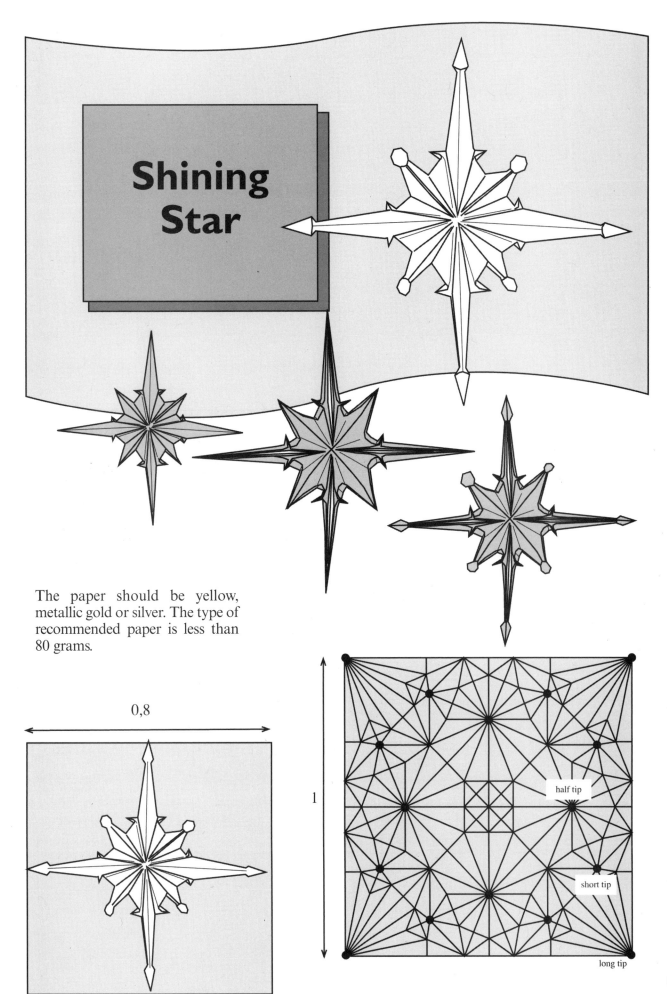

Shining Star

The paper should be yellow, metallic gold or silver. The type of recommended paper is less than 80 grams.

0,8

1

half tip

short tip

long tip

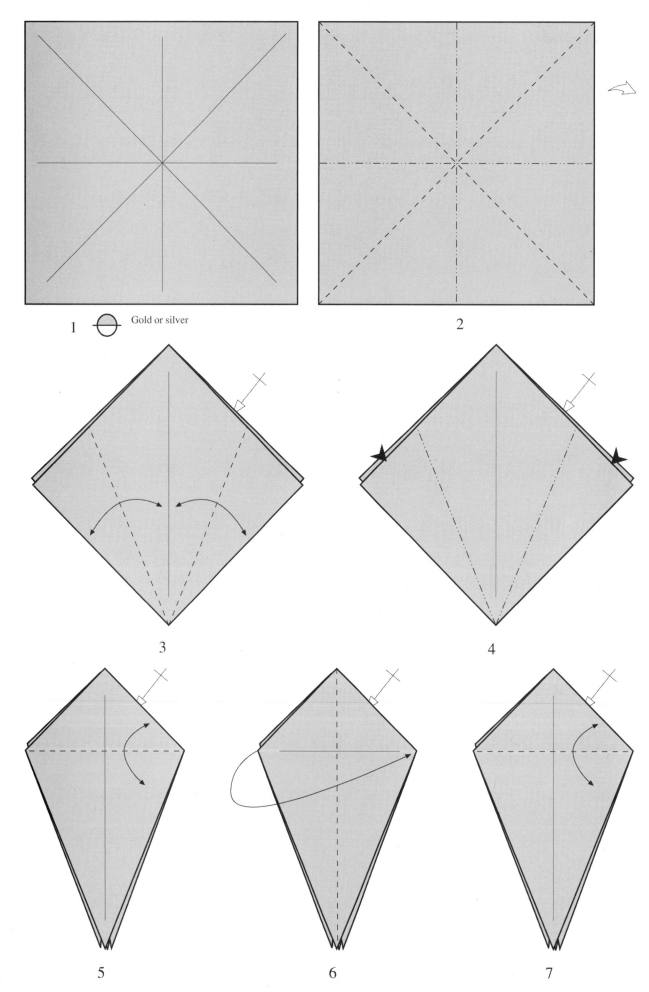

1 Gold or silver

2

3

4

5

6

7

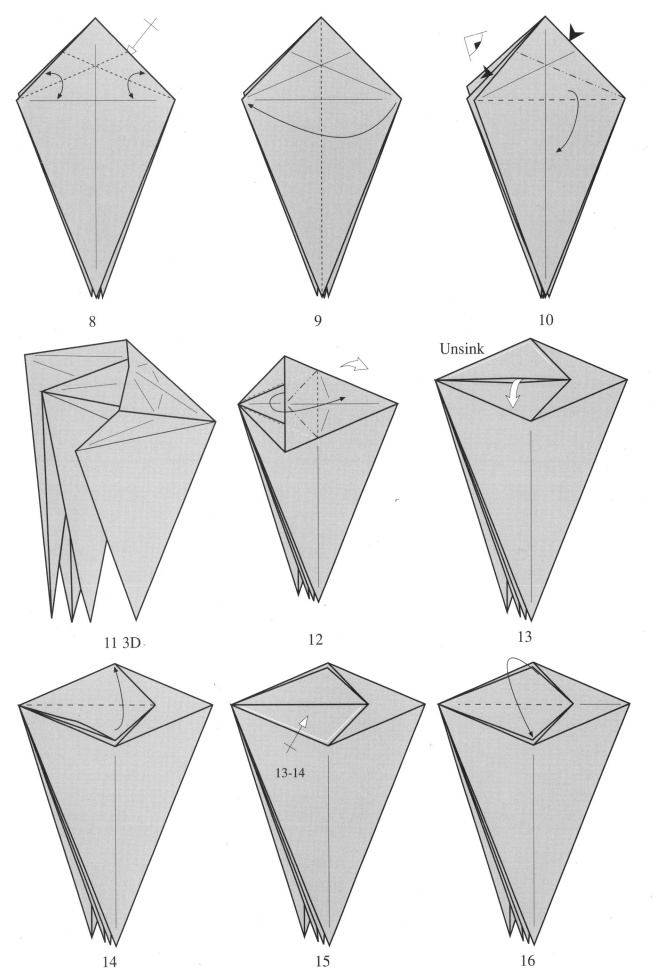

8

9

10

11 3D

12

Unsink

13

14

15

13-14

16

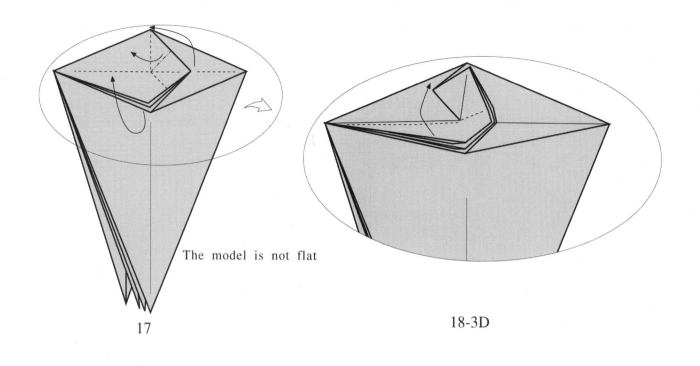

The model is not flat

17

18-3D

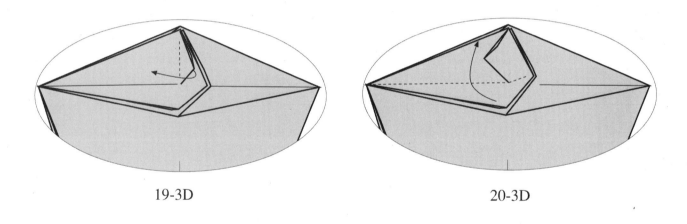

19-3D

20-3D

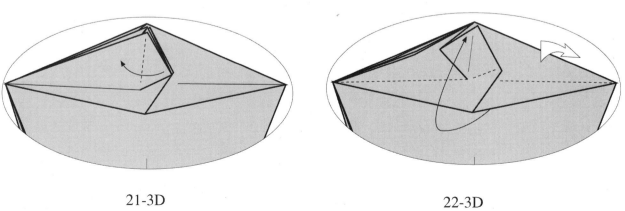

21-3D

22-3D

94

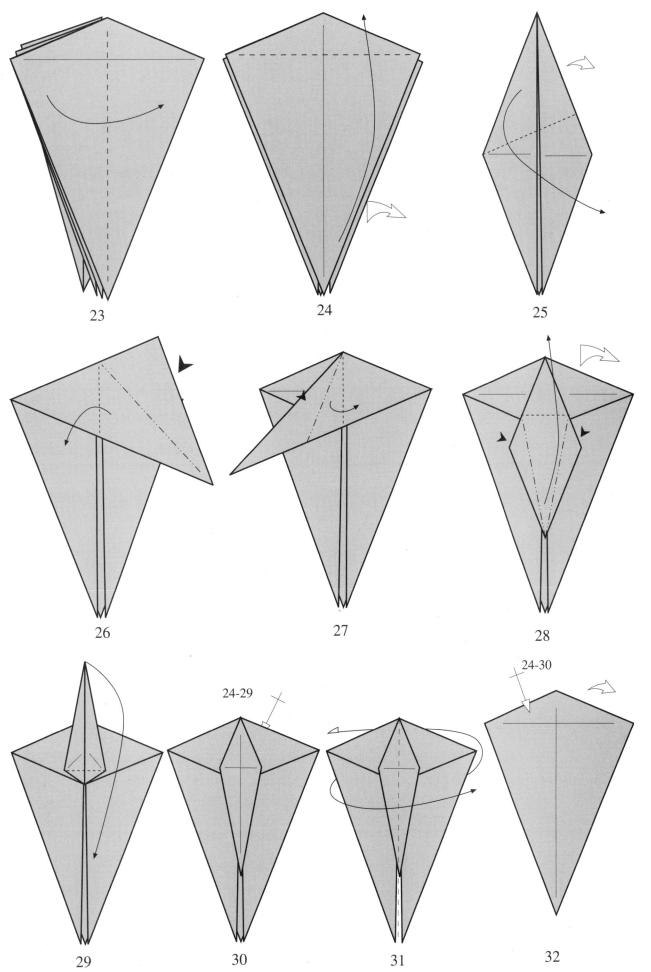

23

24

25

26

27

28

24-29

24-30

29

30

31

32

95

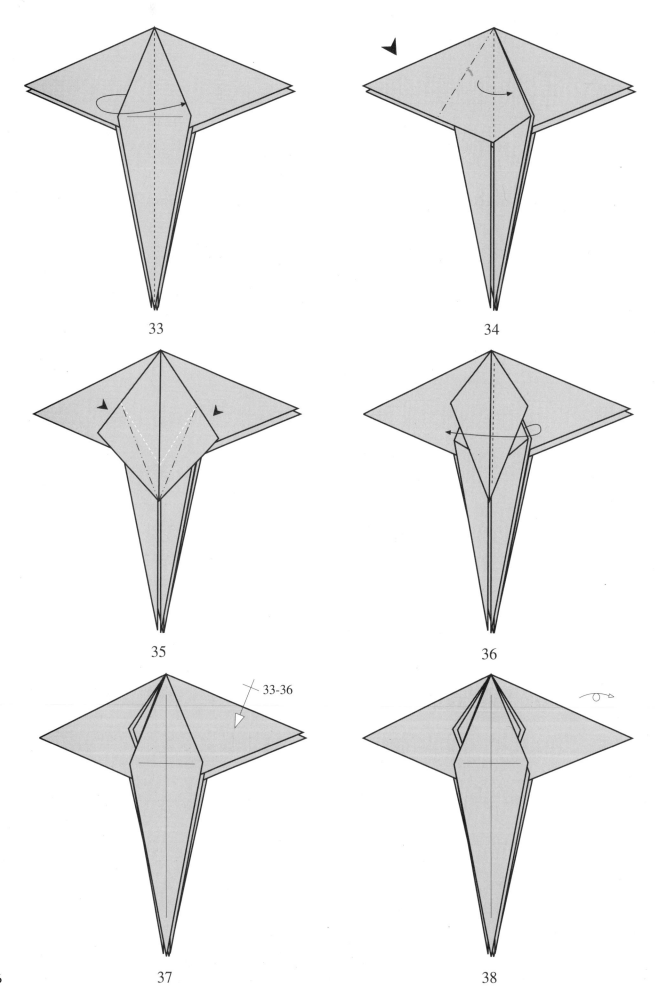

33

34

35

36

33-36

37

38

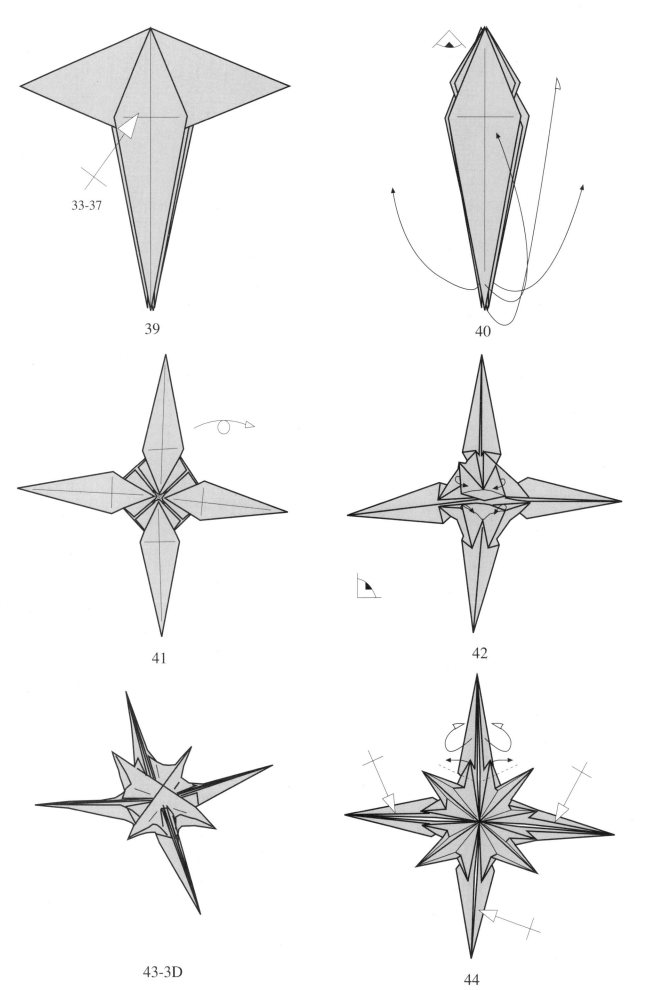

33-37

39

40

41

42

43-3D

44

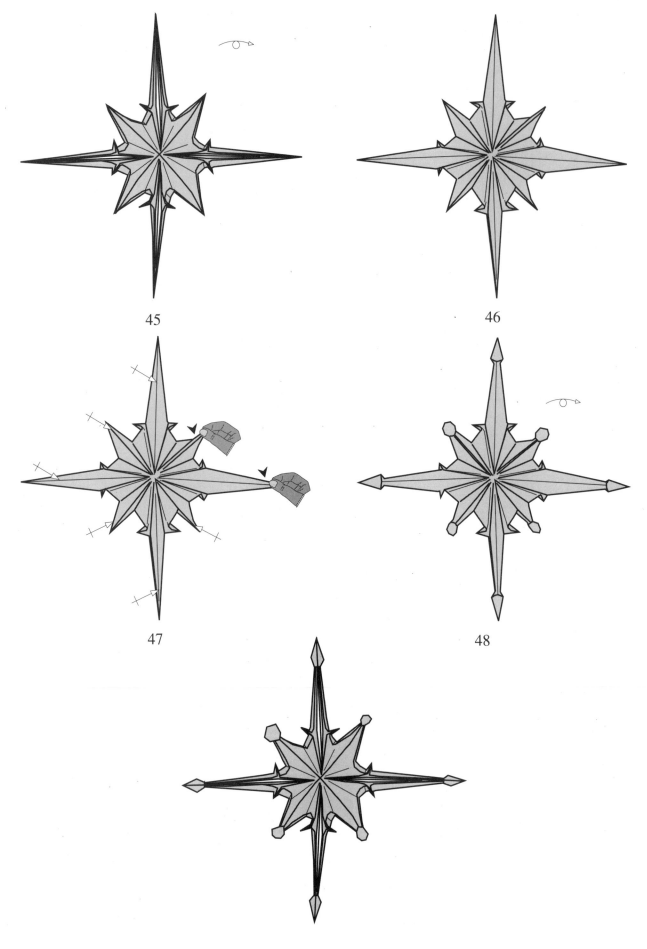

45

46

47

48

49

Black Swan and White Swan

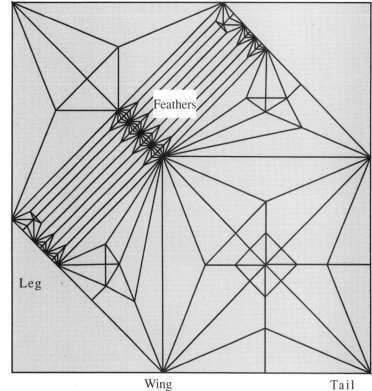

The paper should be white and orange for the white swan. Red and black for the black swan. It should be less than 40 grams, double silk or of the type "sandwich" and 13.75x13.75 inches (35x35 cm) or bigger.

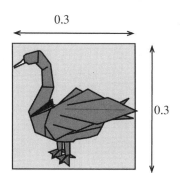

0.3

0.3

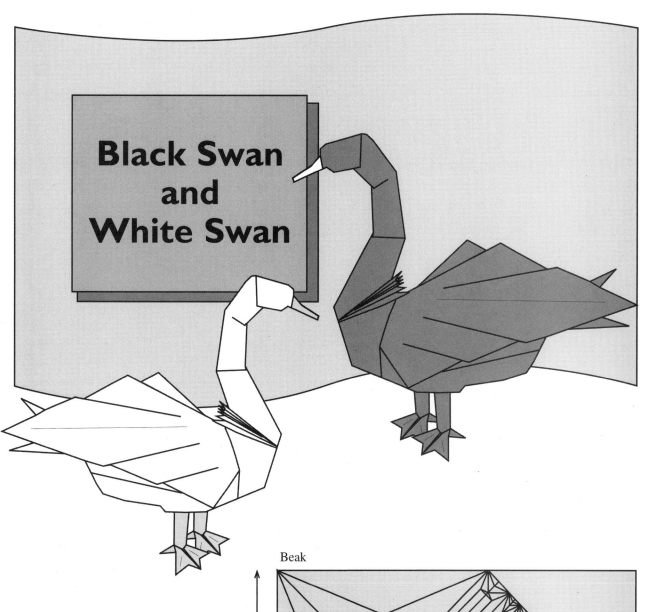

Beak

Feathers

1

Leg

Wing

Tail

Black Swan

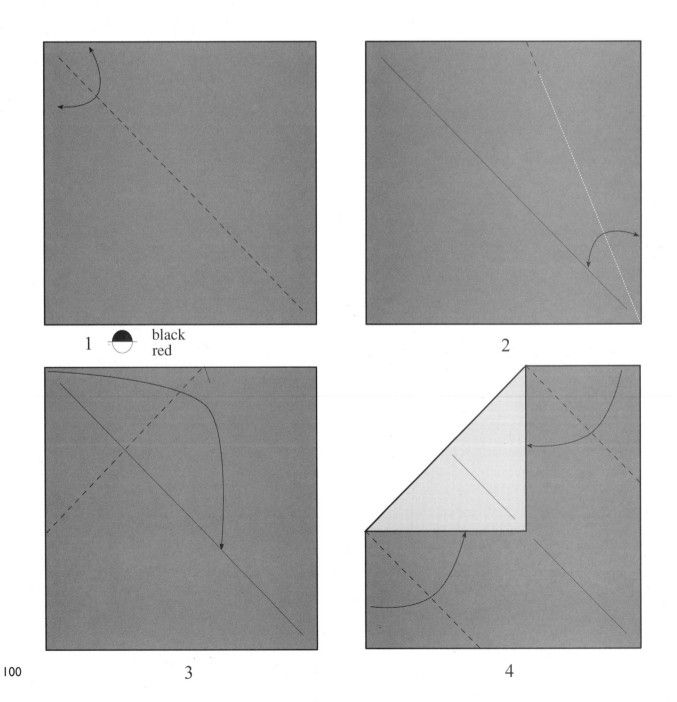

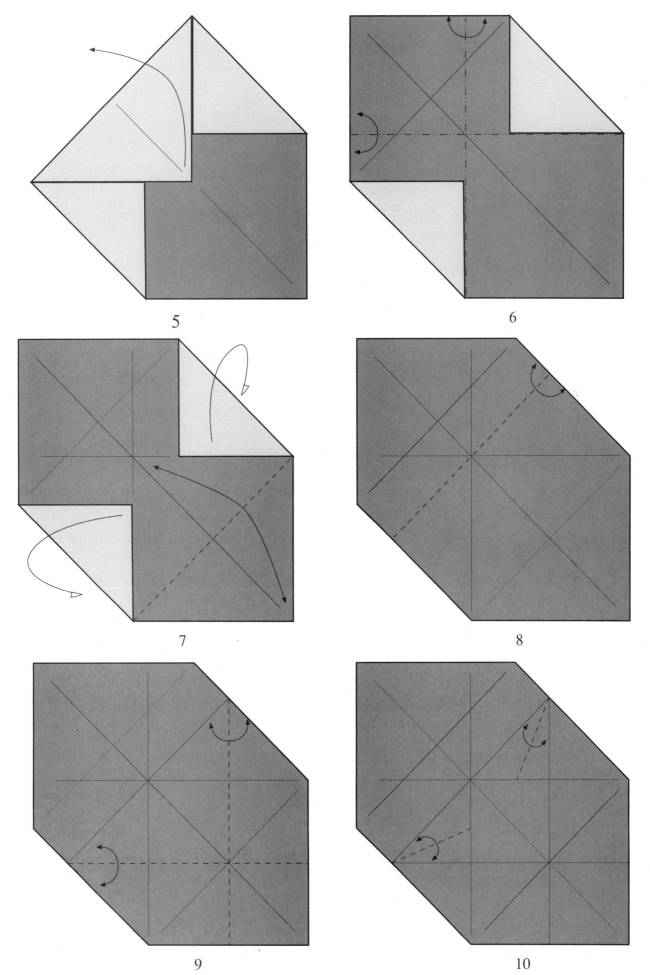

5

6

7

8

9

10

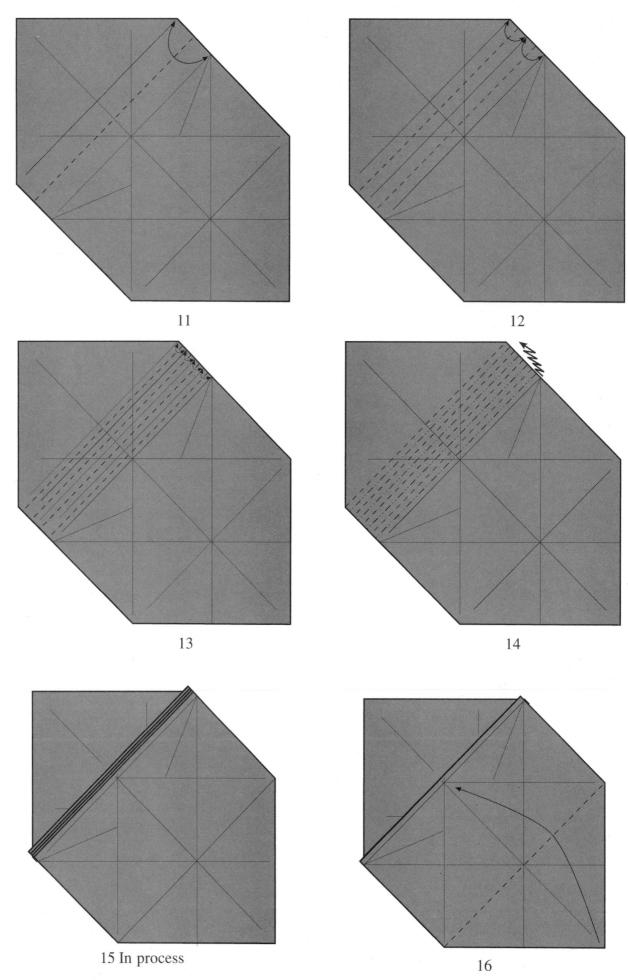

11

12

13

14

15 In process

16

102

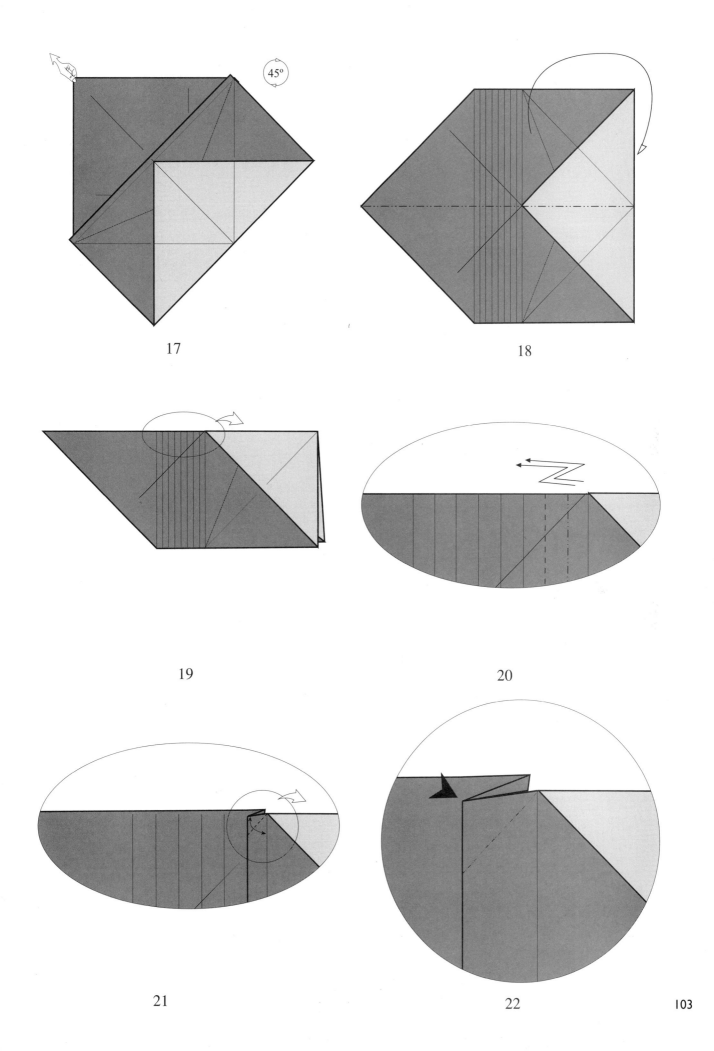

17

18

19

20

21

22

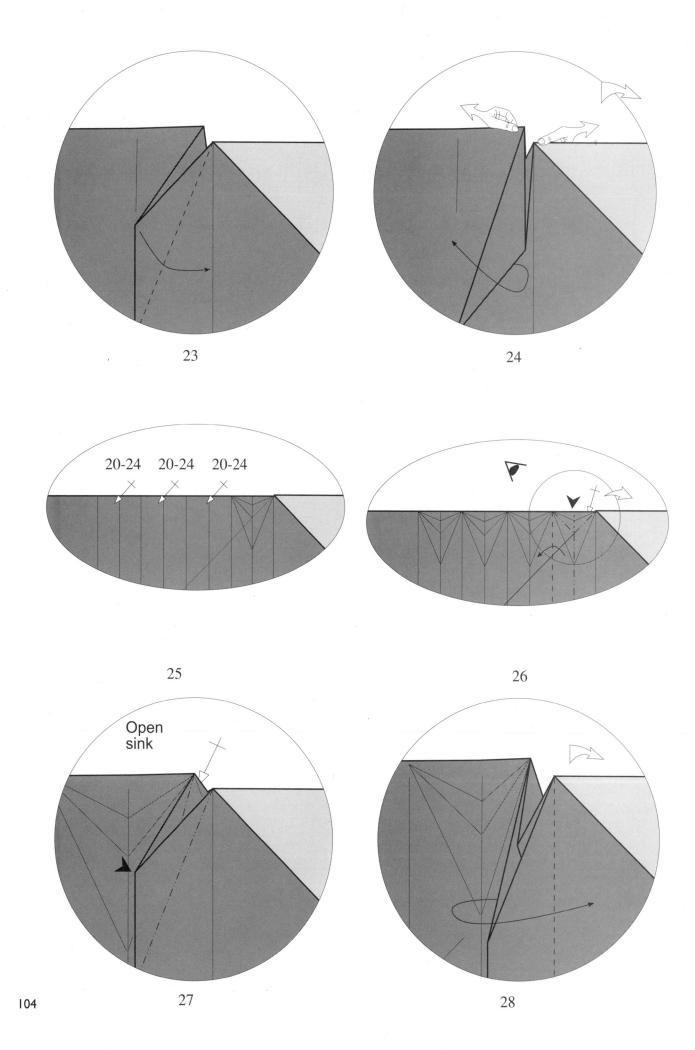

23

24

20-24 20-24 20-24

25

26

Open
sink

27

28

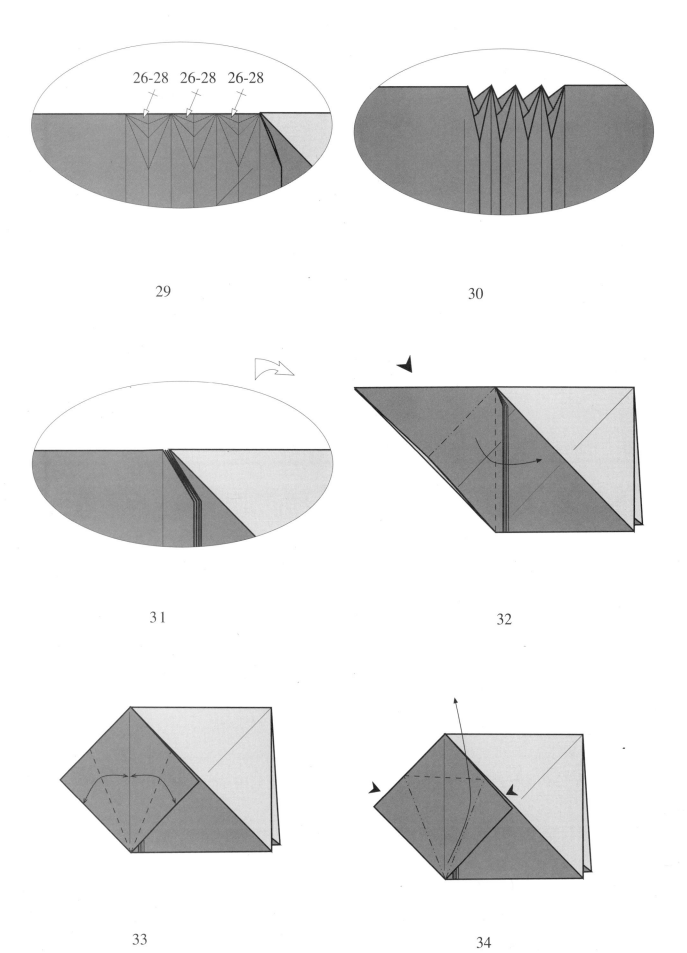

26-28　26-28　26-28

29

30

31

32

33

34

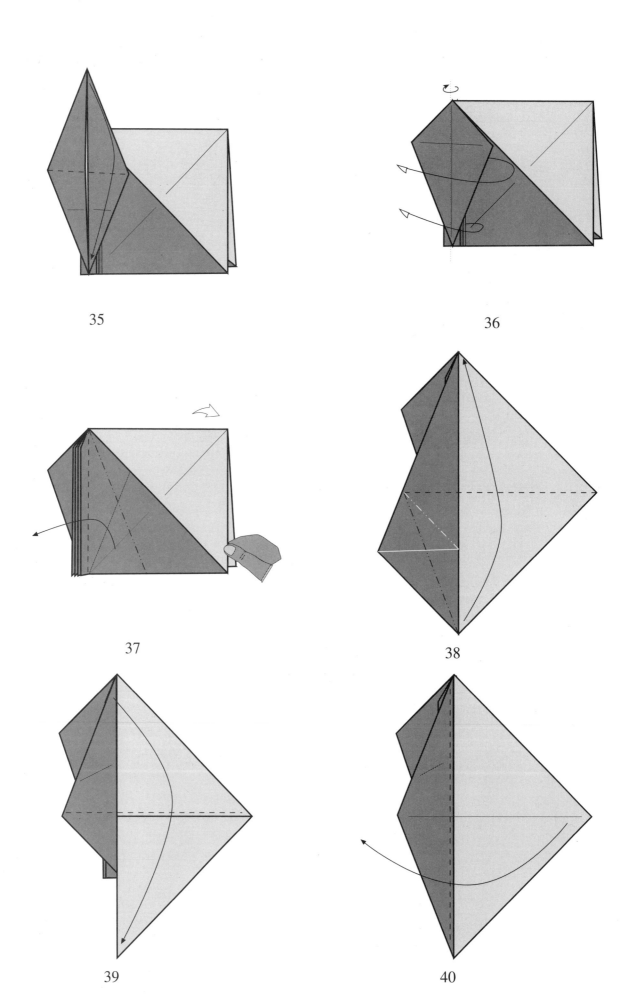

35

36

37

38

39

40

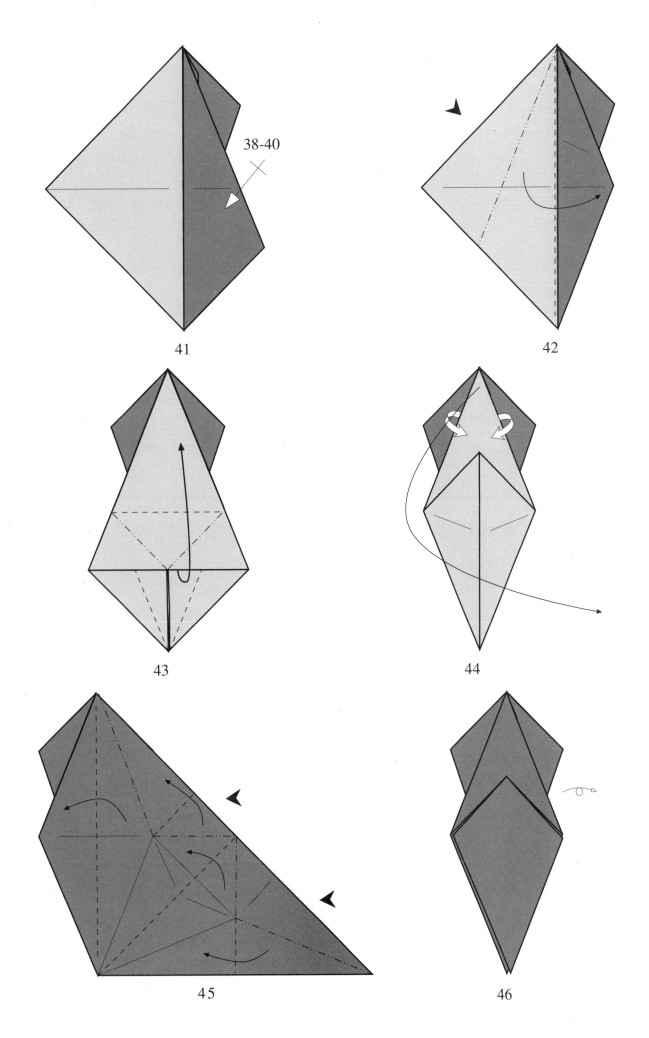

41

42

43

44

45

46

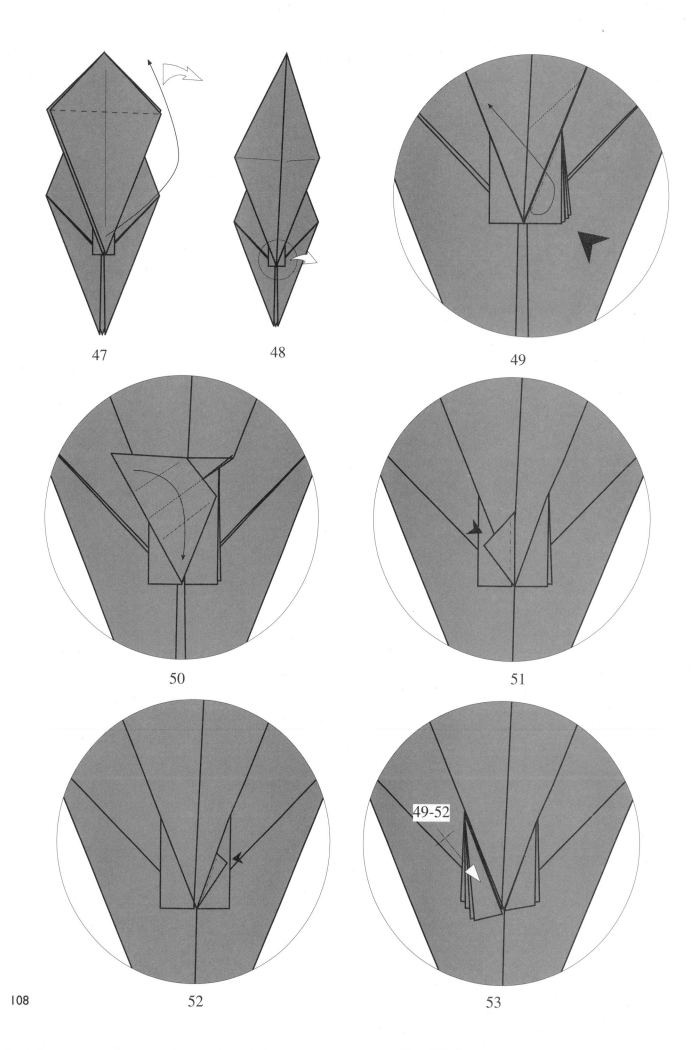

47

48

49

50

51

52

49-52

53

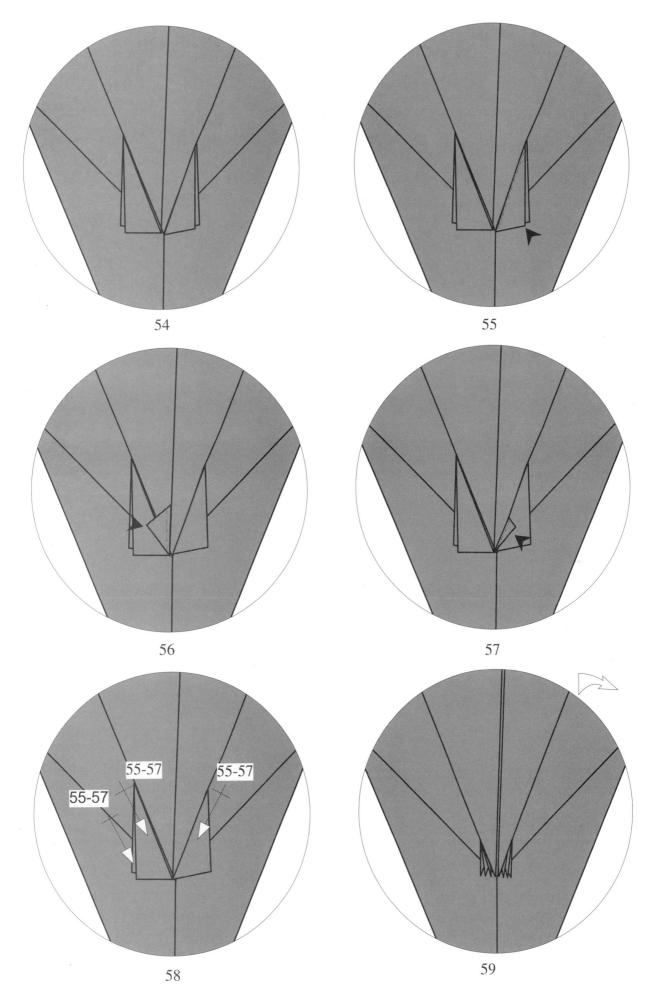

54

55

56

57

58

55-57   55-57

55-57

59

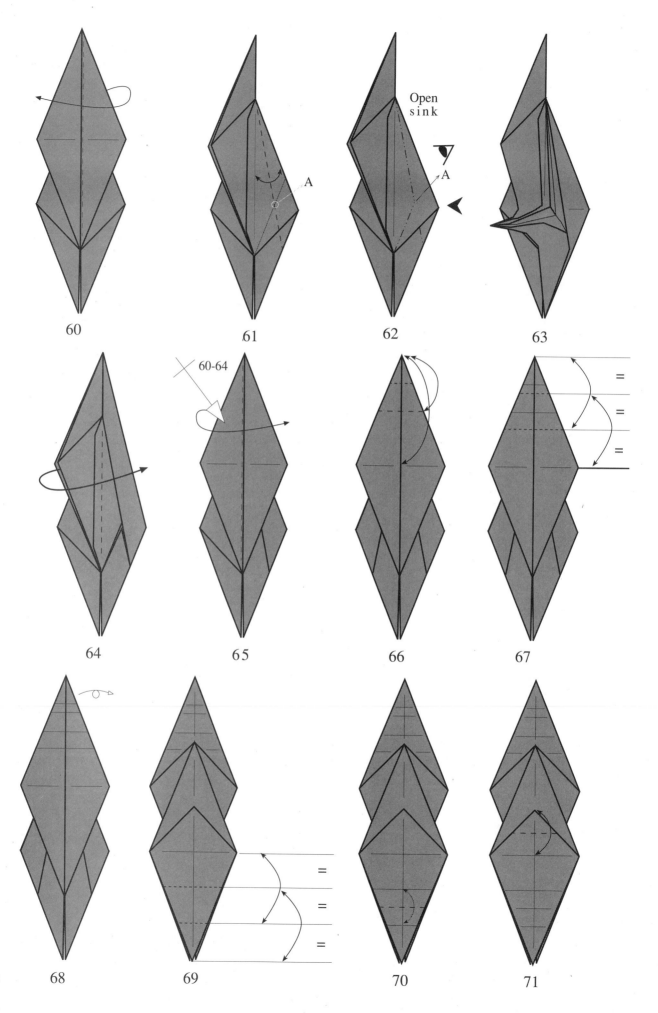

60

61

A

62

Open
sink

A

63

64

65

60-64

66

67

=
=
=

68

69

=
=
=

70

71

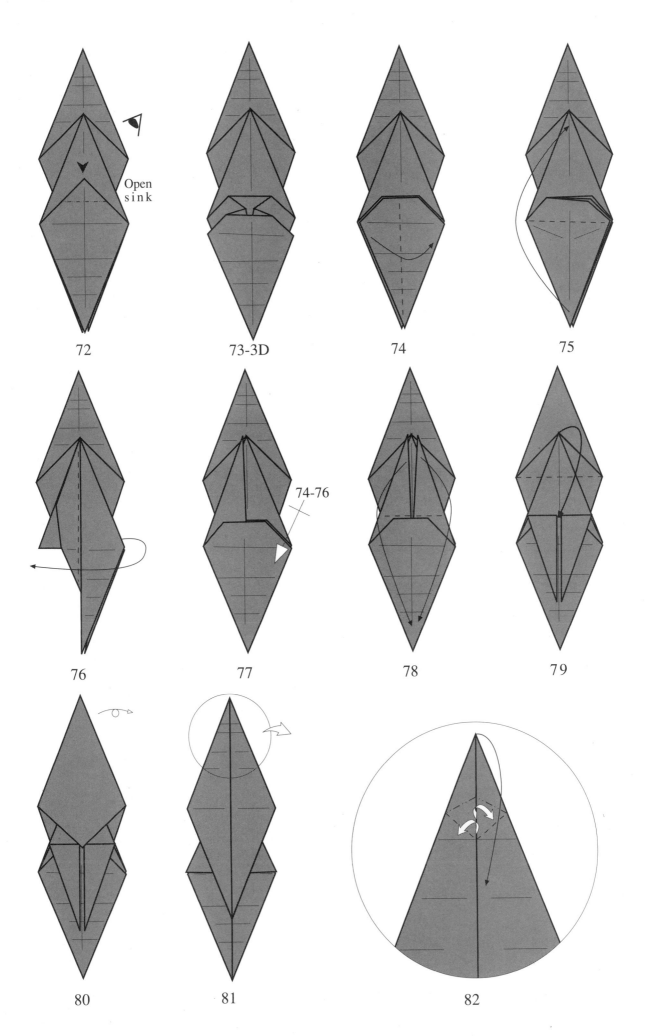

72

Open
sink

73-3D

74

75

76

77

74-76

78

79

80

81

82

111

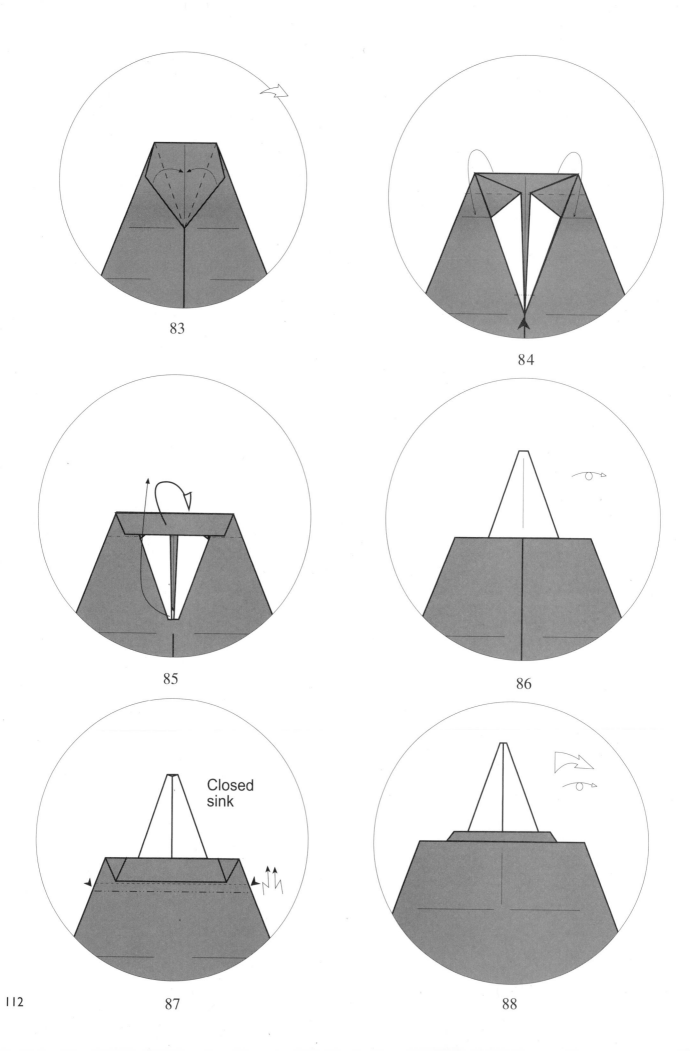

83

84

85

86

Closed
sink

87

88

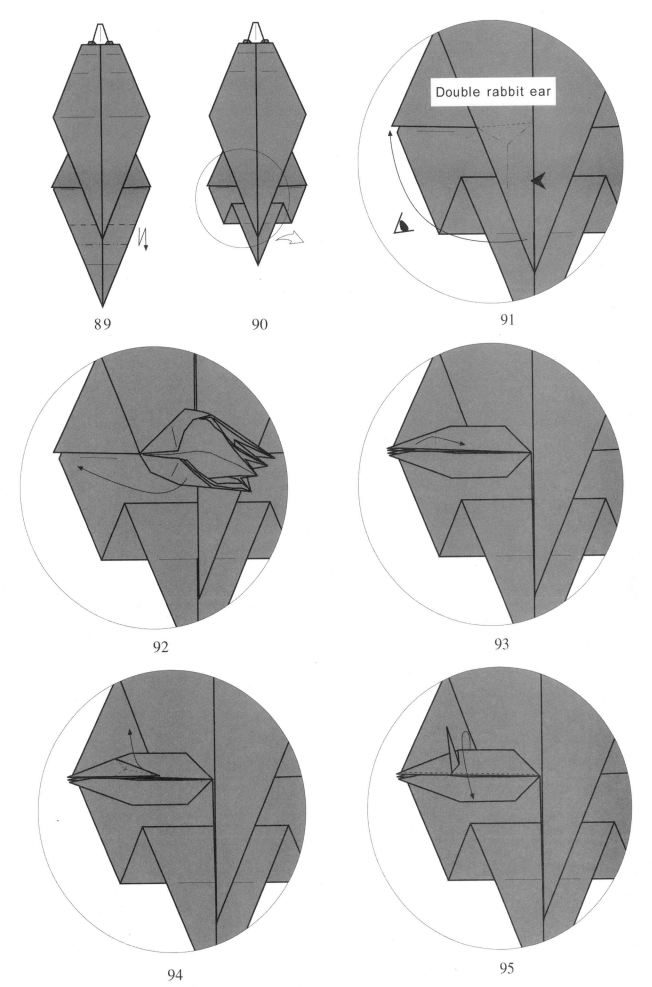

89

90

91

Double rabbit ear

92

93

94

95

113

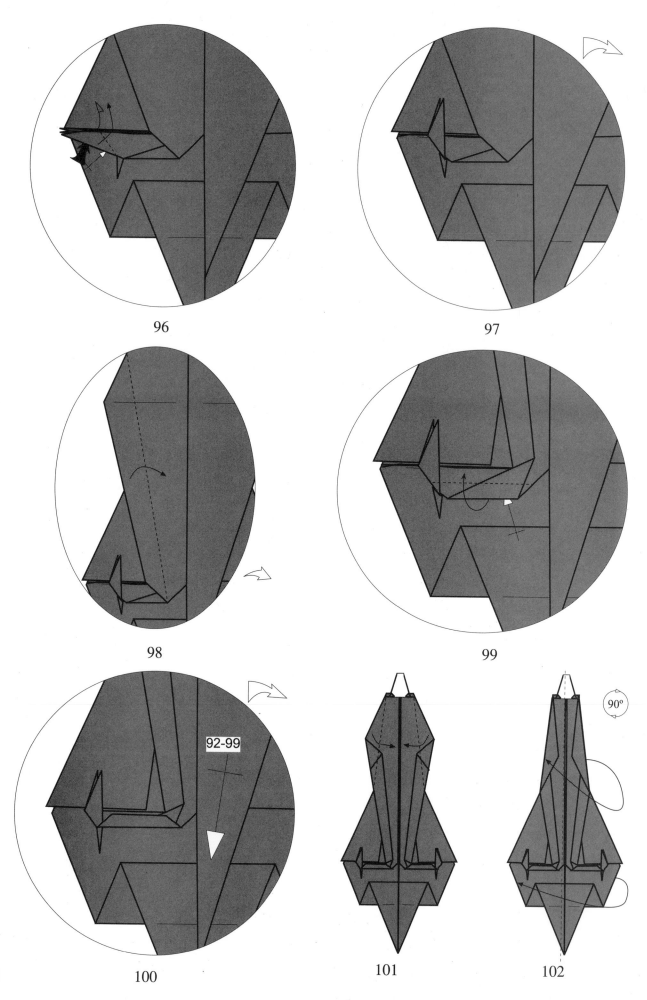

96

97

98

99

92-99

100

101

102

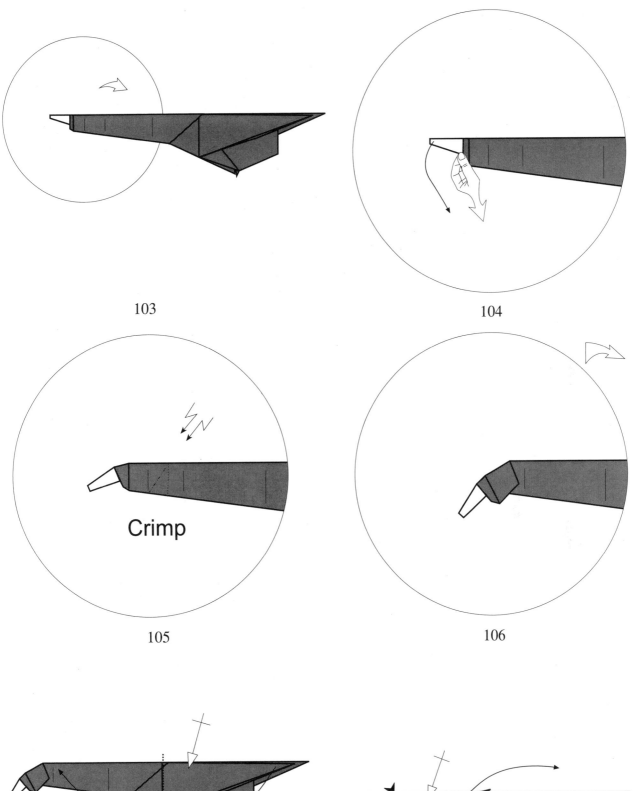

103

104

Crimp

105

106

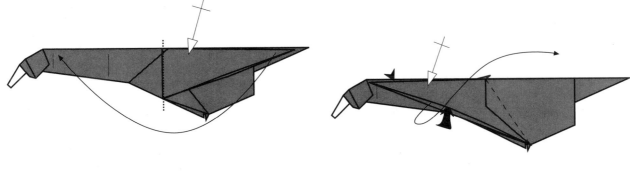

107

108

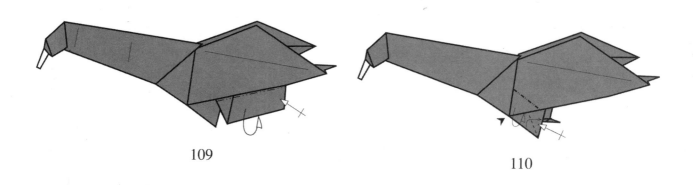

109

110

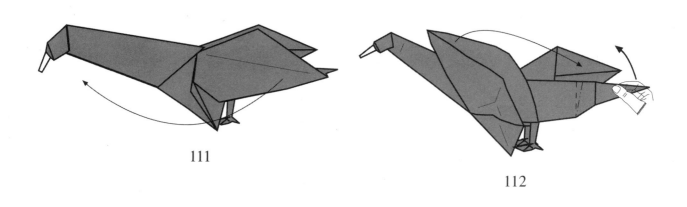

111

112

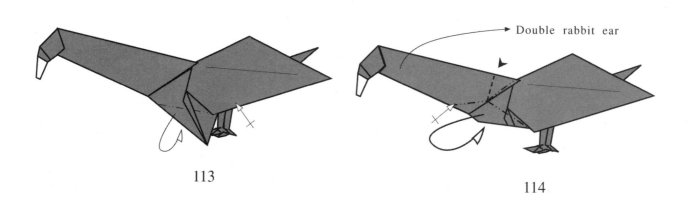

Double rabbit ear

113

114

115

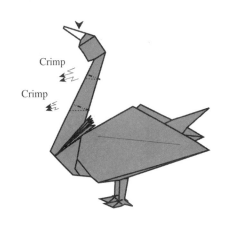

Crimp

Crimp

116

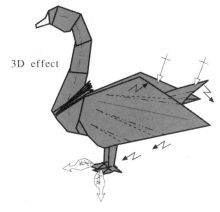

3D effect

117

118

White Swan

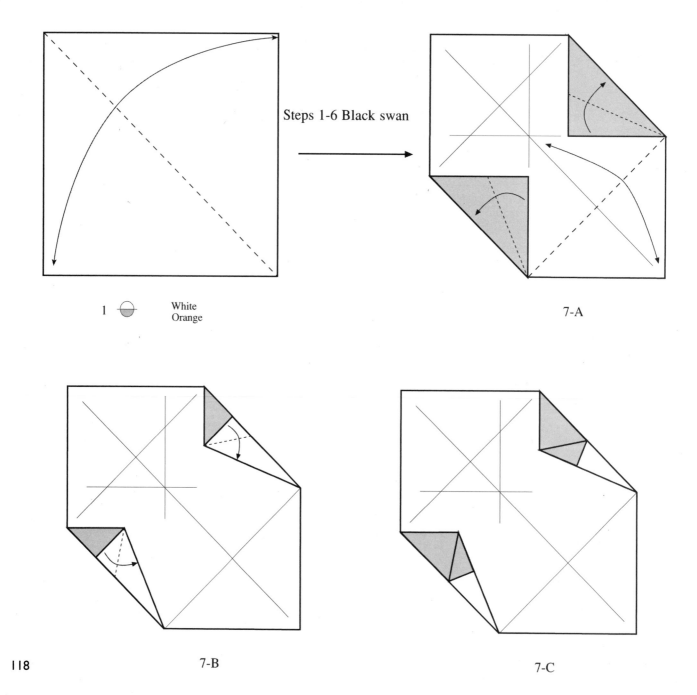

Steps 1-6 Black swan

1 White Orange

7-A

7-B

7-C

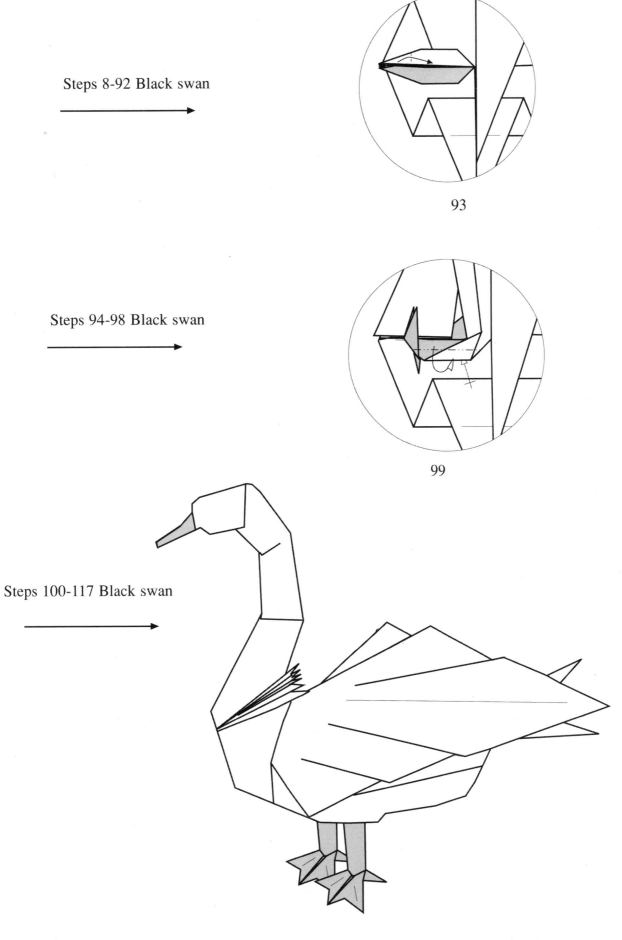

Steps 8-92 Black swan

93

Steps 94-98 Black swan

99

Steps 100-117 Black swan

118

119

Walking Stick

The paper should be green. Fine paper is recommended, less than 30 grams, silk, banana tree, lokta, metallic, or "sandwich" of 7.9x7.9 inches (20x20 cm) or bigger.

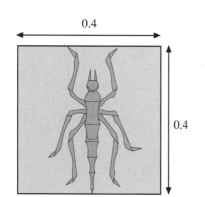

0.4

0.4

Ovoposit

3rd Hindleg

2nd Hindleg

1

Abdomen

1st Foreleg

Antennae

Head

120

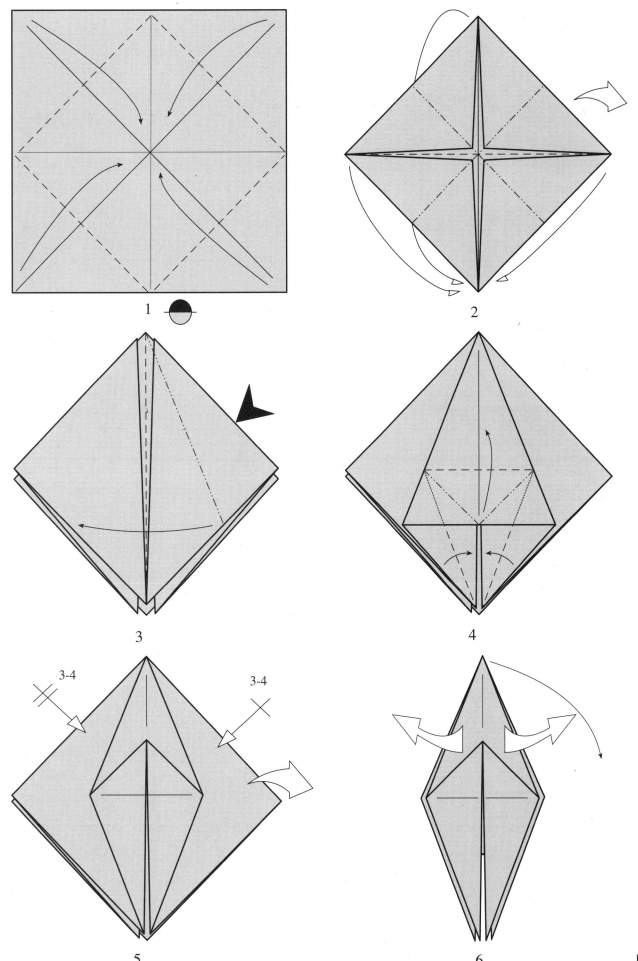

1

2

3

3-4   3-4

4

5

6

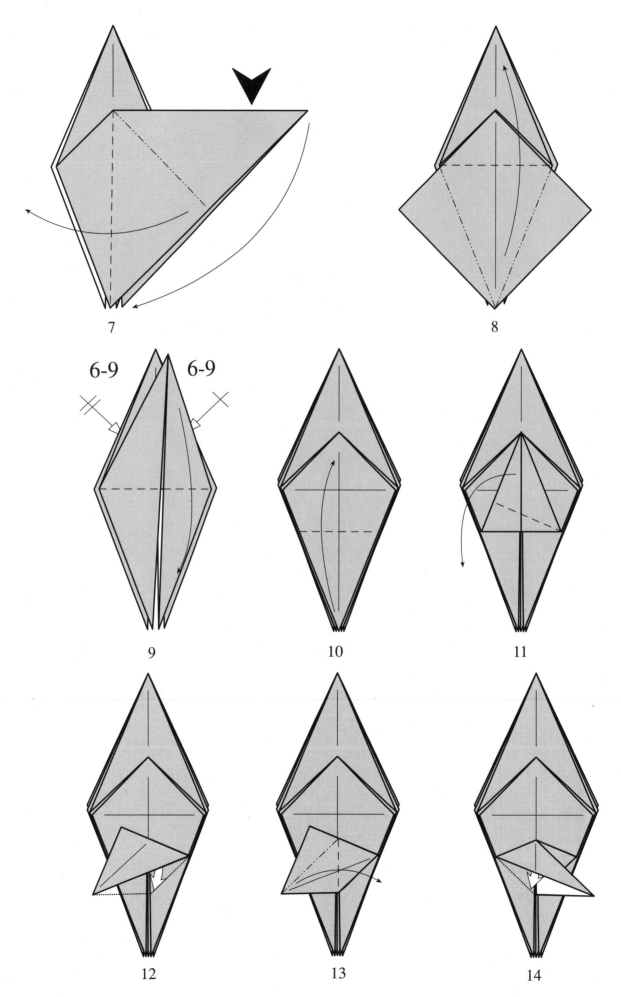

7

8

6-9 6-9

9

10

11

12

13

14

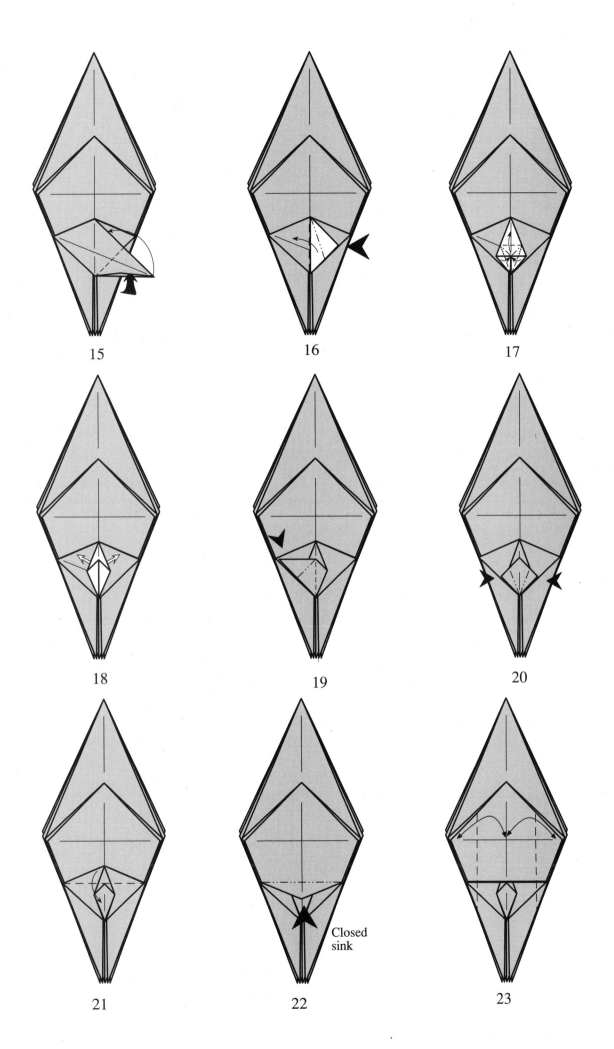

15

16

17

18

19

20

21

22

Closed
sink

23

123

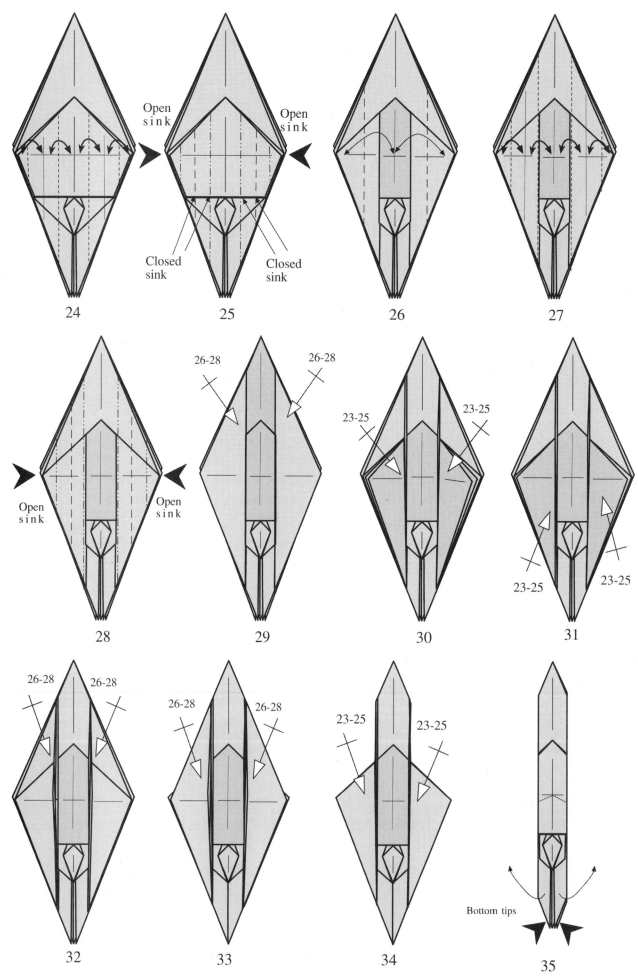

Open sink

Open sink

Closed sink

Closed sink

24

25

26

27

Open sink

Open sink

26-28

26-28

23-25

23-25

23-25

23-25

28

29

30

31

26-28

26-28

26-28

26-28

23-25

23-25

Bottom tips

32

33

34

35

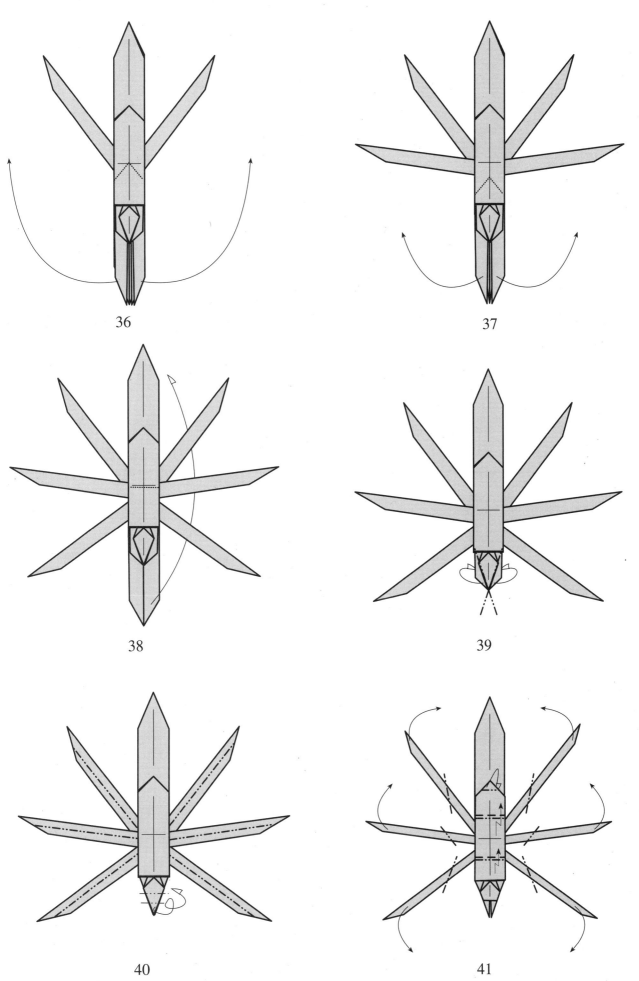

36

37

38

39

40

41

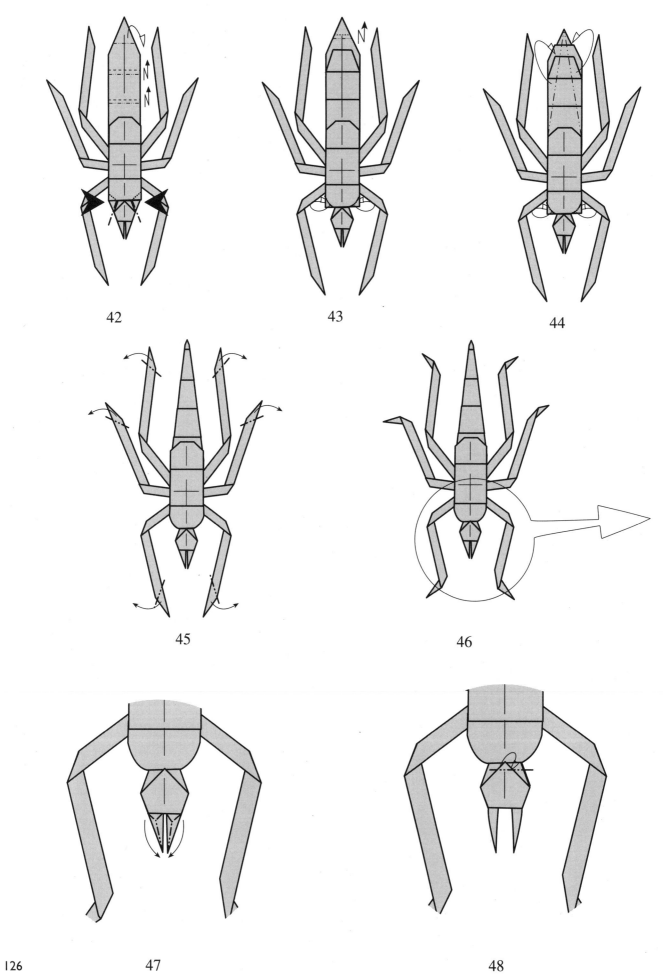

42

43

44

45

46

47

48

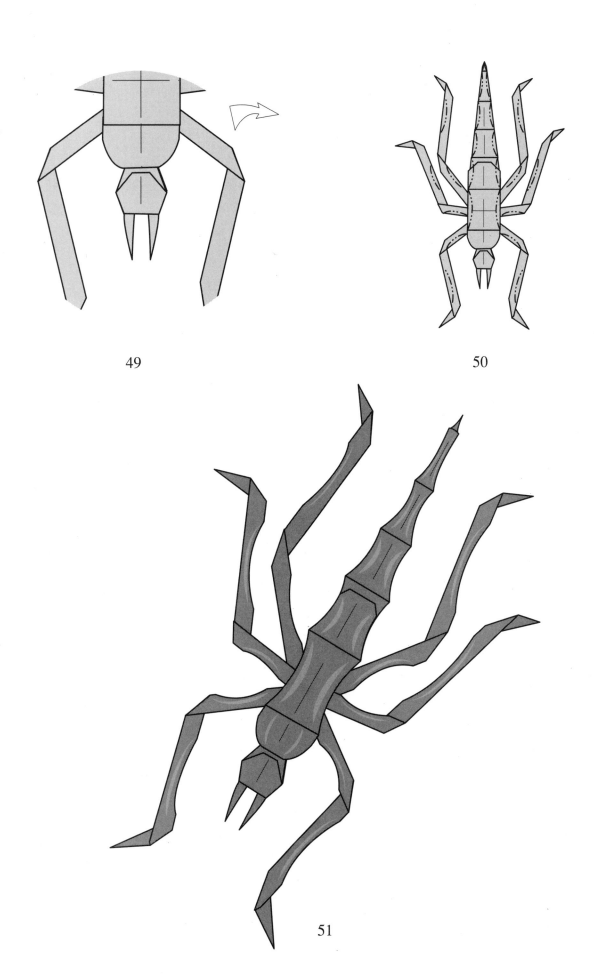

49

50

51

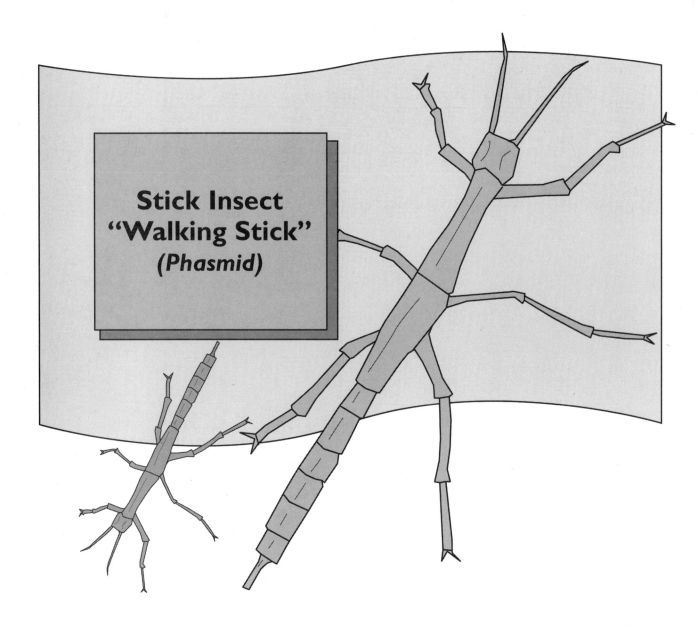

**Stick Insect
"Walking Stick"
(Phasmid)**

An appropriate color for paper would be light-brown, dark-brown or green. It is recommended to use paper 15.7x15.7 inches (40x40 cm) or bigger and weight less than 30 gr/m².

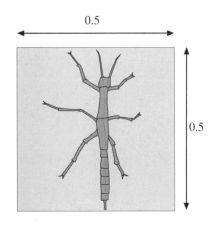

0.5

0.5

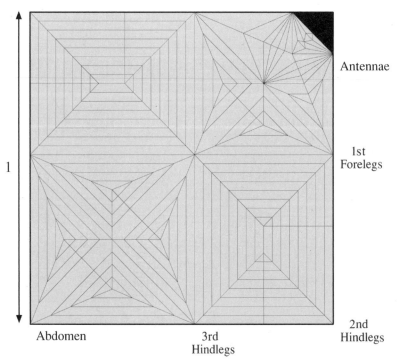

Antennae

1st
Forelegs

2nd
Hindlegs

Abdomen

3rd
Hindlegs

1

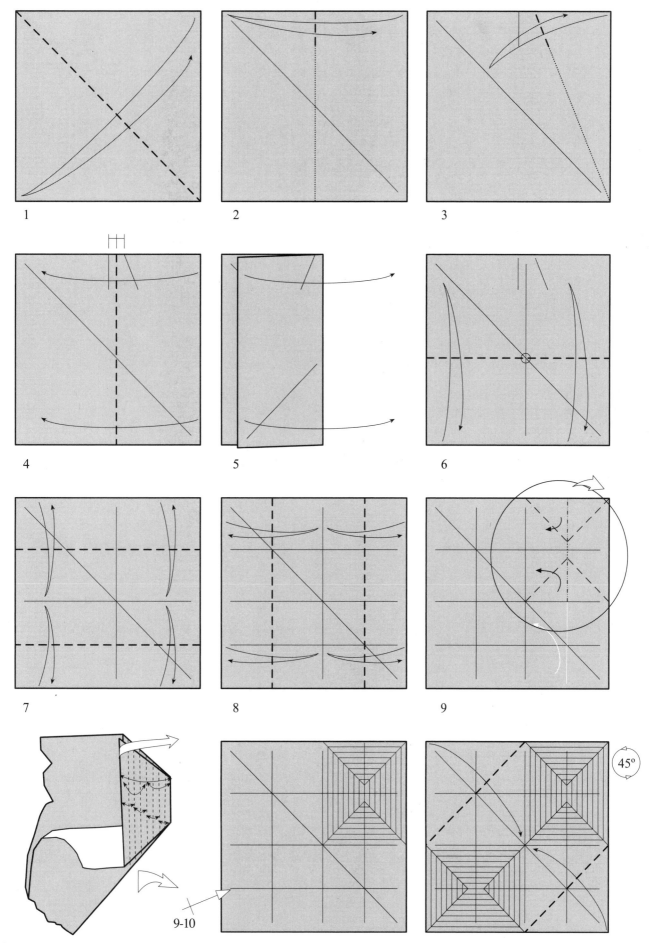

1

2

3

4

5

6

7

8

9

10

9-10

11

12

45°

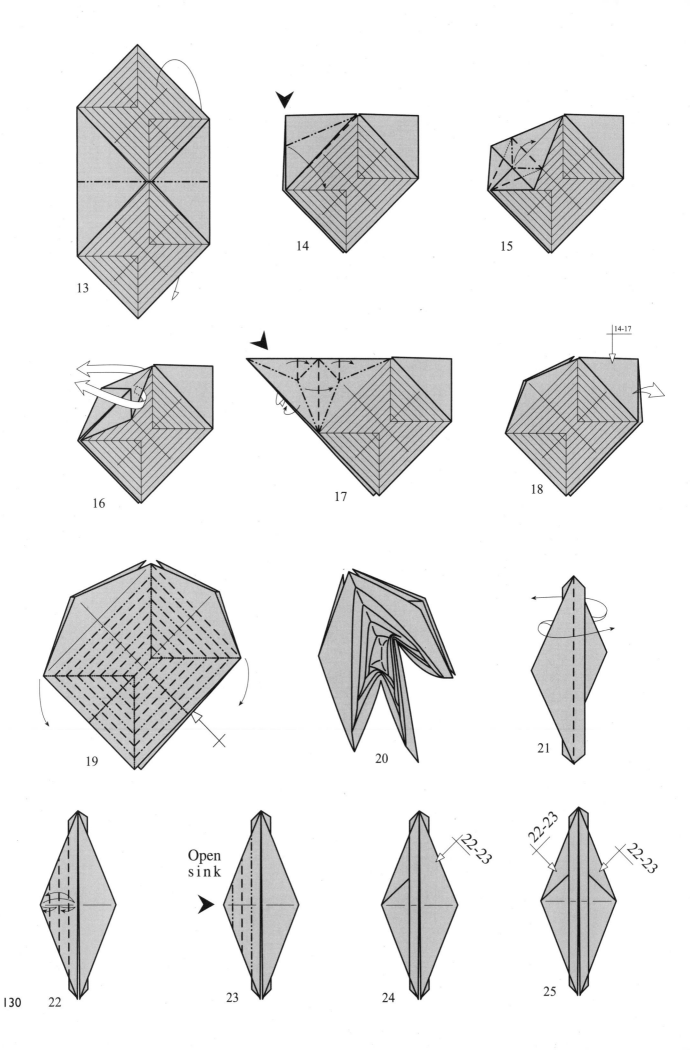

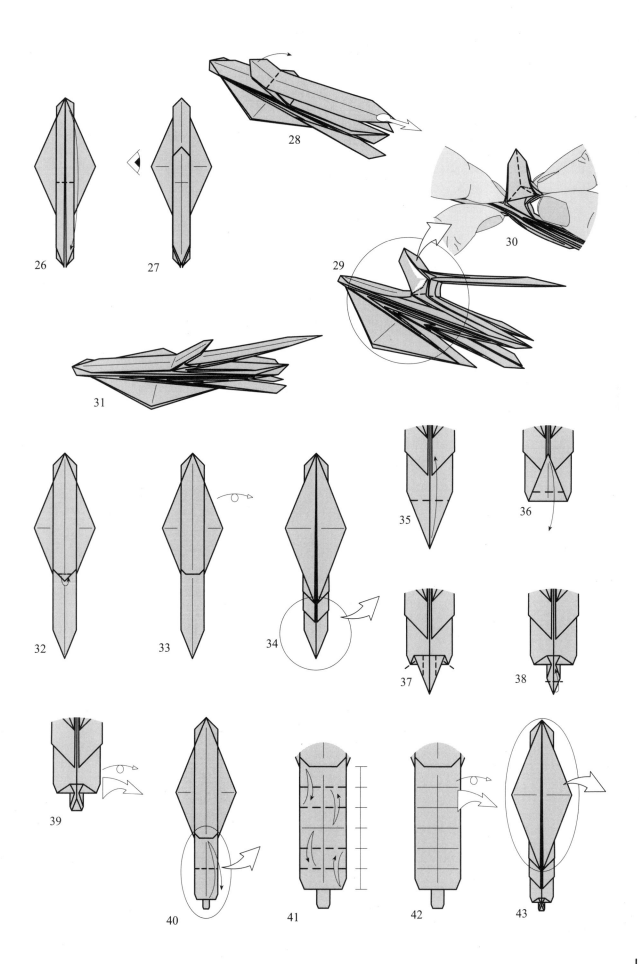

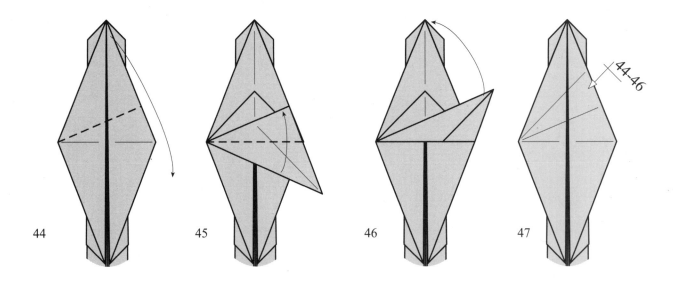

44

45

46

47   44-46

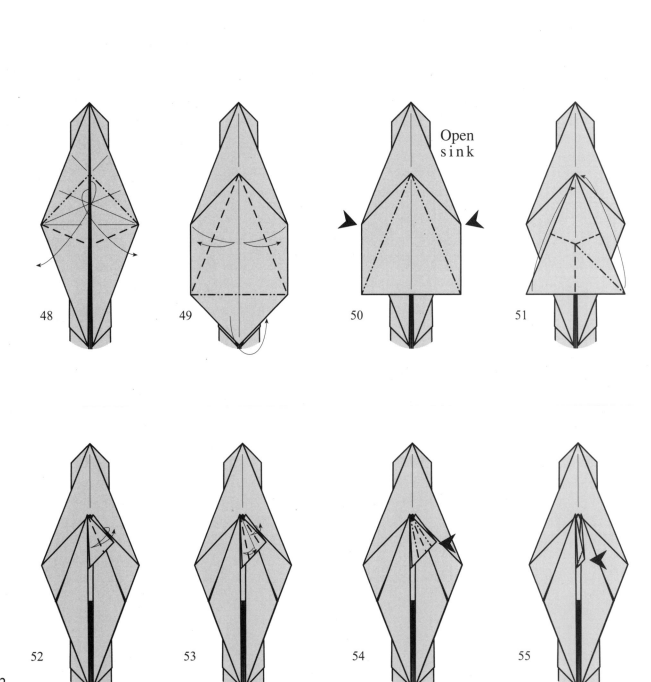

48

49

50   Open sink

51

52

53

54

55

132

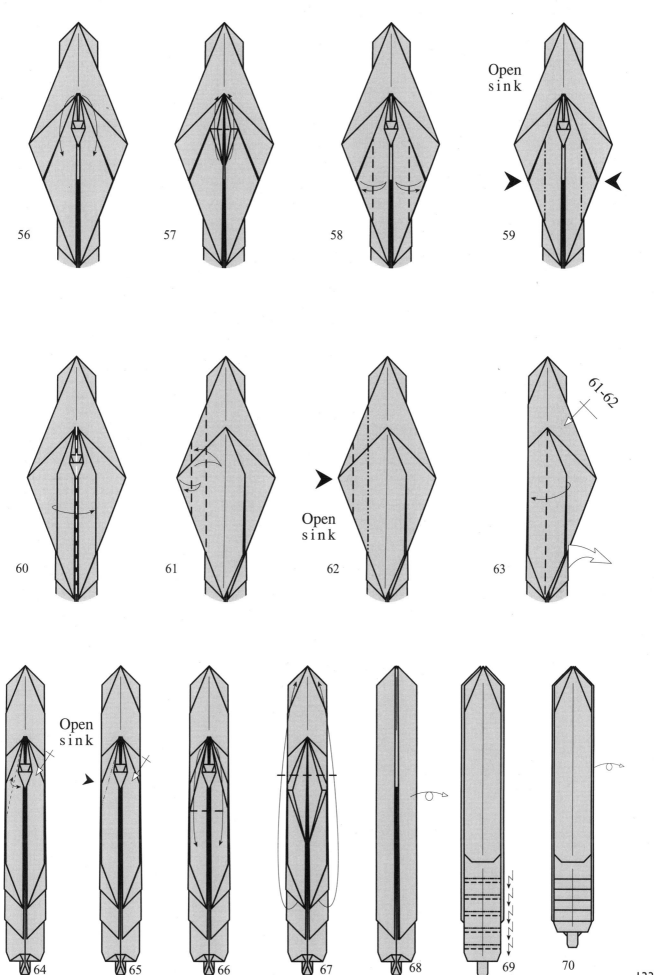

56

57

58

Open
sink

59

60

61

Open
sink

62

61-62

63

Open
sink

64

65

66

67

68

69

70

133

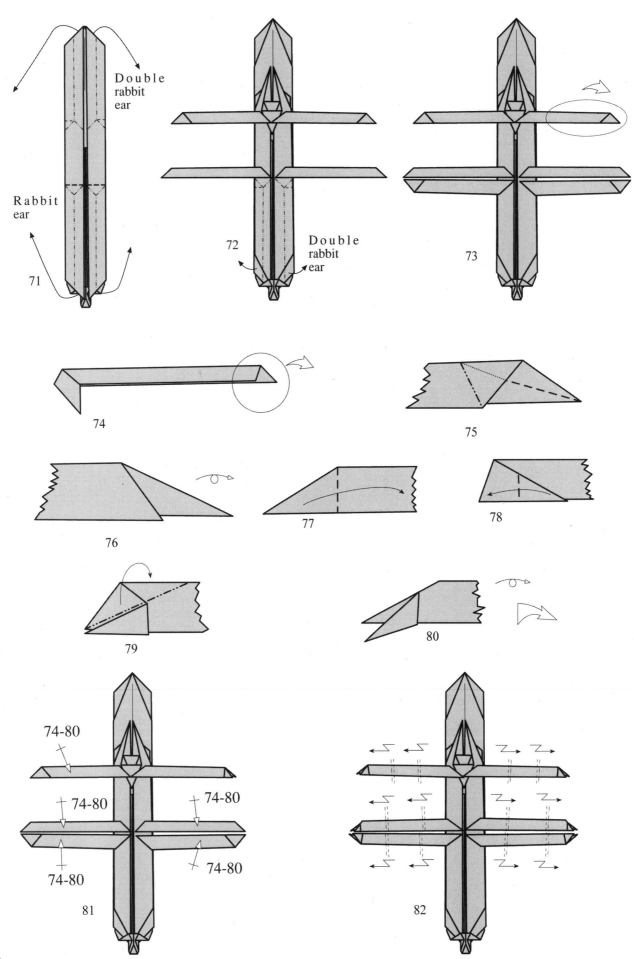

Double
rabbit
ear

Rabbit
ear

71

72

Double
rabbit
ear

73

74

75

76

77

78

79

80

74-80

74-80

74-80

74-80

74-80

81

82

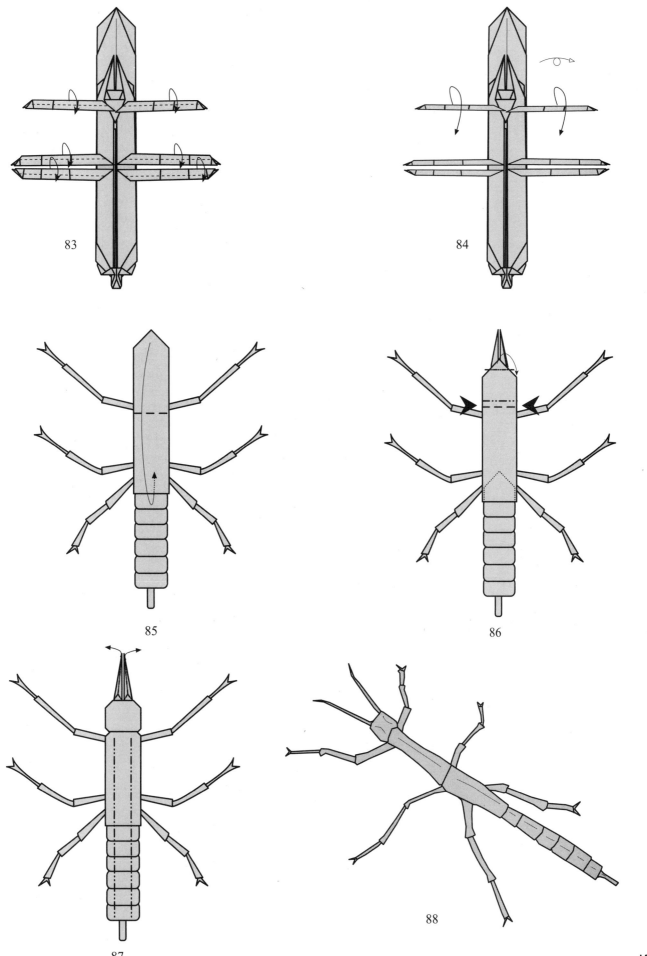

83

84

85

86

87

88

Leaf Mantis

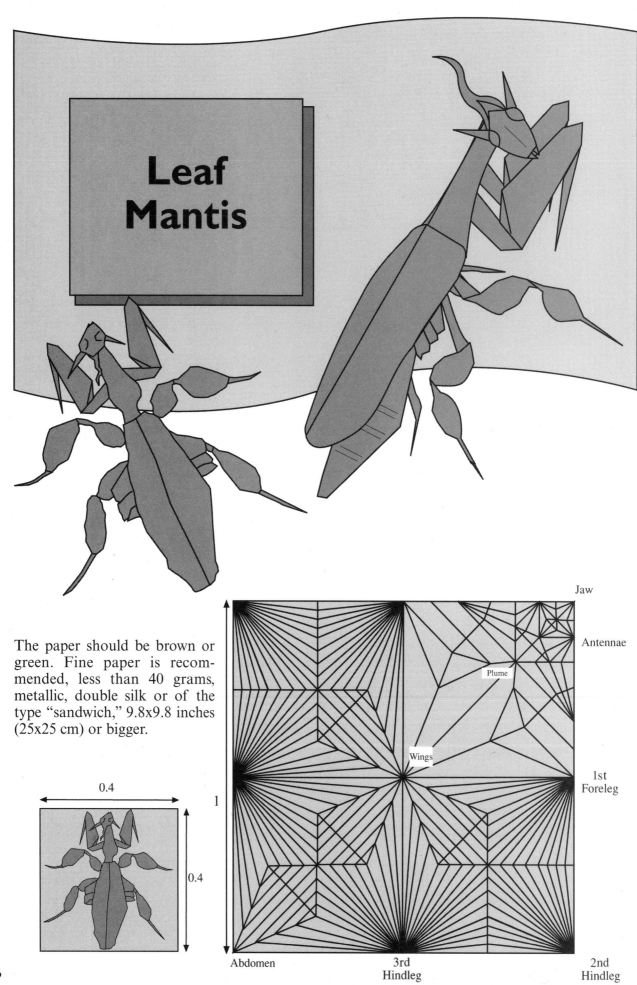

The paper should be brown or green. Fine paper is recommended, less than 40 grams, metallic, double silk or of the type "sandwich," 9.8x9.8 inches (25x25 cm) or bigger.

0.4

0.4

1

Jaw

Antennae

Plume

Wings

1st Foreleg

Abdomen

3rd Hindleg

2nd Hindleg

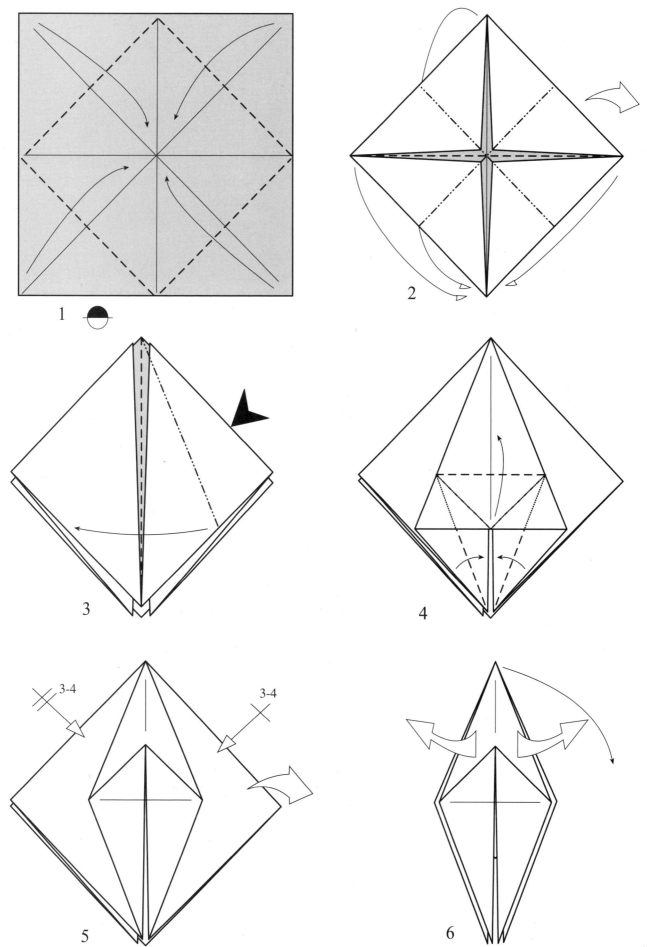

1

2

3

4

5

3-4   3-4

6

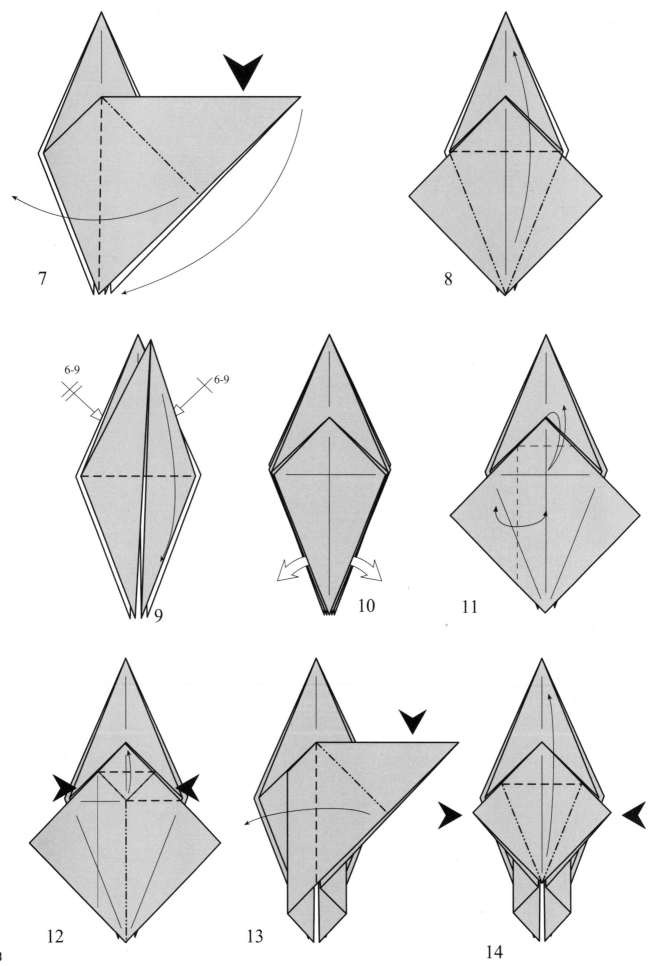

7

8

9

6-9

6-9

10

11

12

13

14

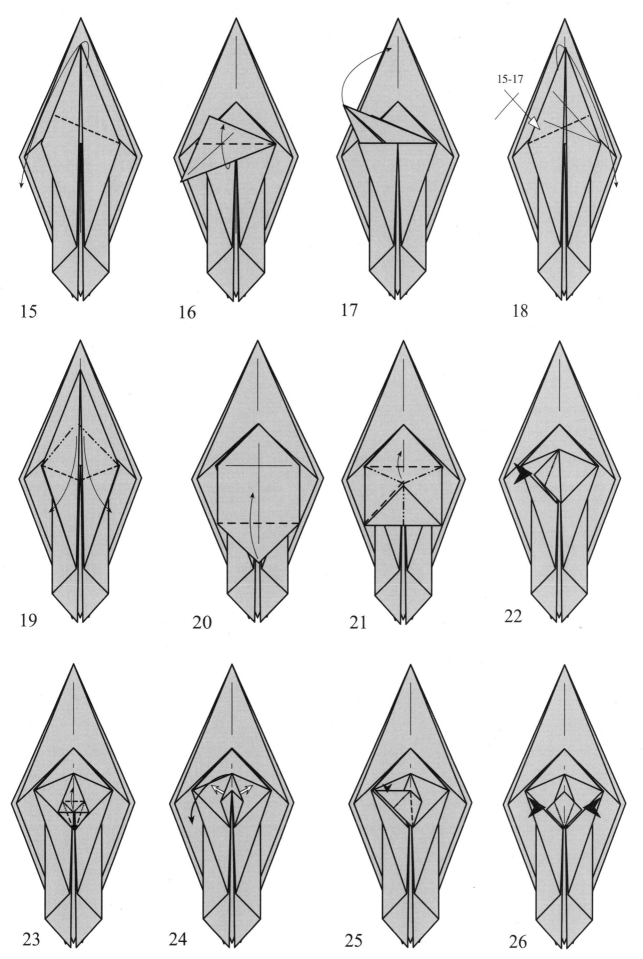

15

16

17

18

19

20

21

22

23

24

25

26

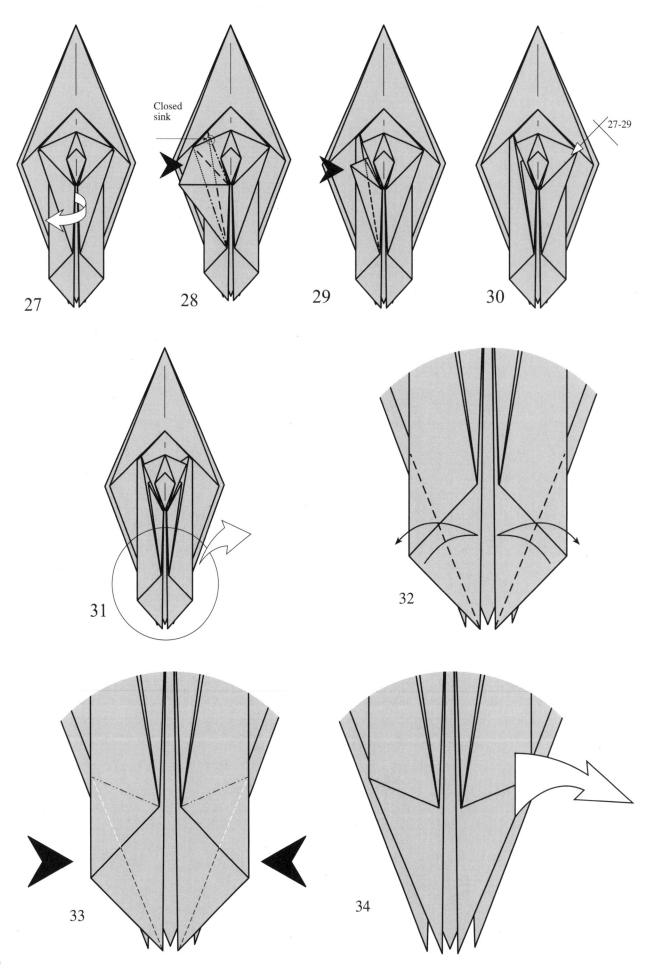

Closed
sink

27-29

27

28

29

30

31

32

33

34

140

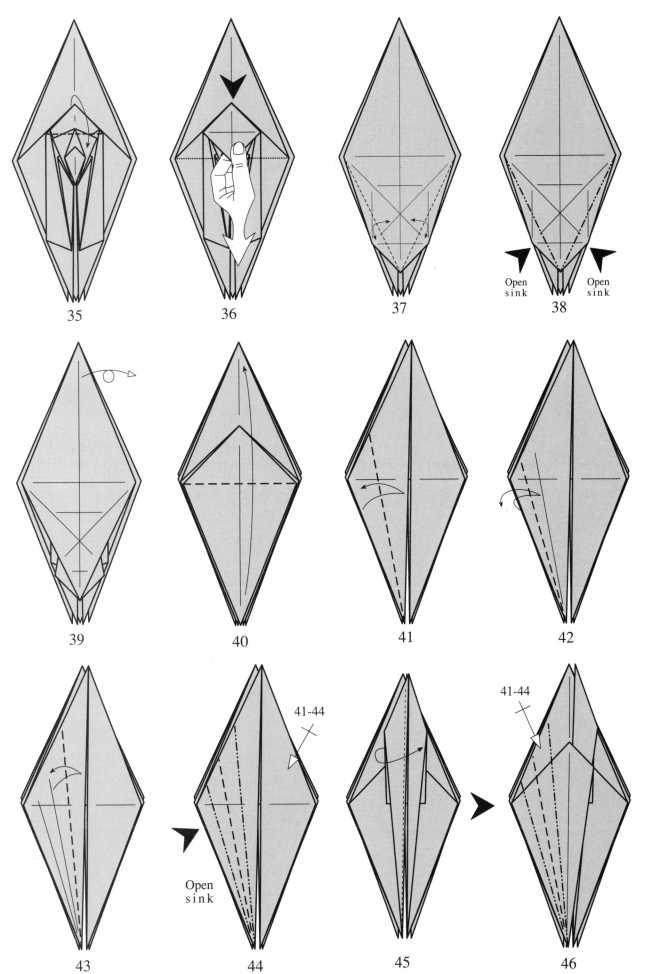

35

36

37

38

Open sink   Open sink

39

40

41

42

43

44

Open sink

45

46

41-44

41-44

141

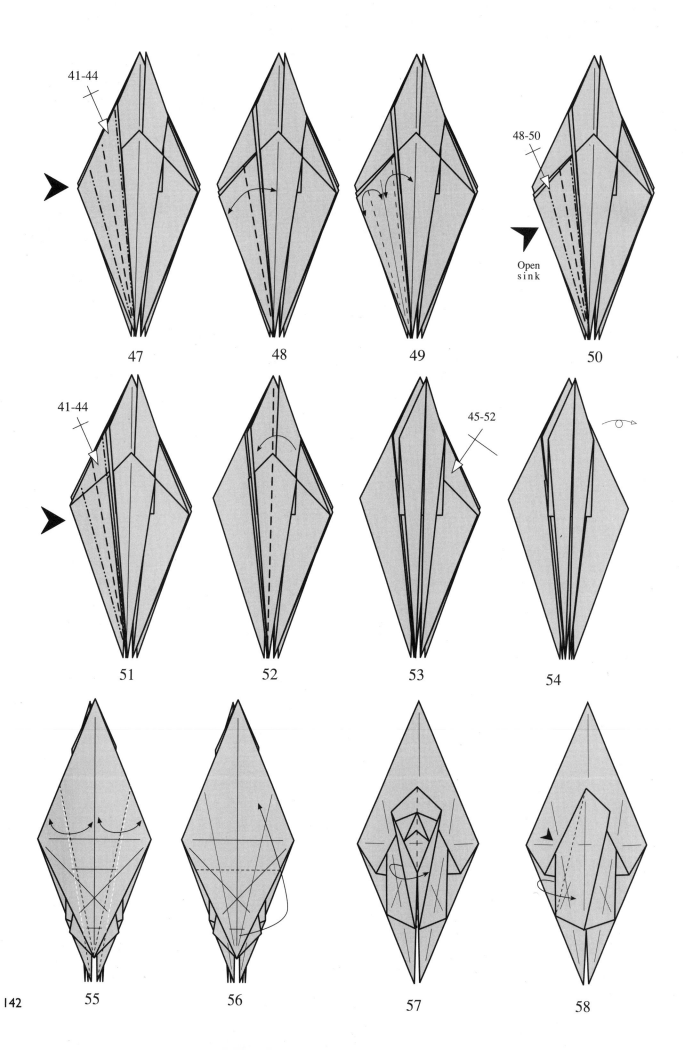

41-44

47

48

49

48-50

Open
sink

50

41-44

51

52

45-52

53

54

55

56

57

58

142

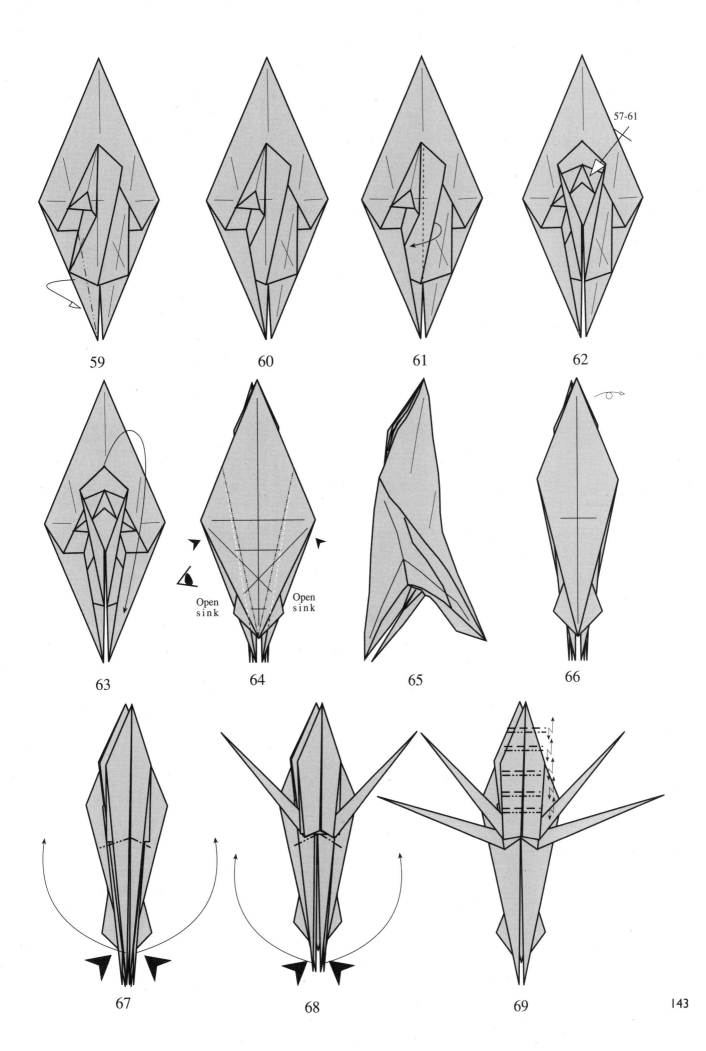

59

60

61

62

57-61

63

64

Open sink   Open sink

65

66

67

68

69

143

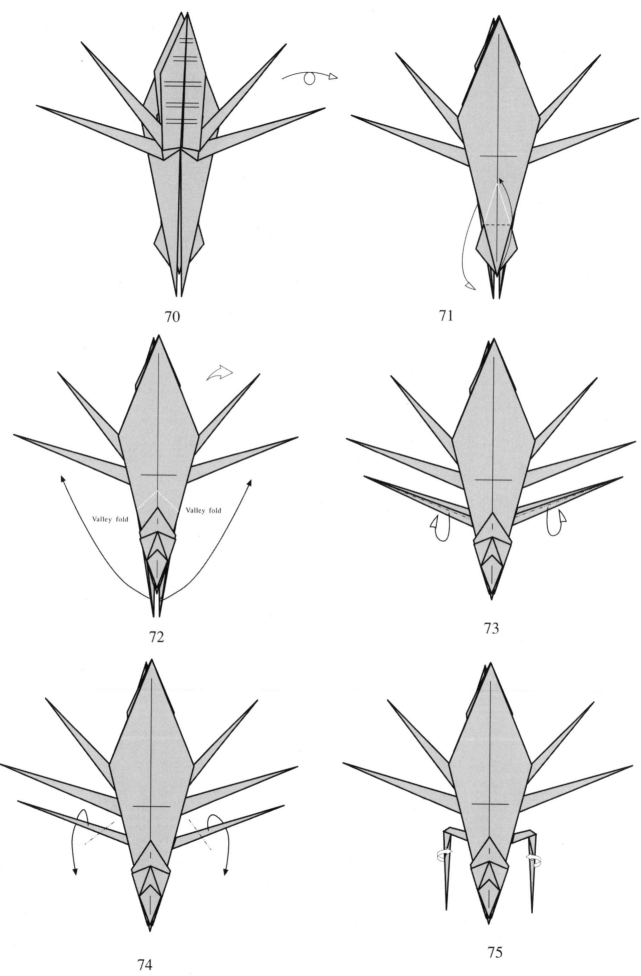

70

71

72

Valley fold   Valley fold

73

74

75

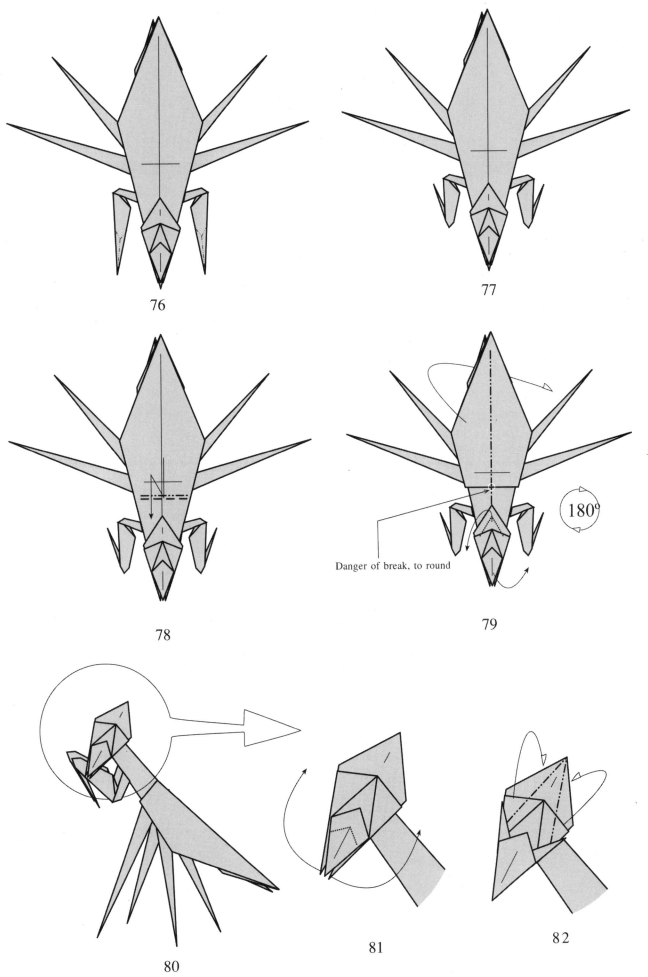

76

77

78

79

Danger of break, to round

180°

80

81

82

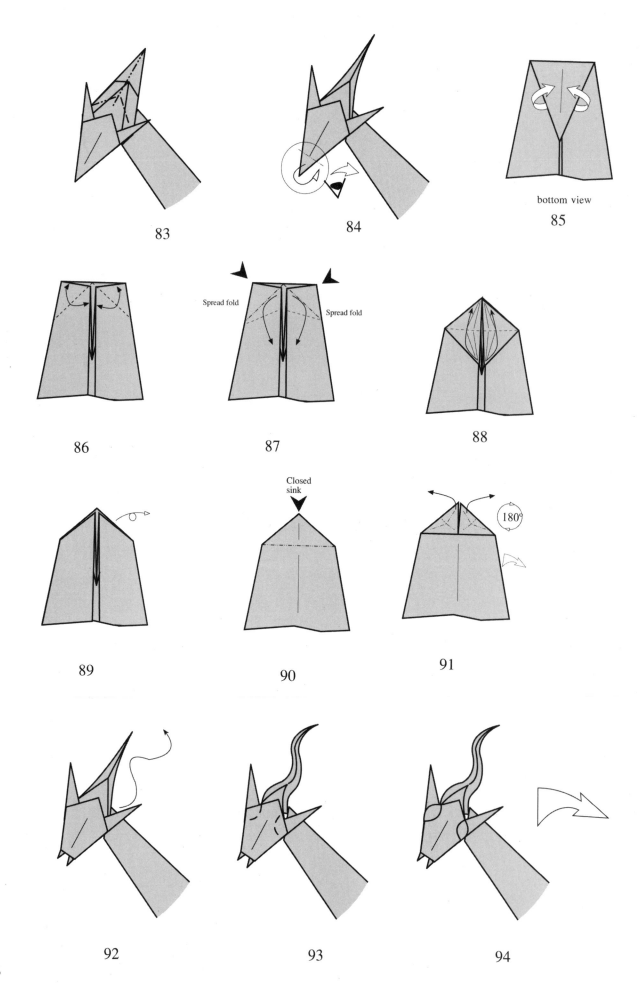

83

84

85
bottom view

86

87
Spread fold　Spread fold

88

89

90
Closed sink

91
180°

92

93

94

146

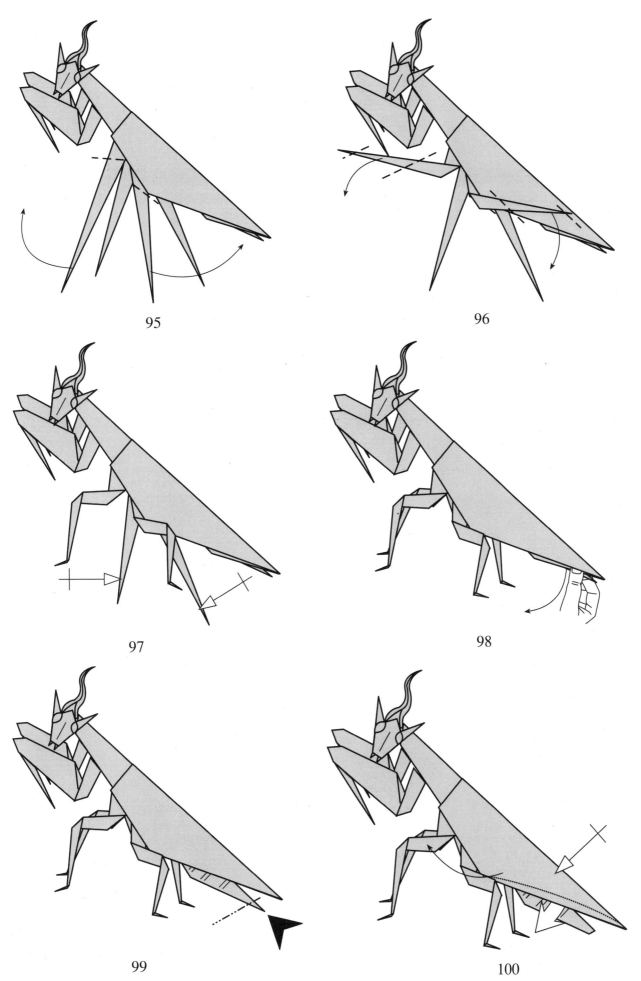

95

96

97

98

99

100

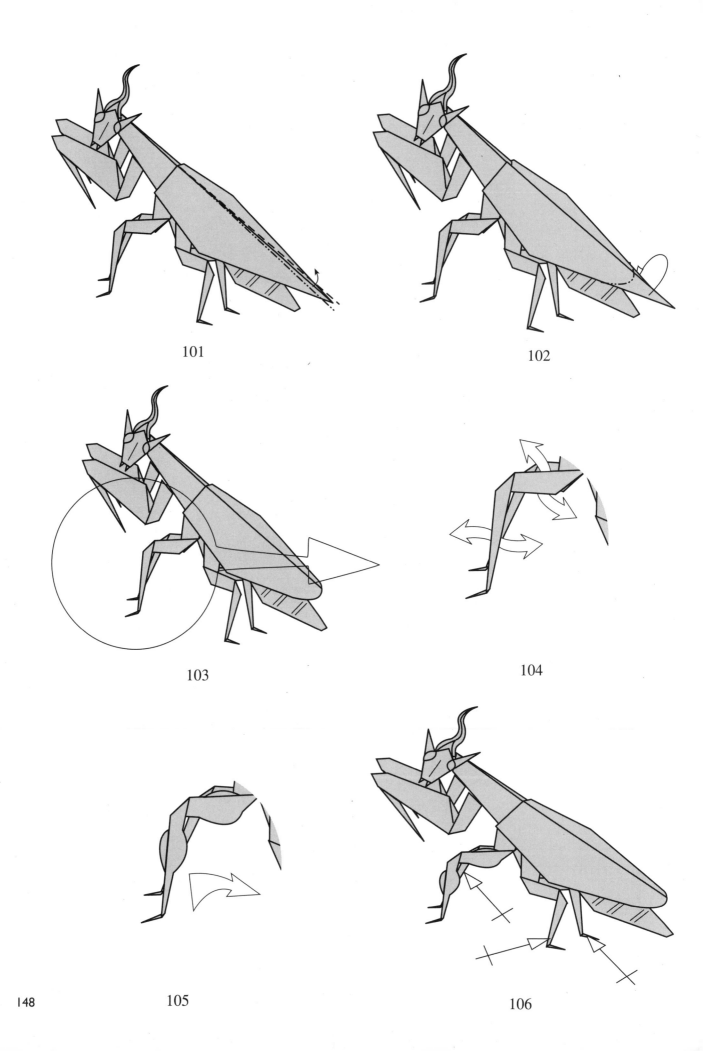

101

102

103

104

105

106

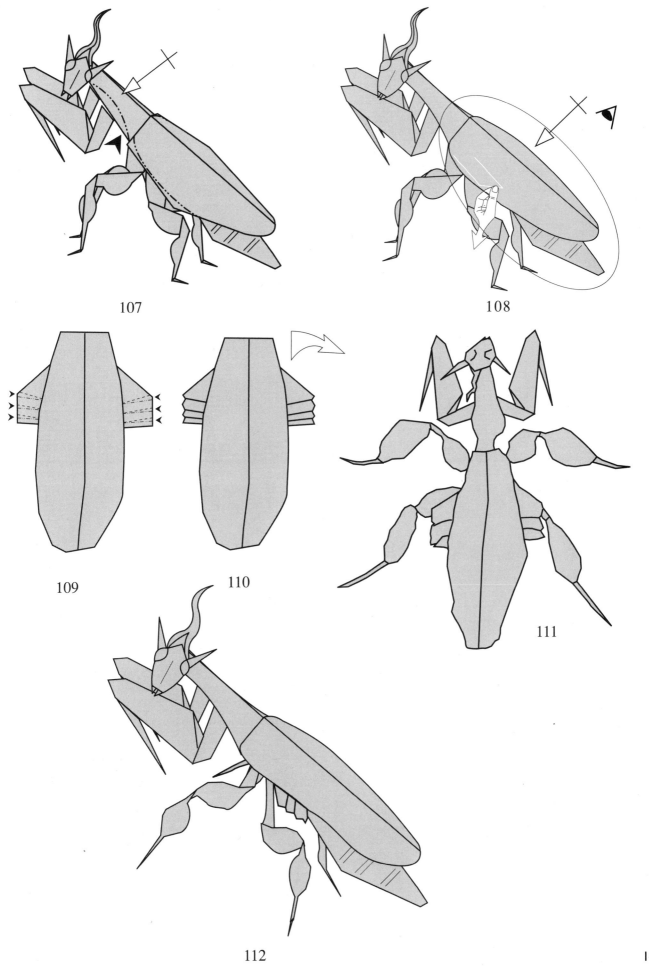

107

108

109

110

111

112

Black Ant

Antennae   1st Forelegs   2nd Hindlegs

The paper should be black. Fine paper is recommended, less than 40 grams, double silk, banana tree, lokta, metallic or "sandwich," 9.8x9.8 inches (25x25 cm) or bigger.

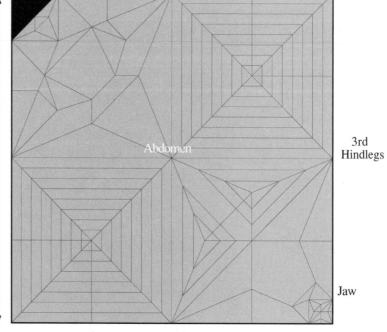

Abdomen

3rd Hindlegs

Jaw

1

1/3

1/3

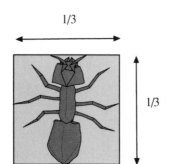

150

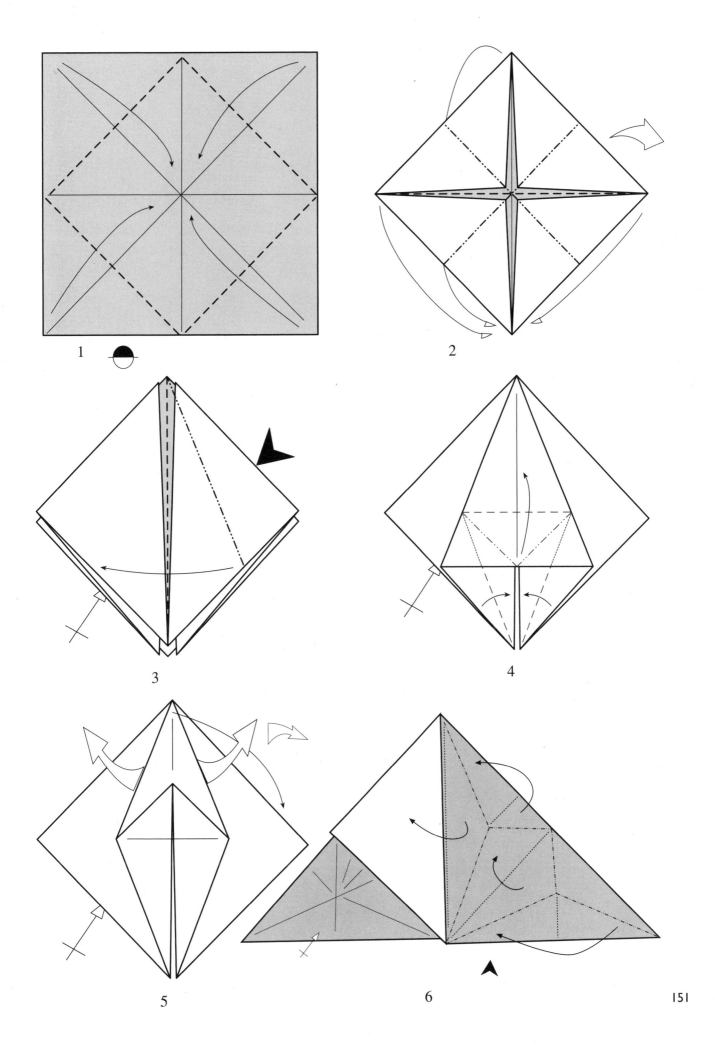

1

2

3

4

5

6

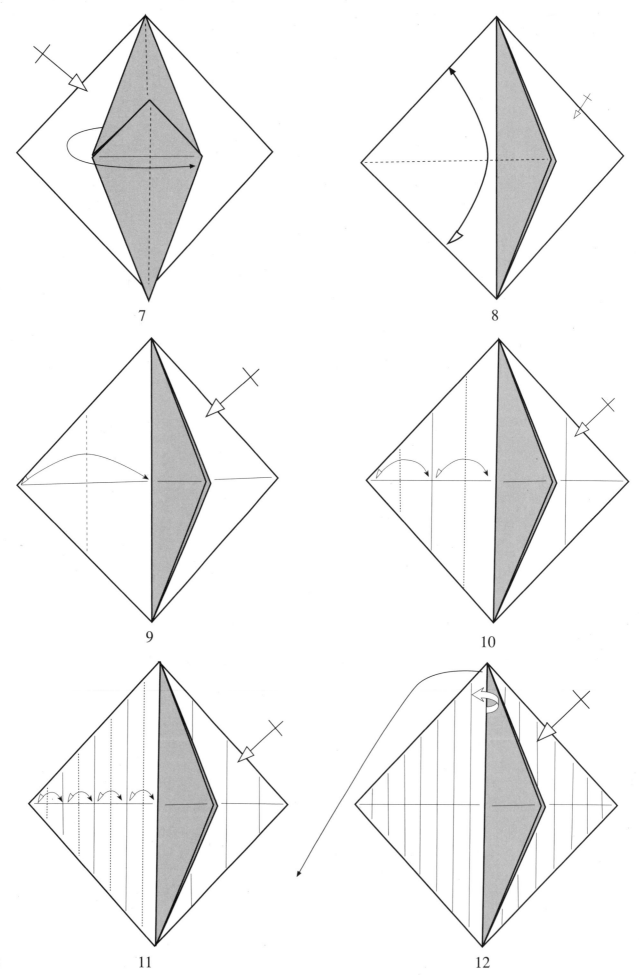

7

8

9

10

11

12

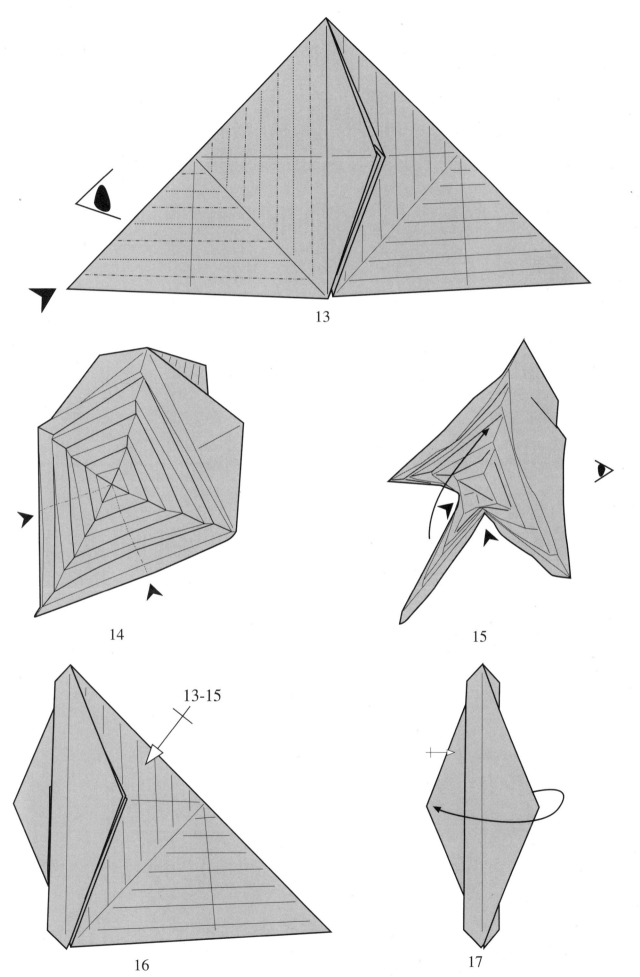

13

14

15

13-15

16

17

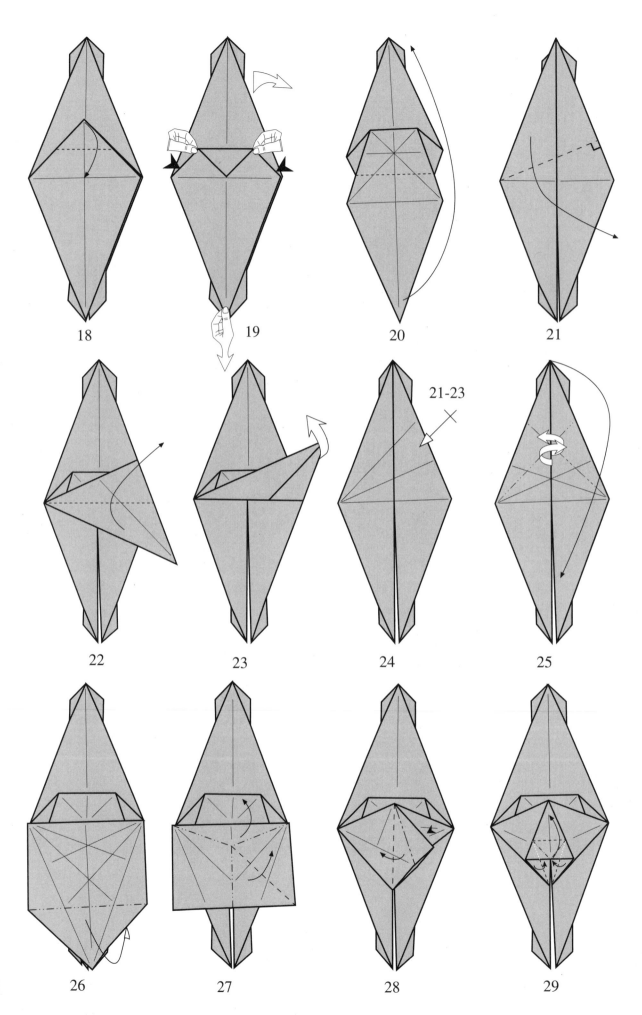

18

19

20

21

22

23

24

21-23

25

26

27

28

29

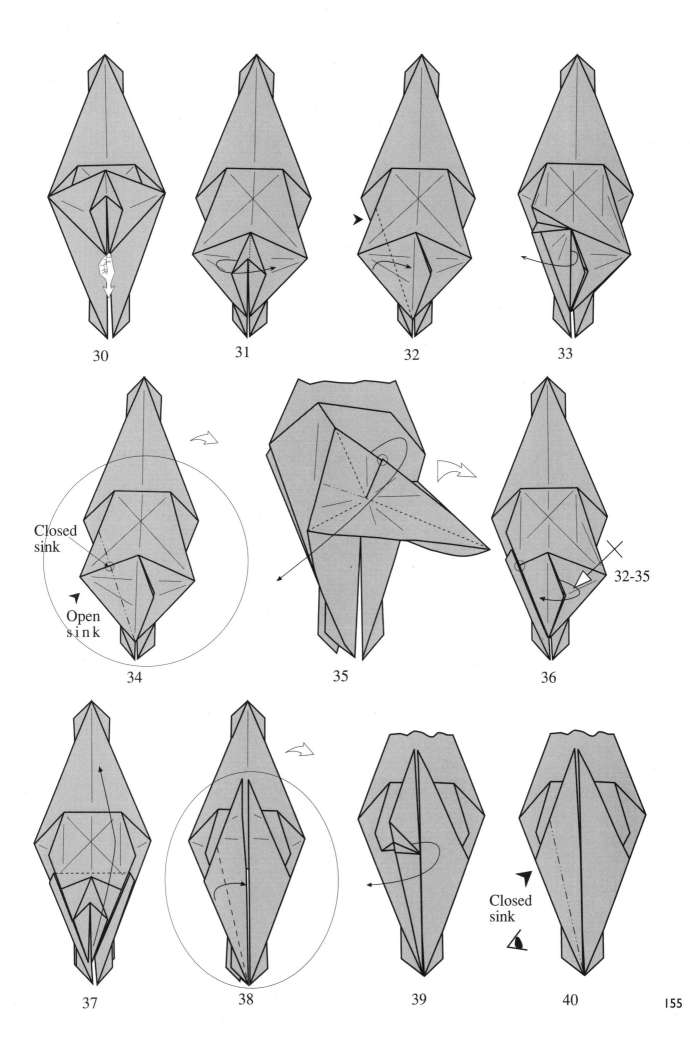

30

31

32

33

Closed
sink

Open
sink

34

35

32-35

36

37

38

Closed
sink

39

40

155

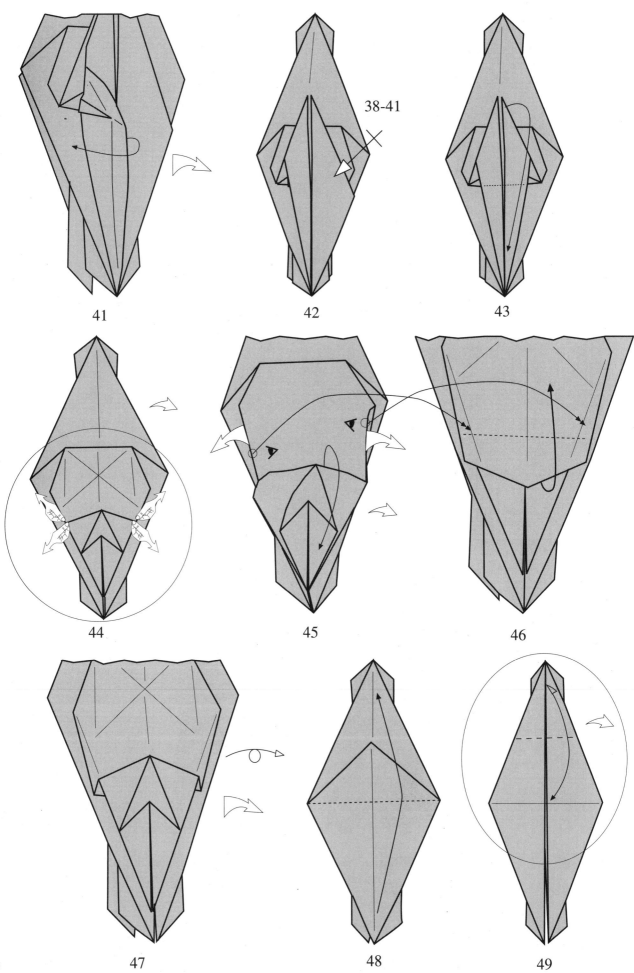

41

42

38-41

43

44

45

46

47

48

49

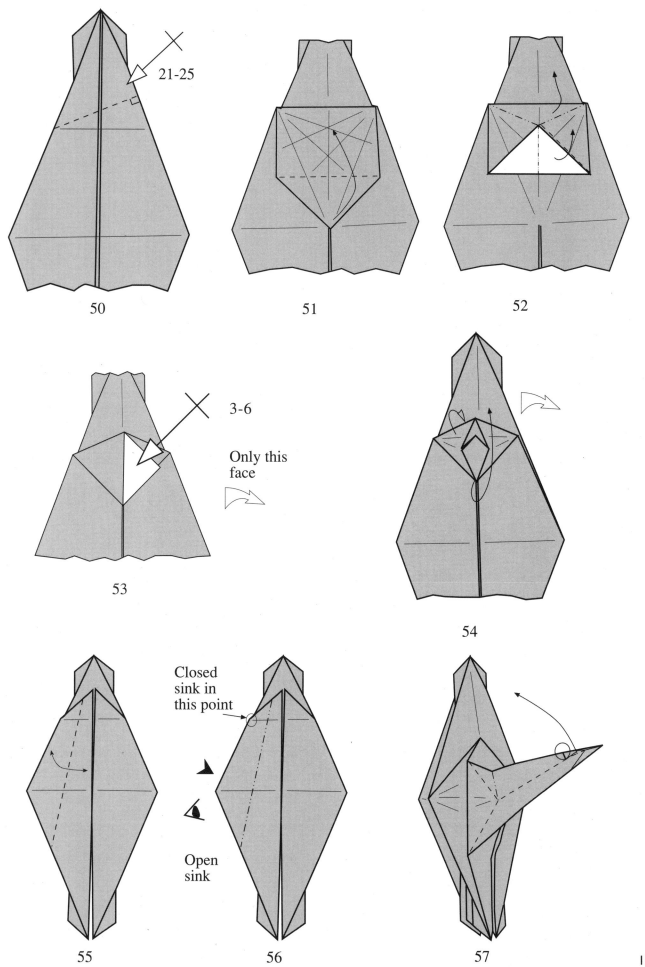

50

51

52

53

3-6

Only this
face

54

55

Closed
sink in
this point

Open
sink

56

57

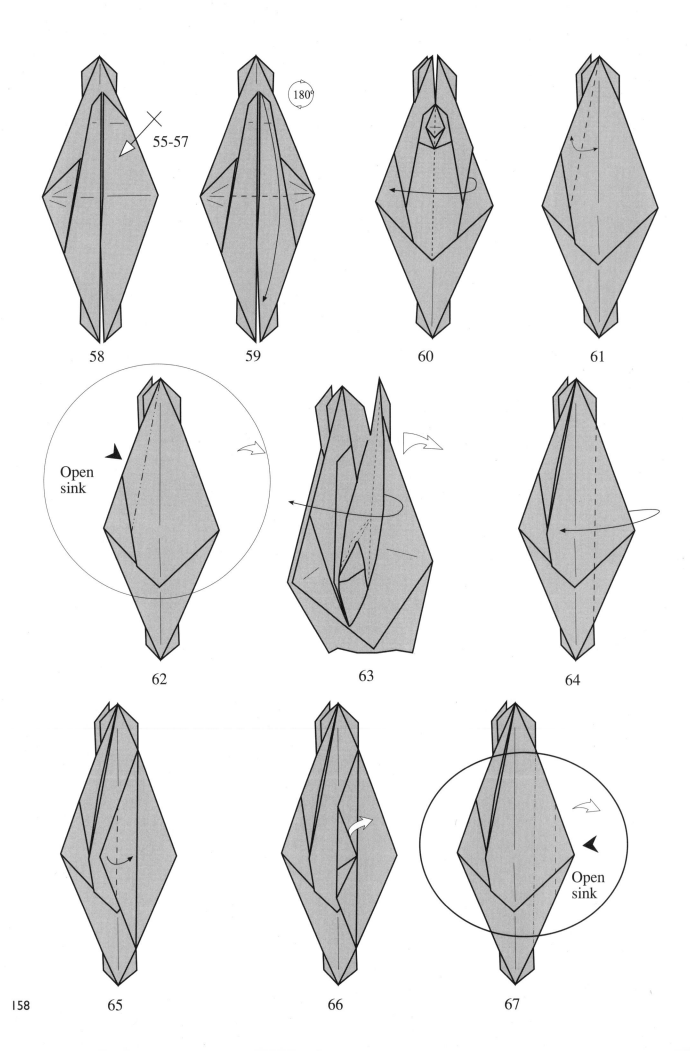

58

59

180°

55-57

60

61

62

Open
sink

63

64

Open
sink

65

66

67

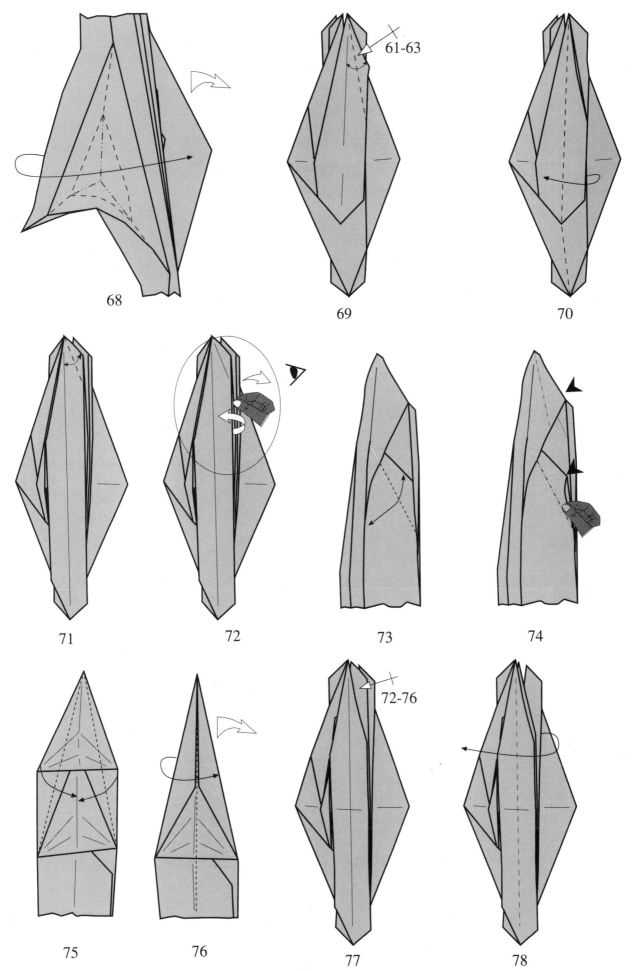

68

69

70

61-63

71

72

73

74

75

76

77

78

72-76

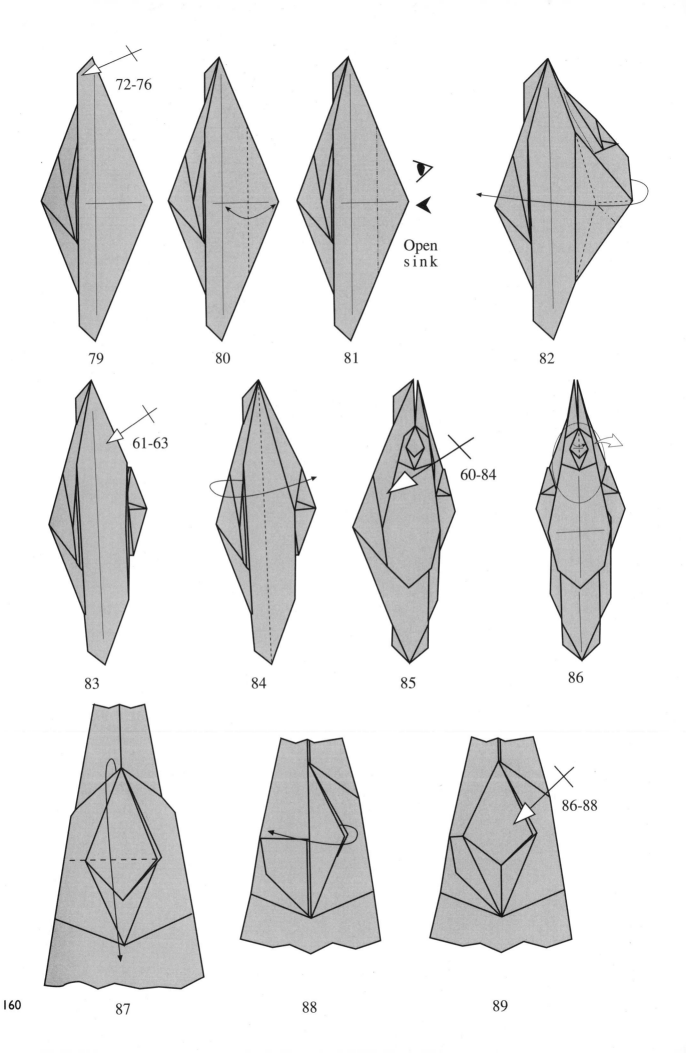

Open
sink

79

80

81

82

72-76

61-63

83

84

85

86

60-84

86-88

87

88

89

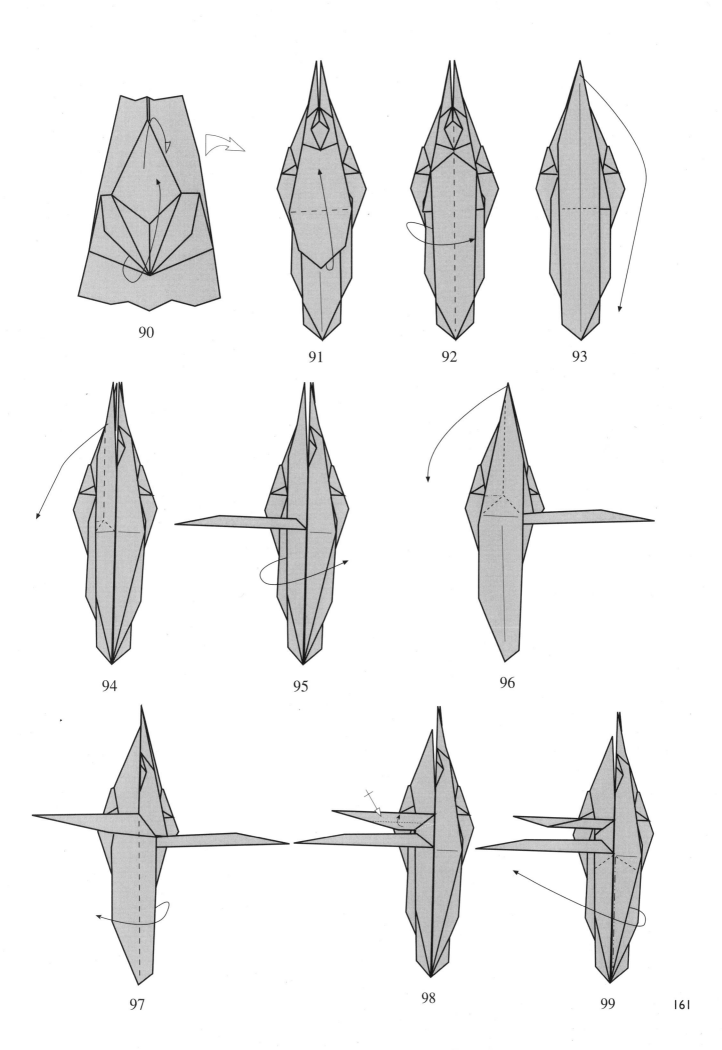

90

91

92

93

94

95

96

97

98

99

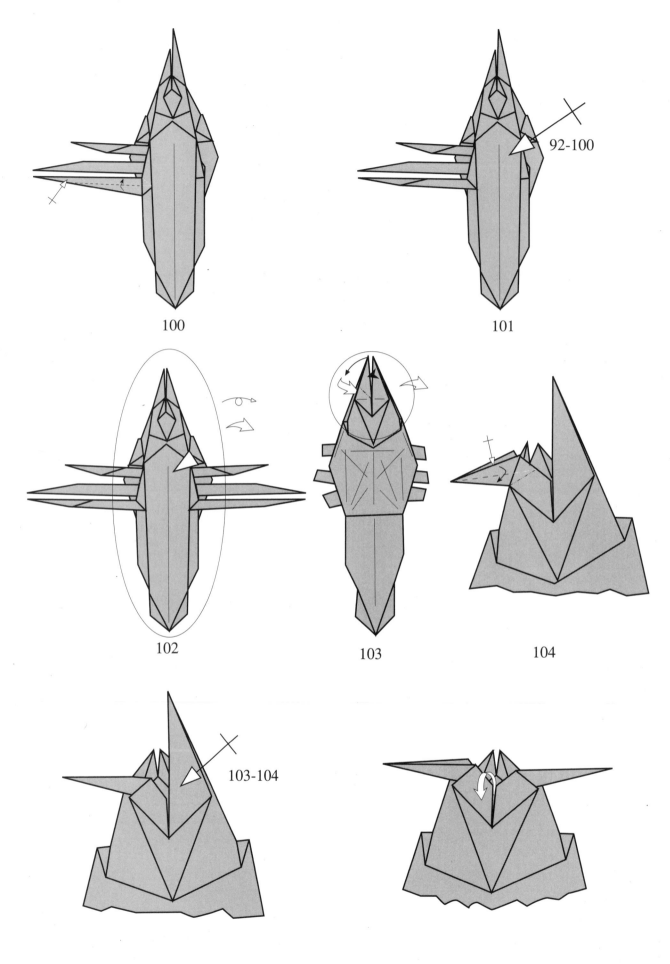

100

101   92-100

102

103

104

105   103-104

106

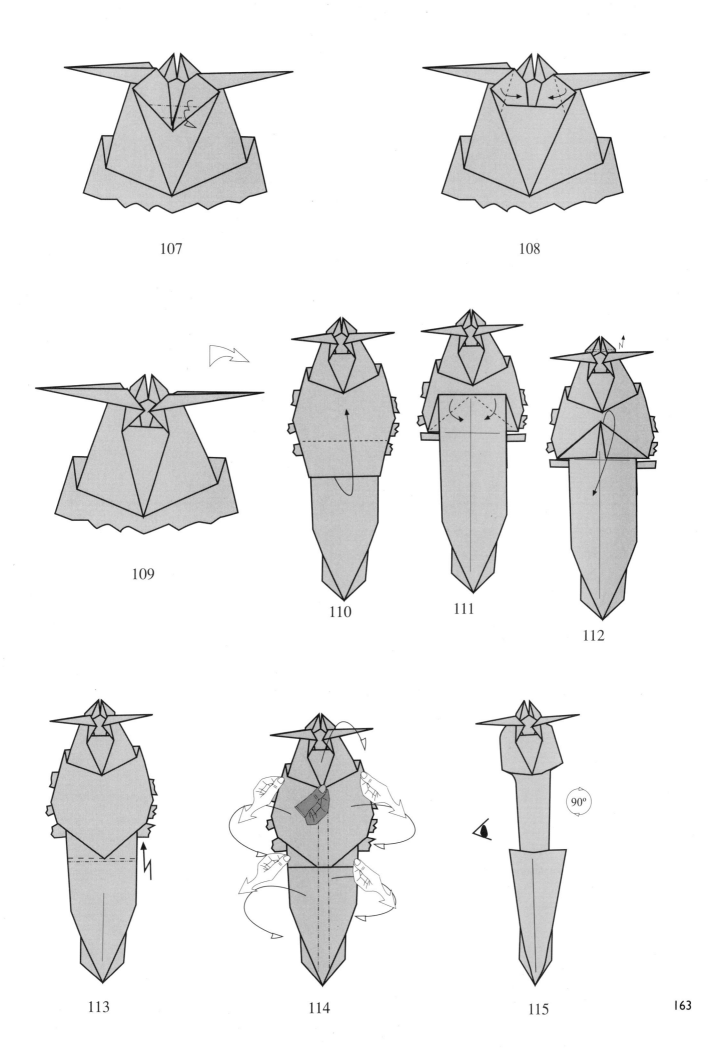

107

108

109

110

111

112

113

114

115

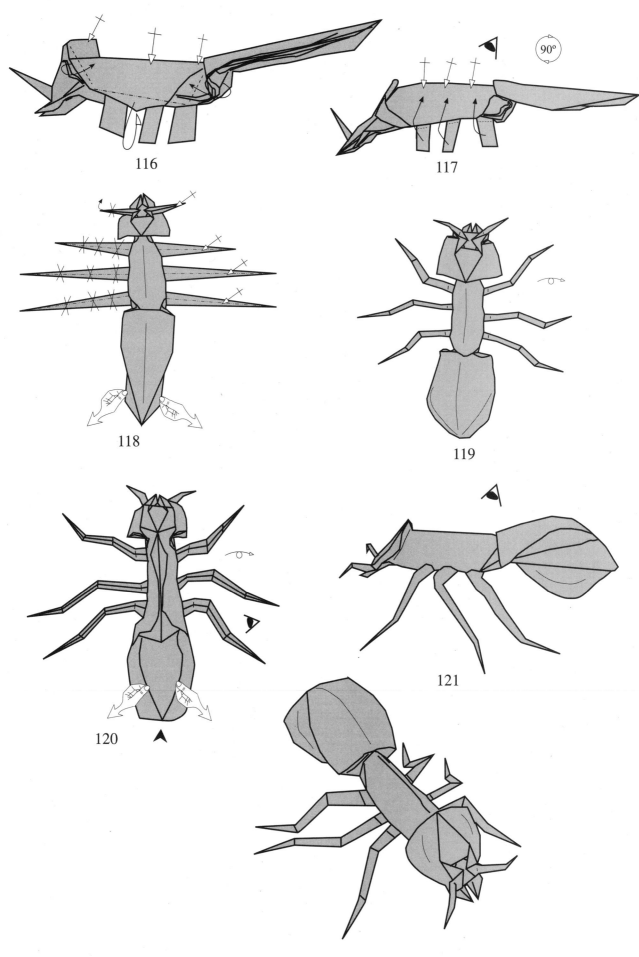

116

117

90°

118

119

120

121

122

Crayfish

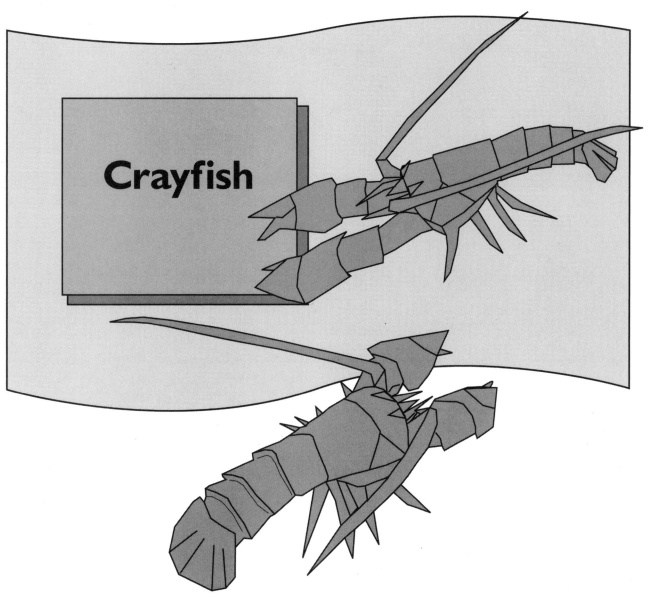

The paper should be dark green or black. Fine paper is recommended, less than 30 grams, double silk, banana tree, lokta, metallic or "sandwich," 11.8x11.8 inches (30x30 cm) or bigger.

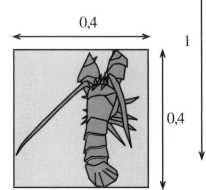

0,4

1

0,4

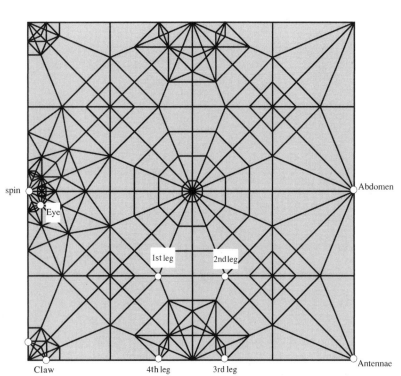

spin

Eye

Abdomen

1st leg

2nd leg

Claw

4th leg

3rd leg

Antennae

165

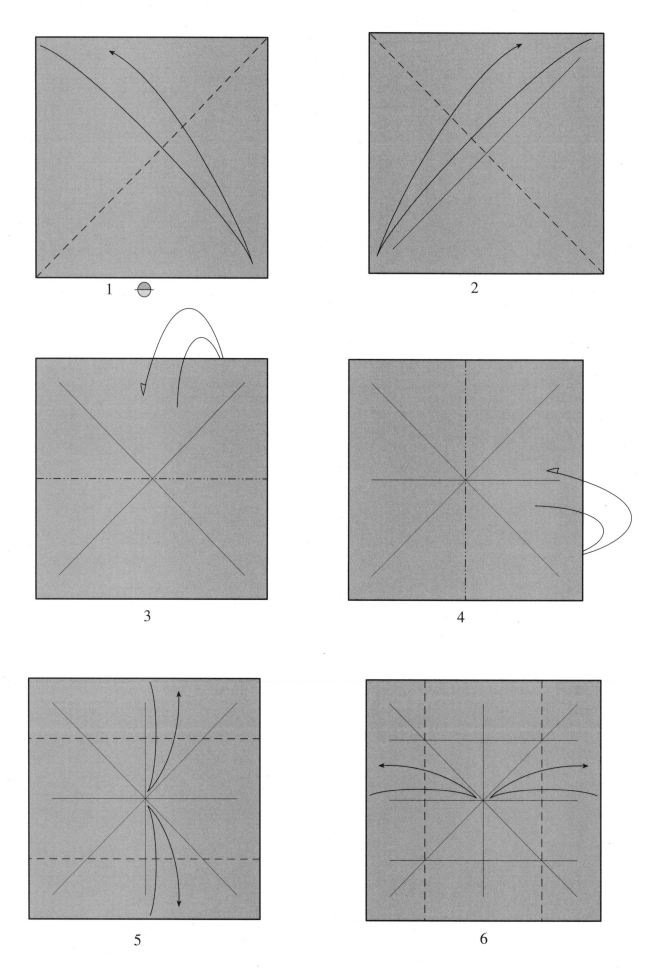

1

2

3

4

5

6

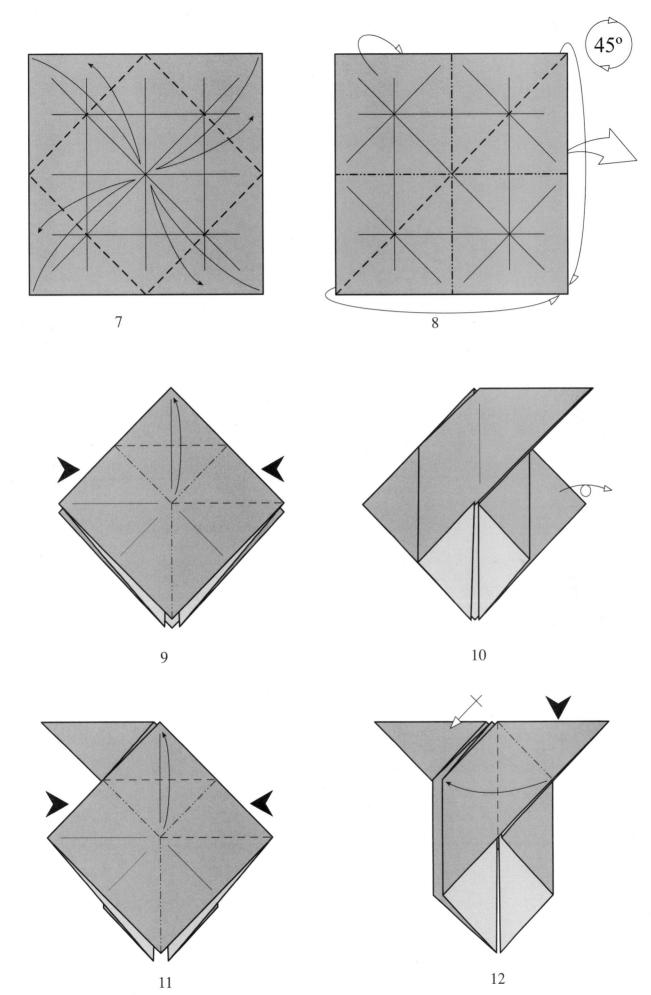

7

8

45°

9

10

11

12

167

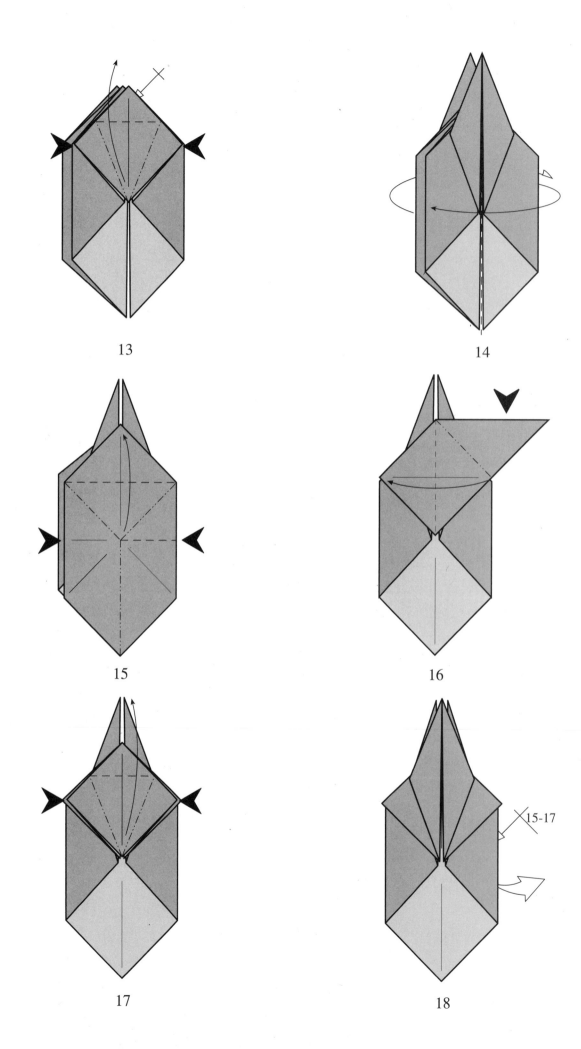

13

14

15

16

17

18

15-17

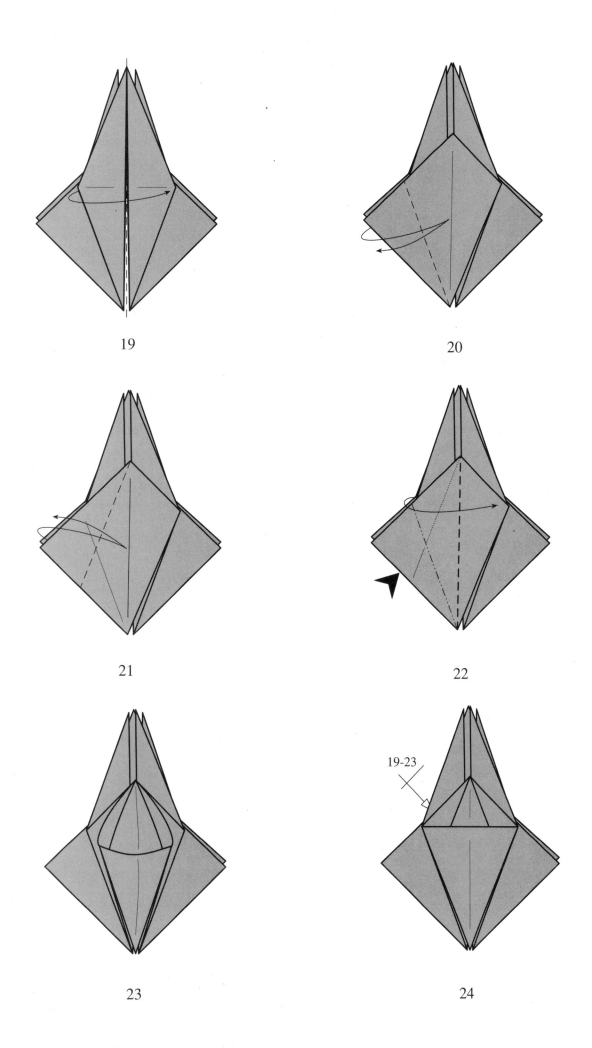

19

20

21

22

23

19-23

24

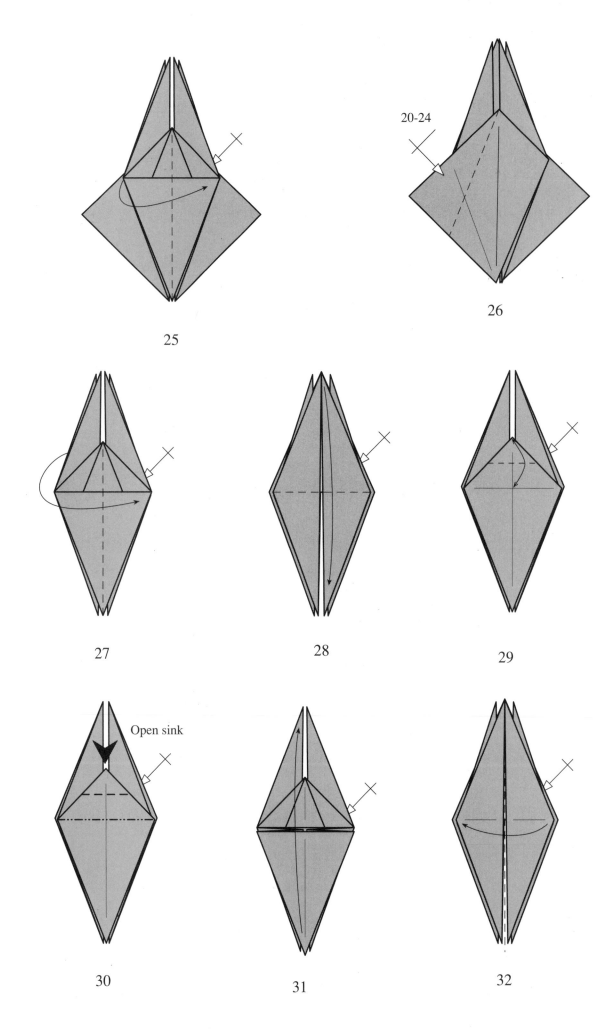

25

20-24

26

27

28

29

Open sink

30

31

32

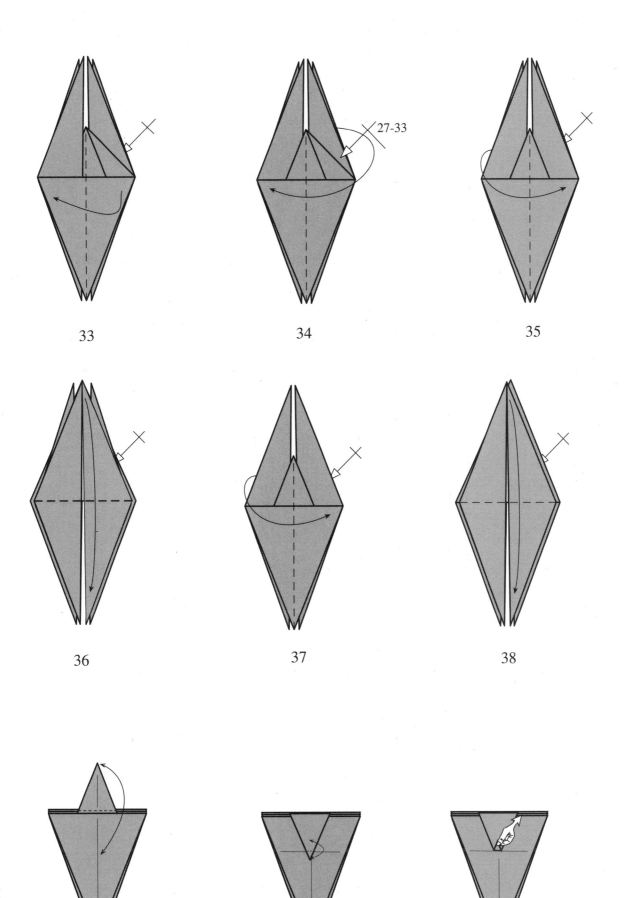

33

34

27-33

35

36

37

38

39

40

41

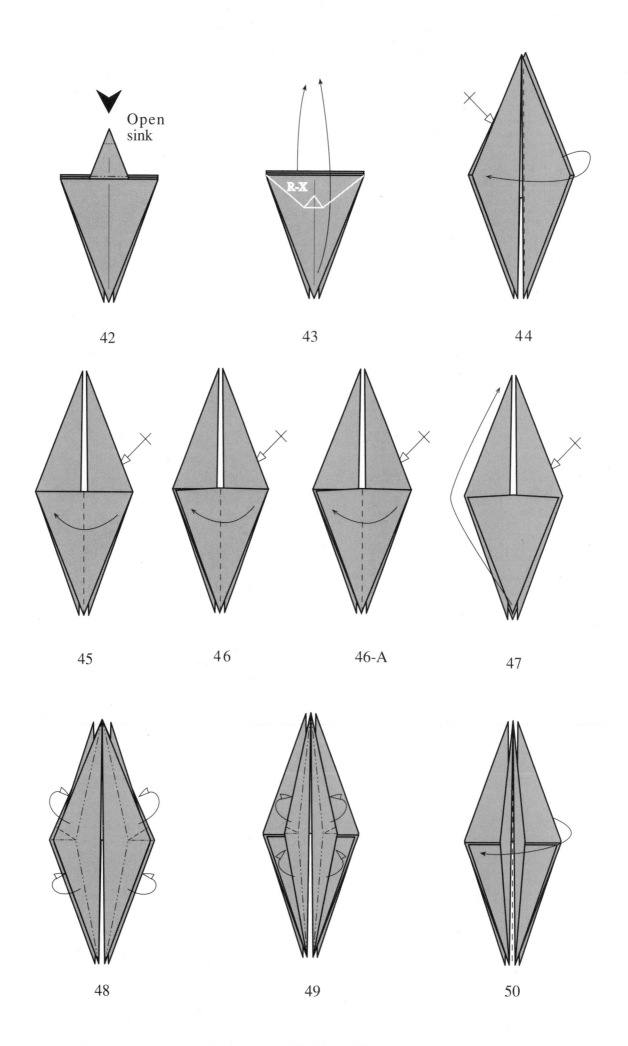

Open
sink

42

R-X

43

44

45

46

46-A

47

48

49

50

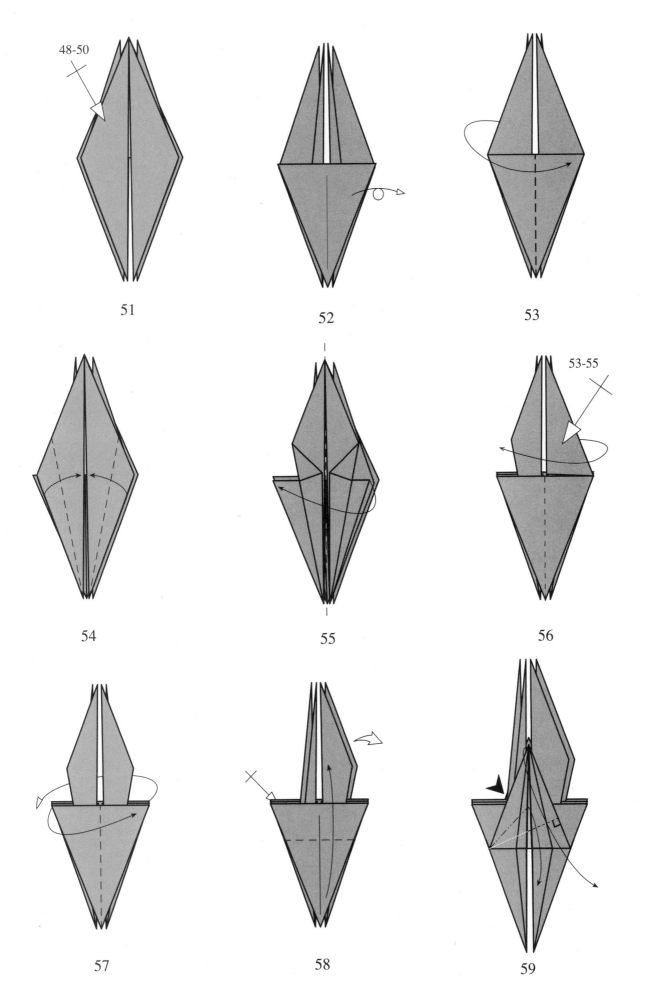

51

52

53

54

55

56

57

58

59

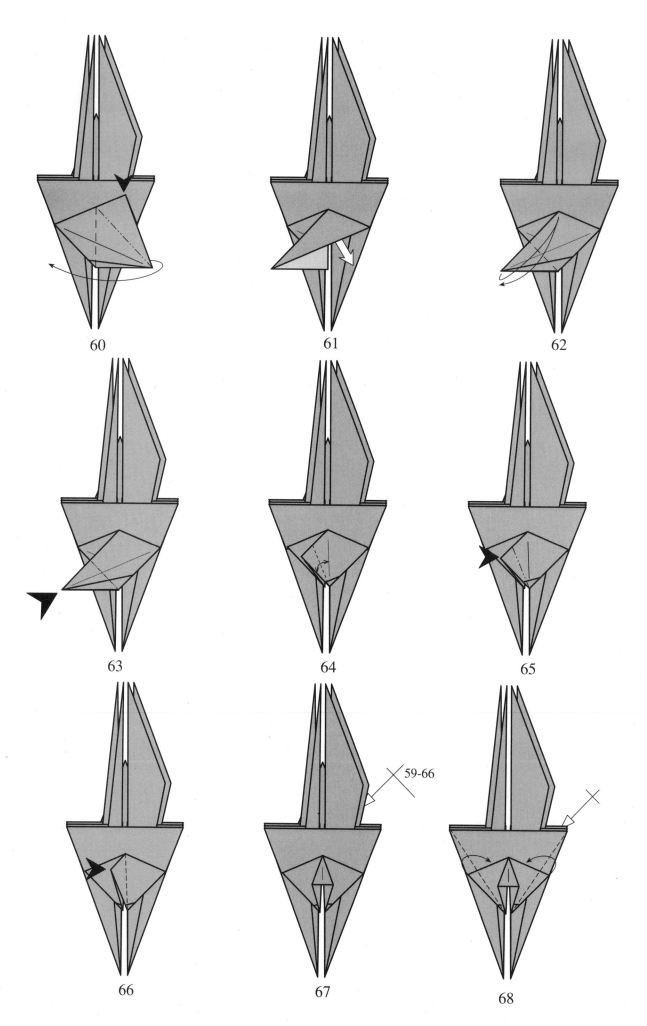

60

61

62

63

64

65

59-66

66

67

68

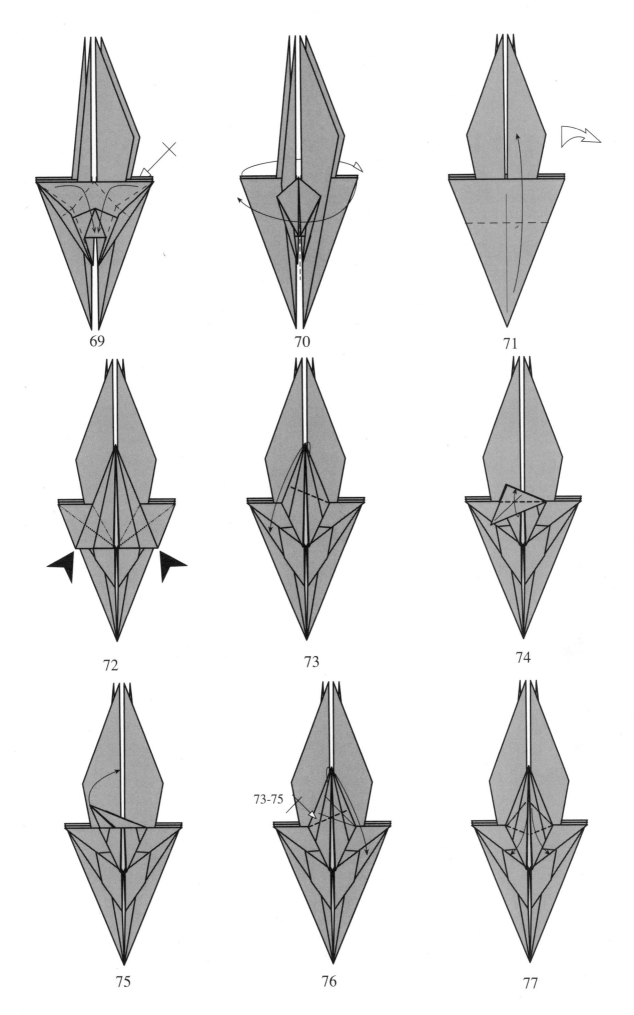

69

70

71

72

73

74

73-75

75

76

77

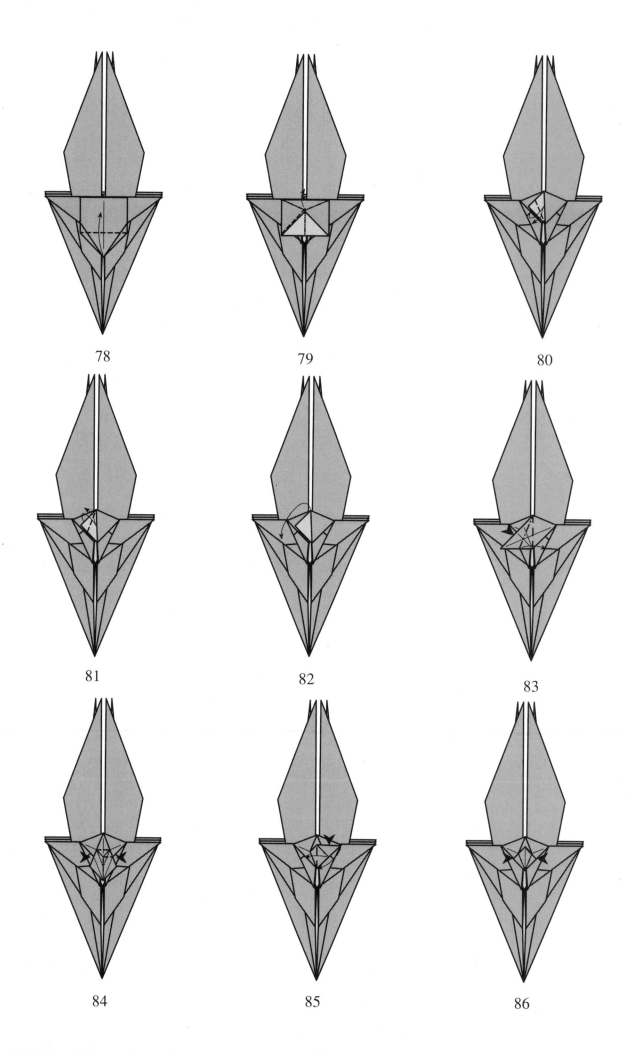

78

79

80

81

82

83

84

85

86

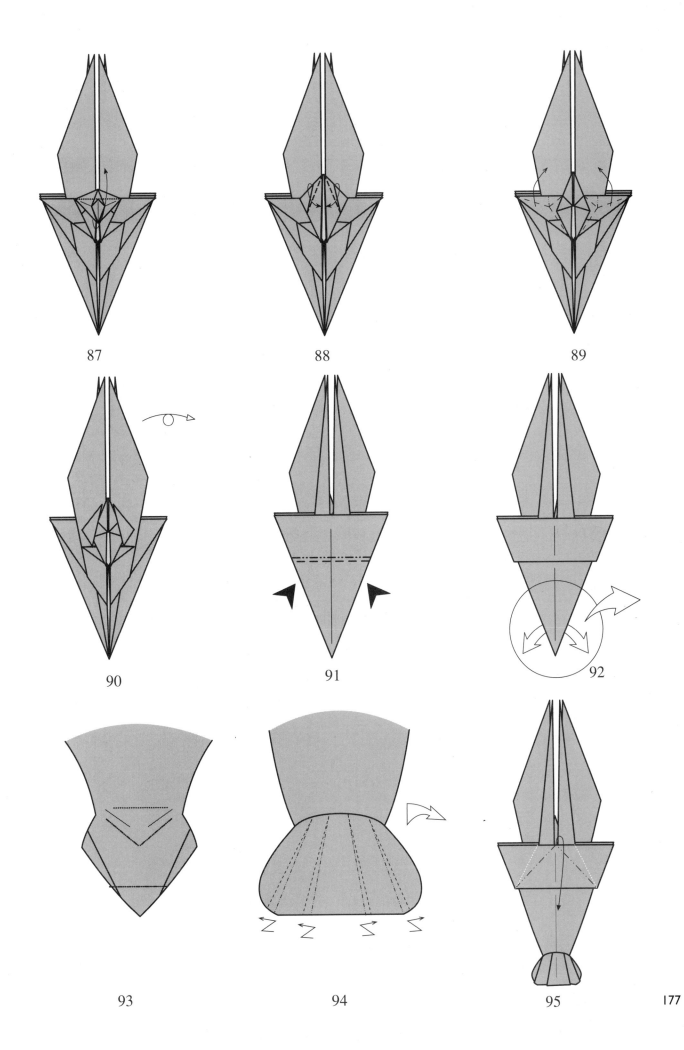

87

88

89

90

91

92

93

94

95

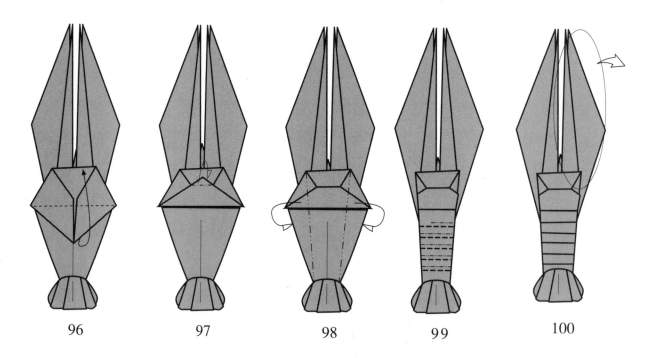

96   97   98   99   100

FOLDING OF THE CLAWS

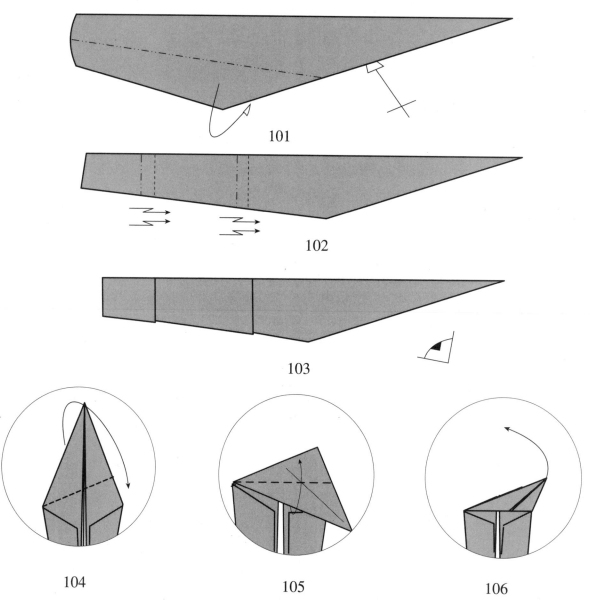

101

102

103

104   105   106

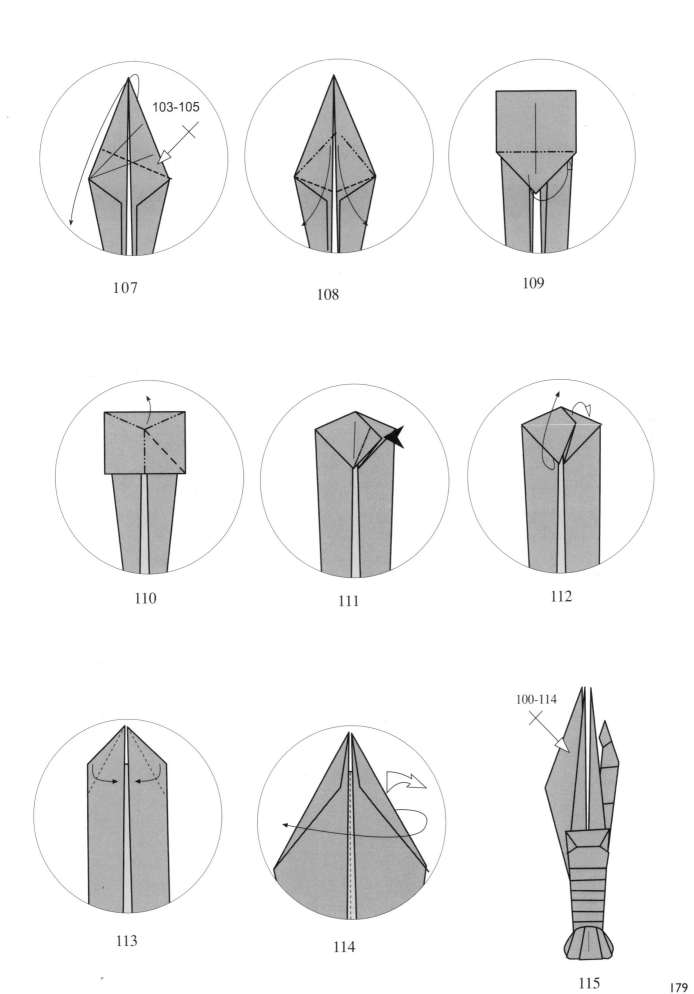

107

103-105

108

109

110

111

112

113

114

115

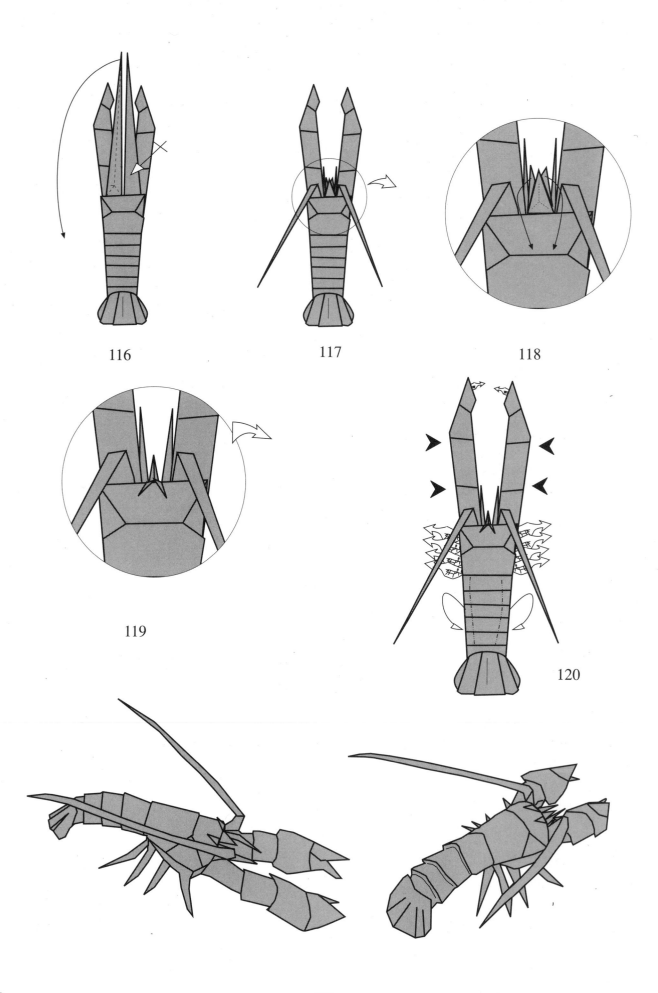

116

117

118

119

120

121

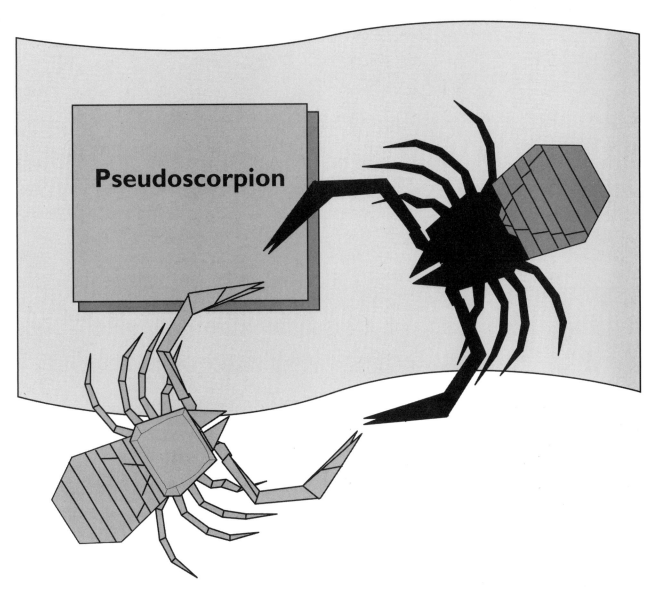

Pseudoscorpion

The paper should be brown. Fine paper is recommended, less than 30 grams, double silk, or "sandwich," 9.8x9.8 inches (25x25 cm) or bigger.

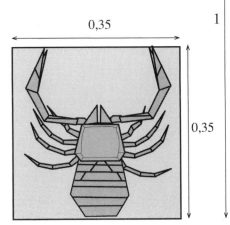

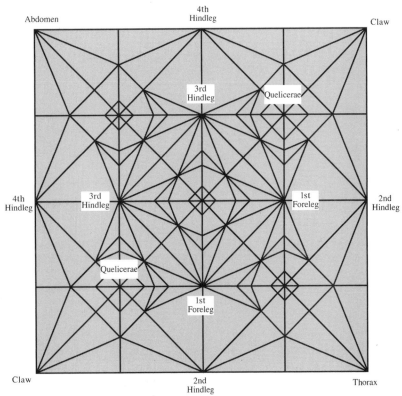

Abdomen · 4th Hindleg · Claw

3rd Hindleg · Quelicerae

4th Hindleg · 3rd Hindleg · 1st Foreleg · 2nd Hindleg

Quelicerae

1st Foreleg

Claw · 2nd Hindleg · Thorax

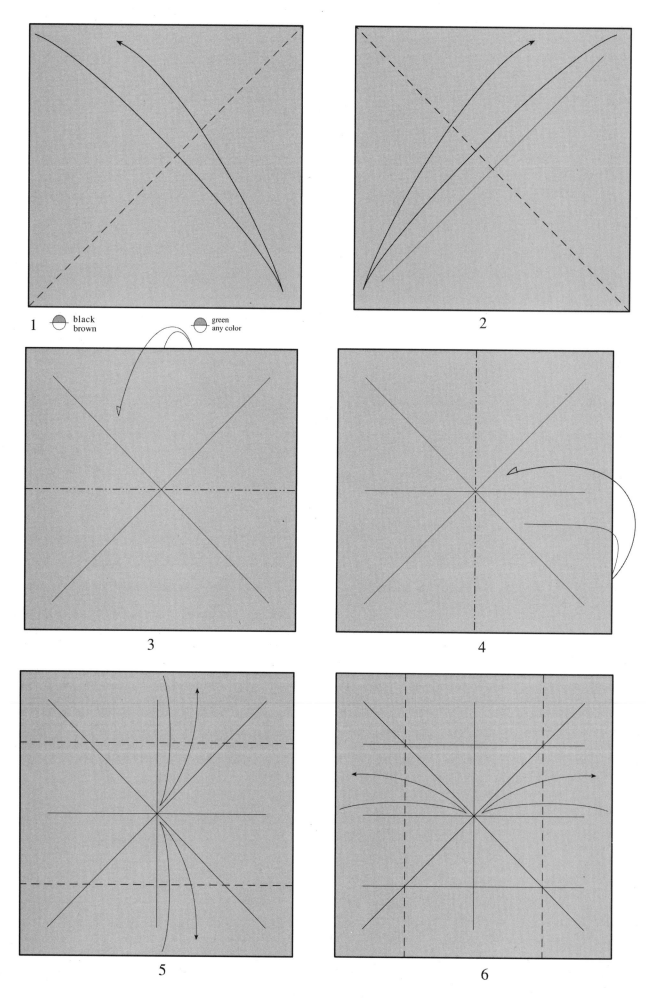

1

black
brown

green
any color

2

3

4

5

6

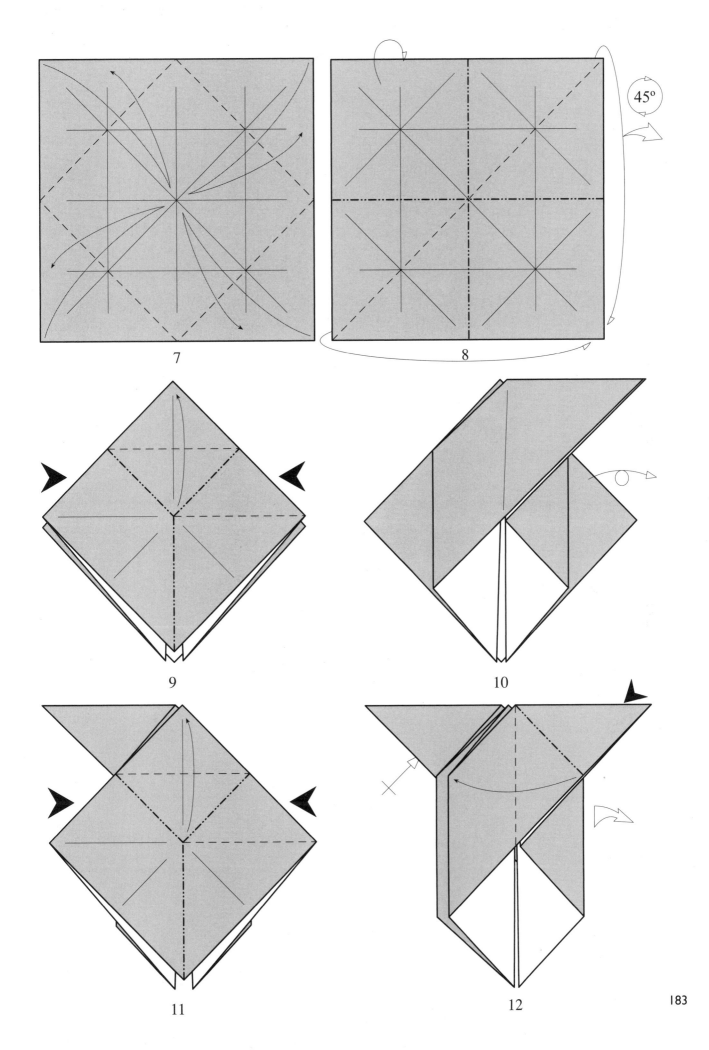

7

8

45°

9

10

11

12

183

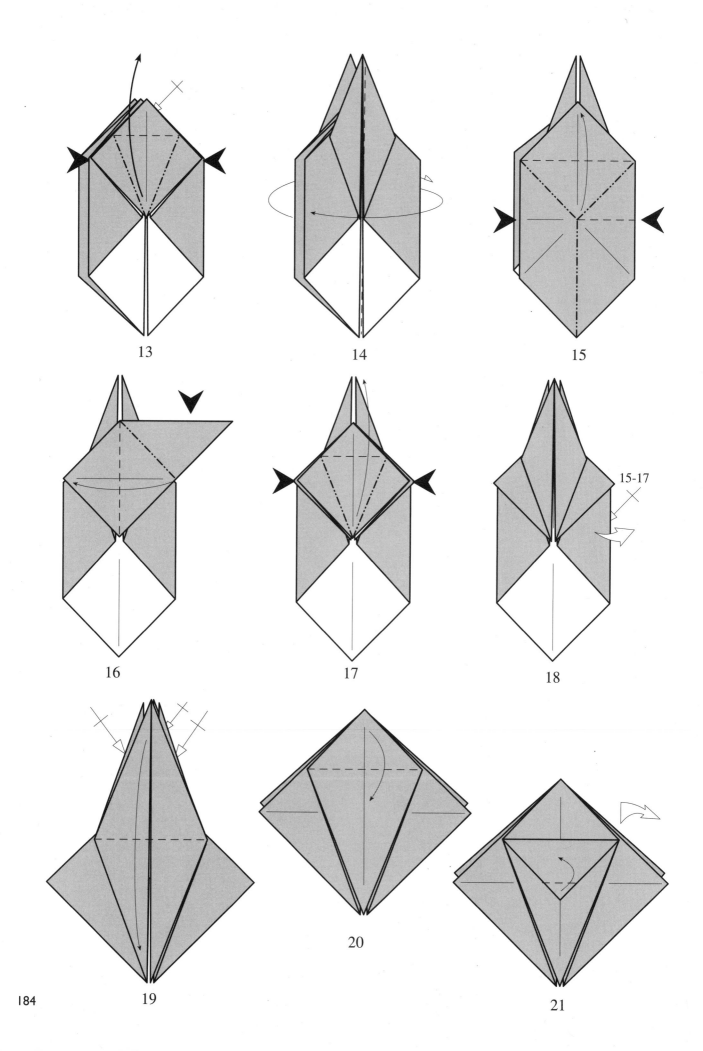

13

14

15

16

17

18

19

20

21

184

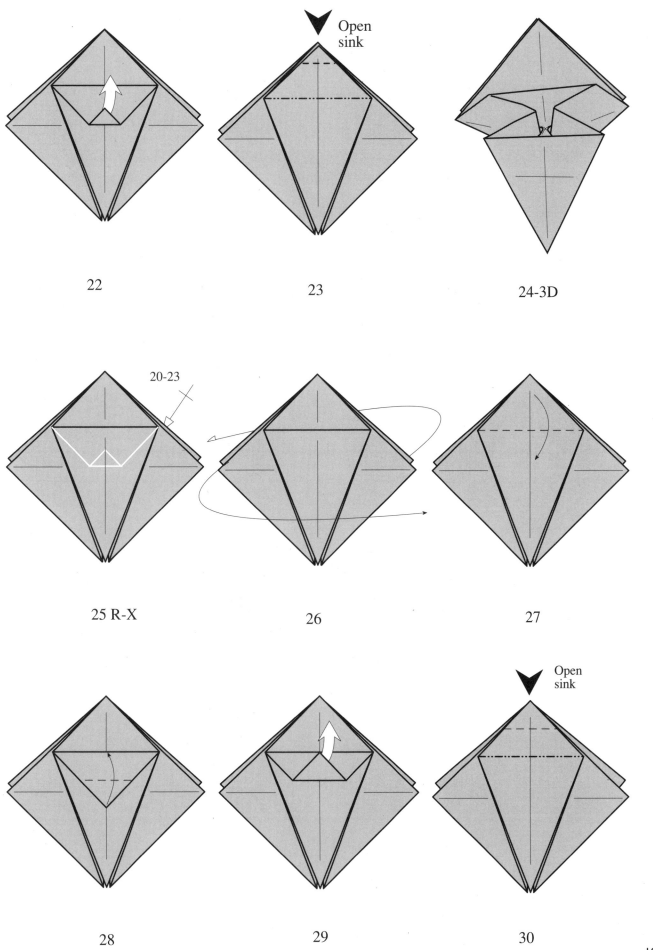

22

23

Open
sink

24-3D

25 R-X

26

27

28

29

30

Open
sink

20-23

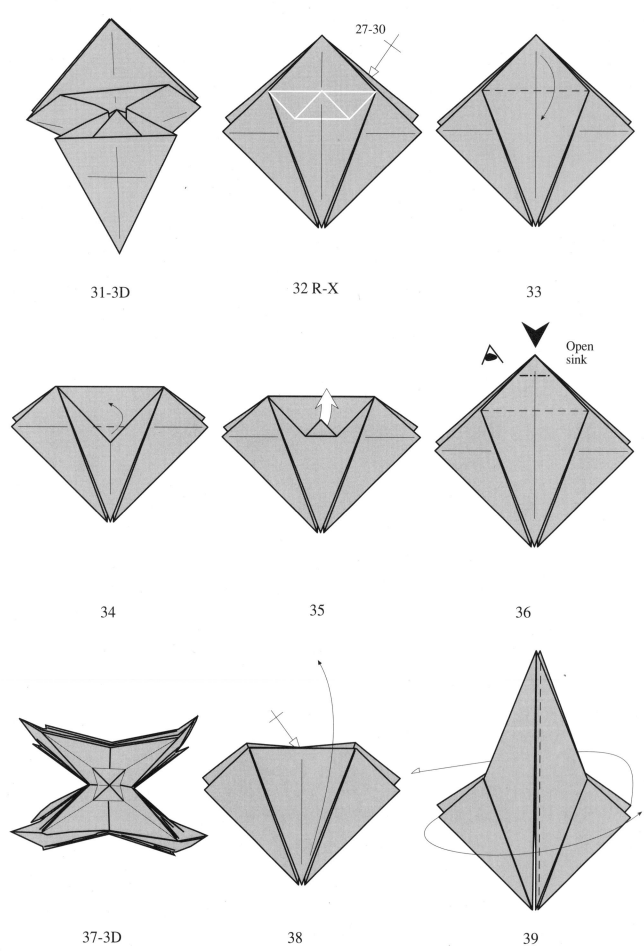

31-3D

32 R-X

33

34

35

36
Open sink

37-3D

38

39

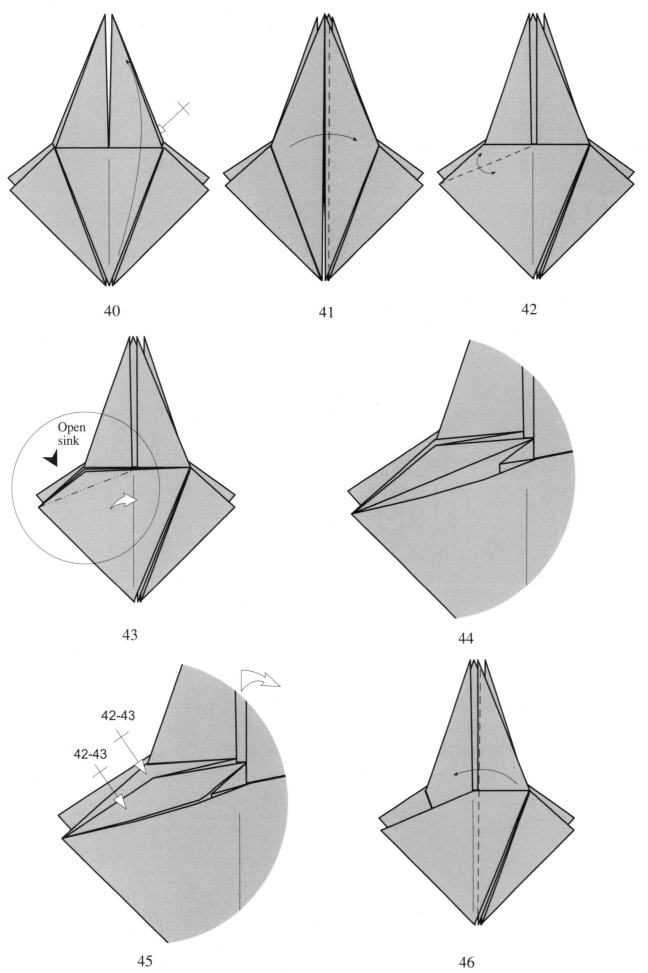

40

41

42

Open
sink

43

44

42-43

42-43

45

46

187

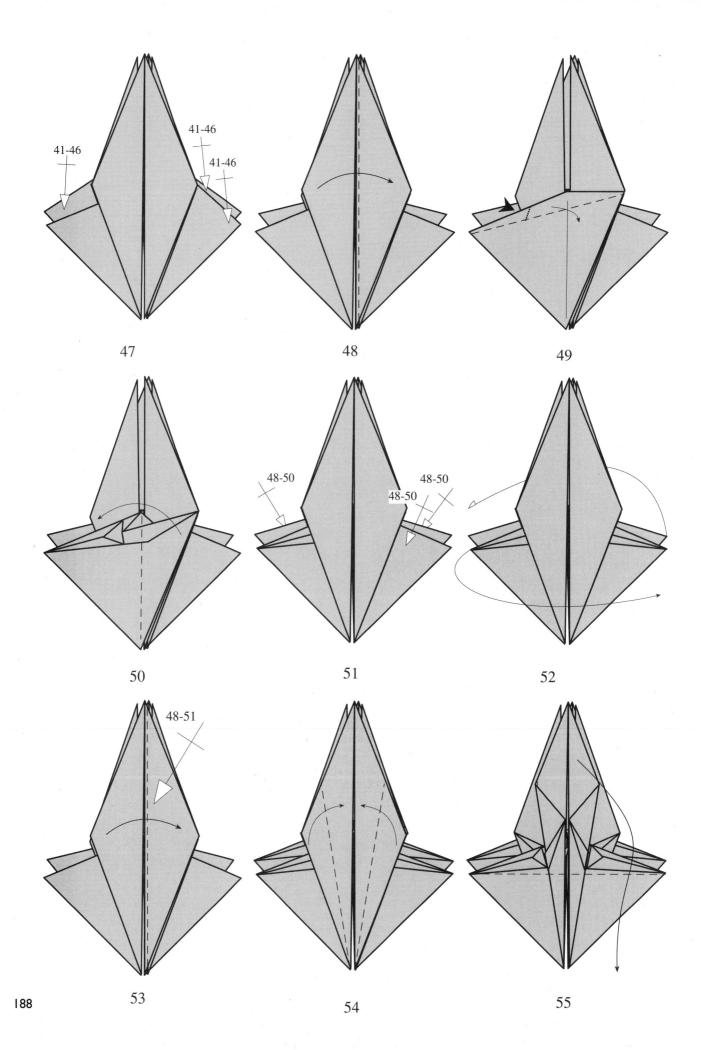

47

48

49

50

51

52

53

54

55

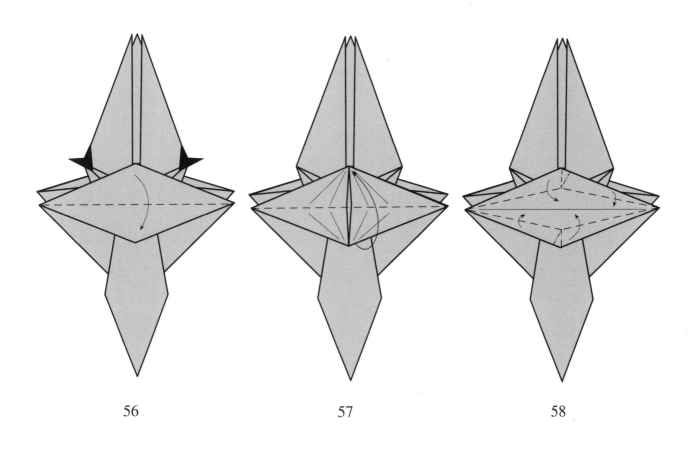

56

57

58

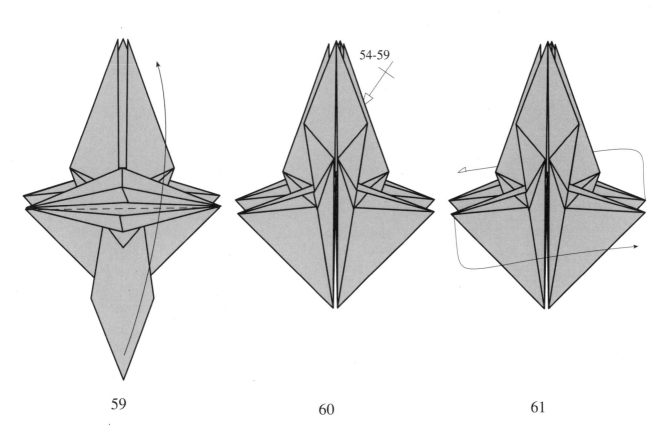

59

60

61

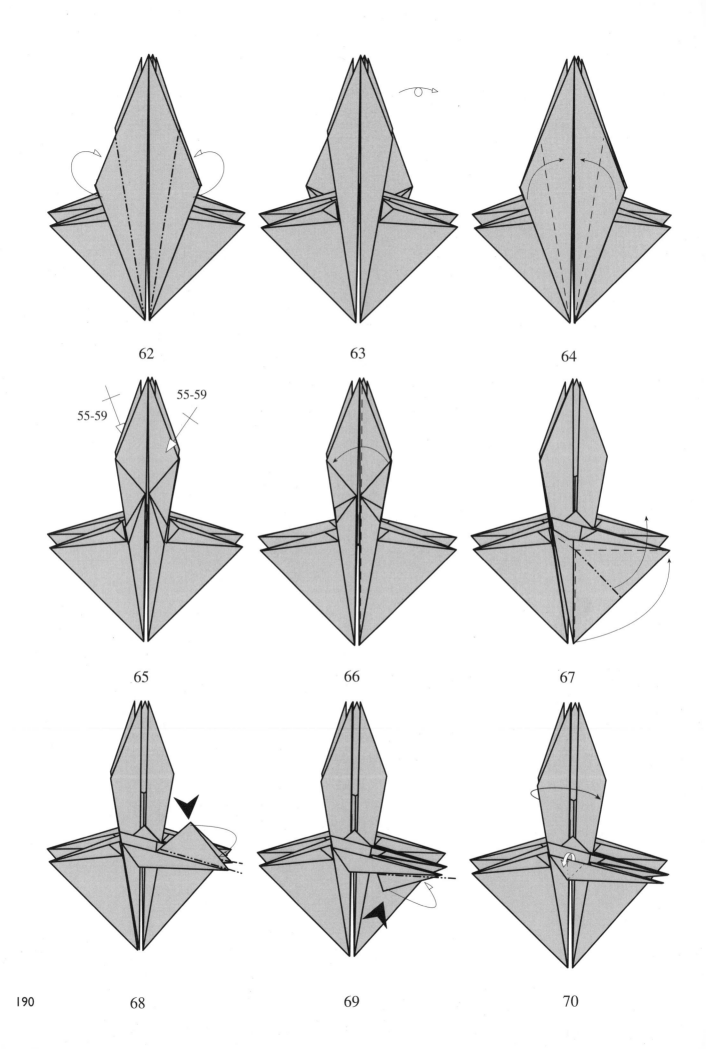

62

63

64

55-59   55-59

65

66

67

68

69

70

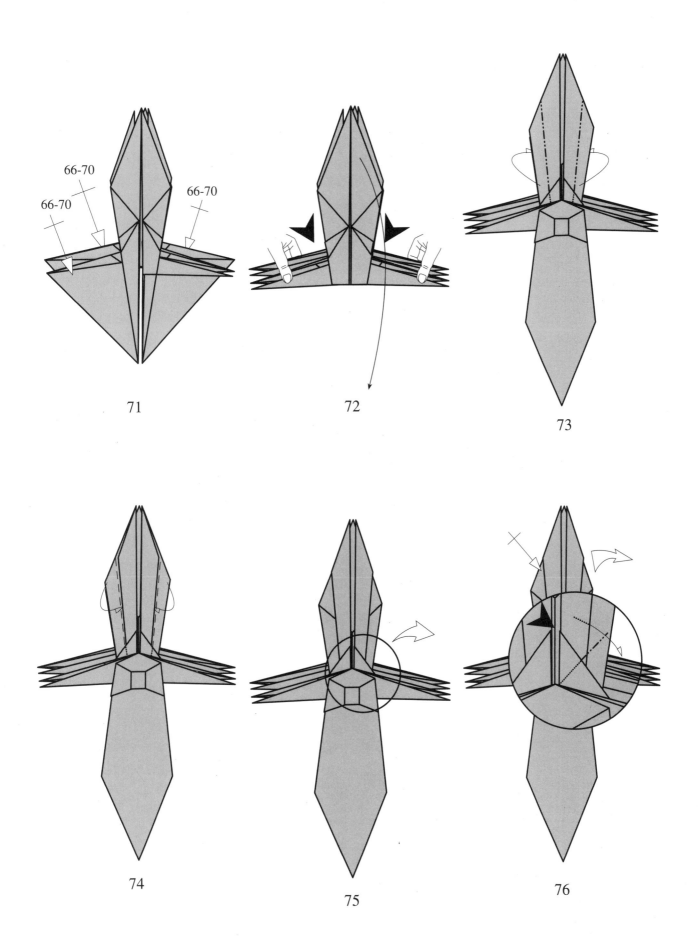

71

72

73

74

75

76

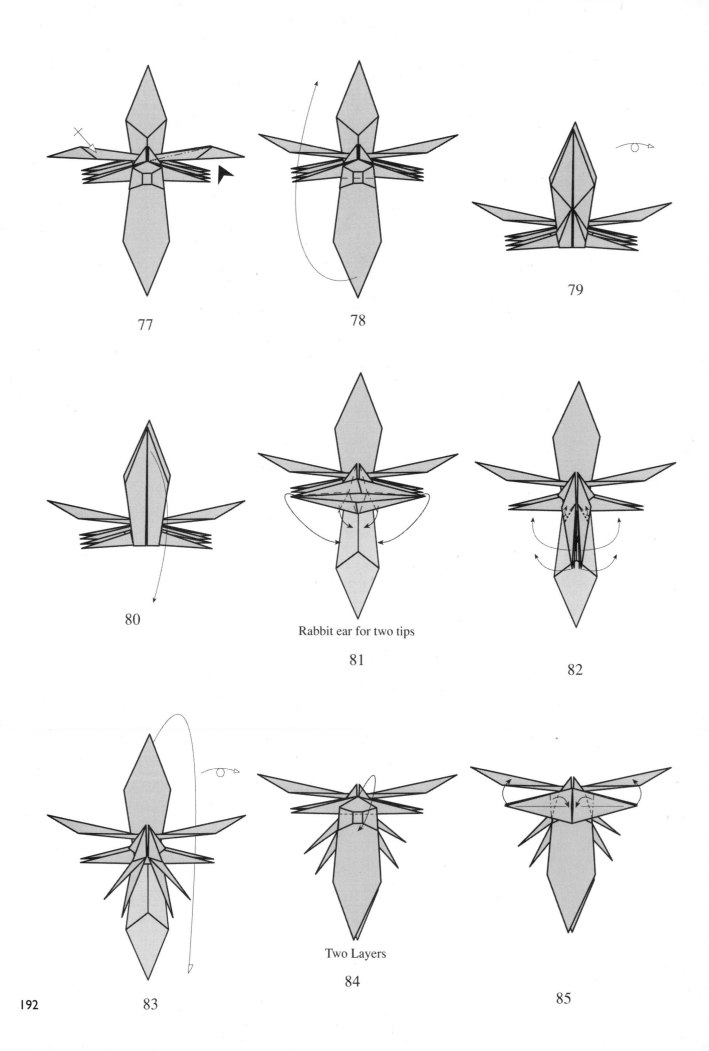

77

78

79

80

81

Rabbit ear for two tips

82

83

84

Two Layers

85

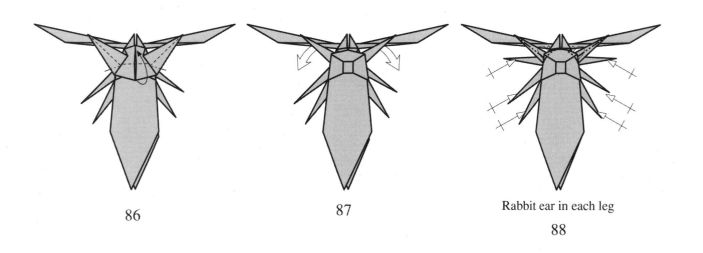

86

87

Rabbit ear in each leg

88

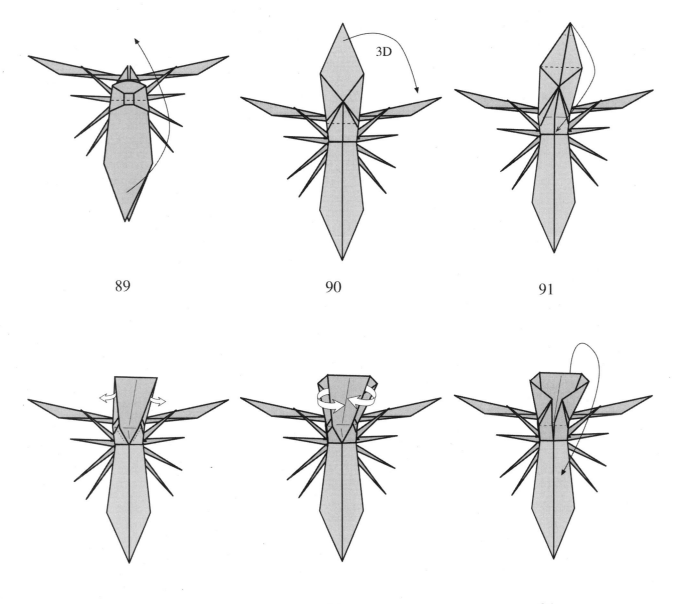

89

90

3D

91

92

93

94

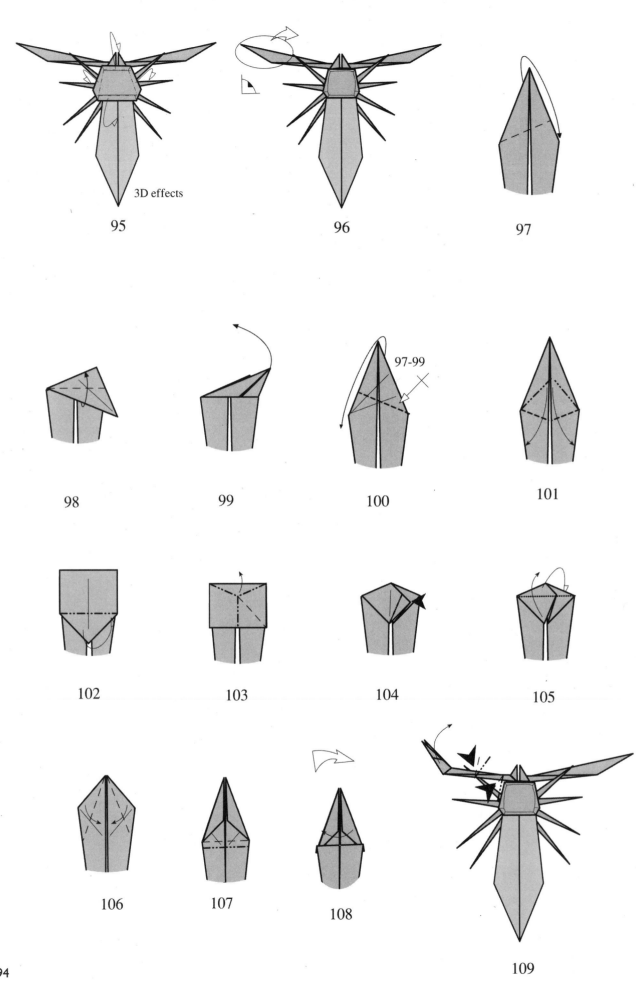

95

3D effects

96

97

98

99

100

97-99

101

102

103

104

105

106

107

108

109

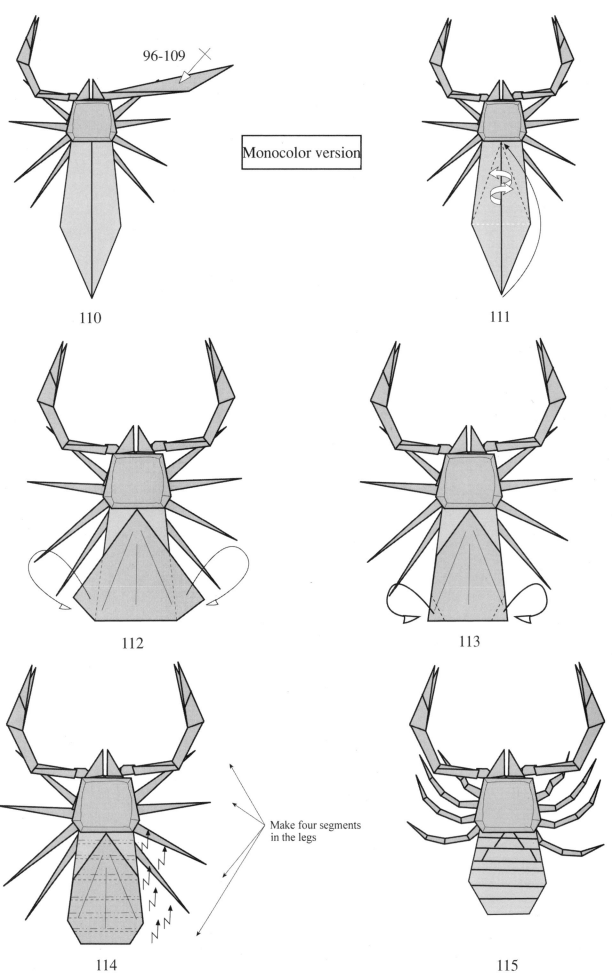

96-109

Monocolor version

110

111

112

113

Make four segments
in the legs

114

115

195

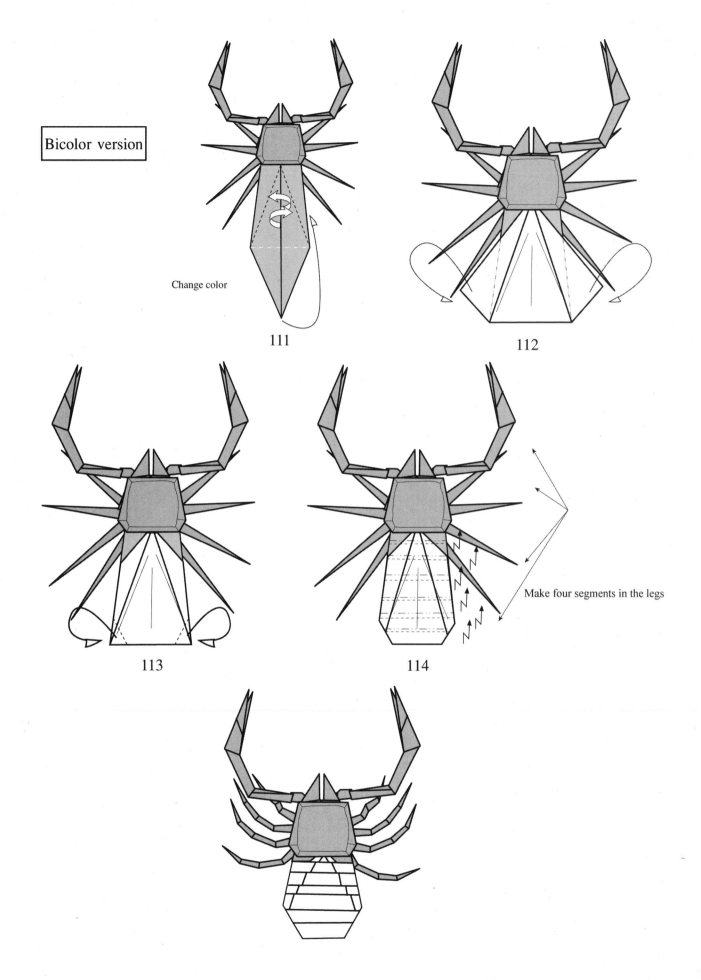

Bicolor version

Change color

111

112

113

114

Make four segments in the legs

115

Scorpion
(Buthus)

The paper should be brown. Fine paper is recommended, less than 30 grams, double silk, or "sandwich," 9.8x9.8 inches (25x25 cm) or bigger.

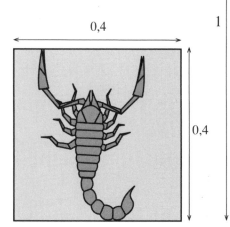

0,4

0,4

1

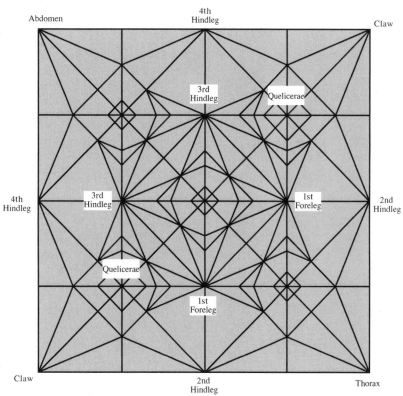

Abdomen

4th Hindleg

Claw

3rd Hindleg

Quelicerae

4th Hindleg

3rd Hindleg

1st Foreleg

2nd Hindleg

Quelicerae

1st Foreleg

Claw

2nd Hindleg

Thorax

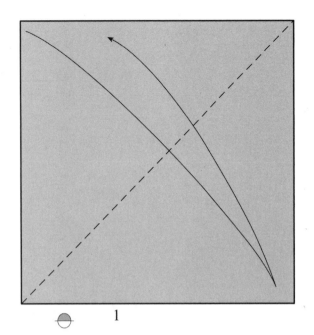

1

Steps 2 until 80 of Pseudoscorpion

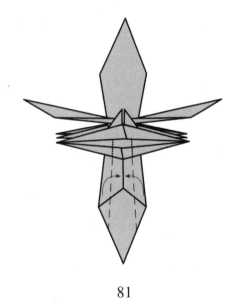

81

Rabbit ear for two tips

82

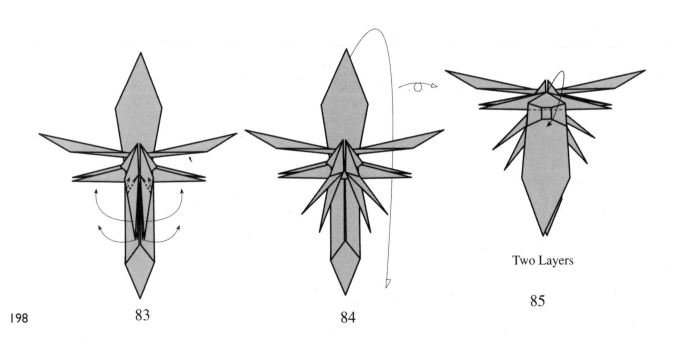

83

84

Two Layers

85

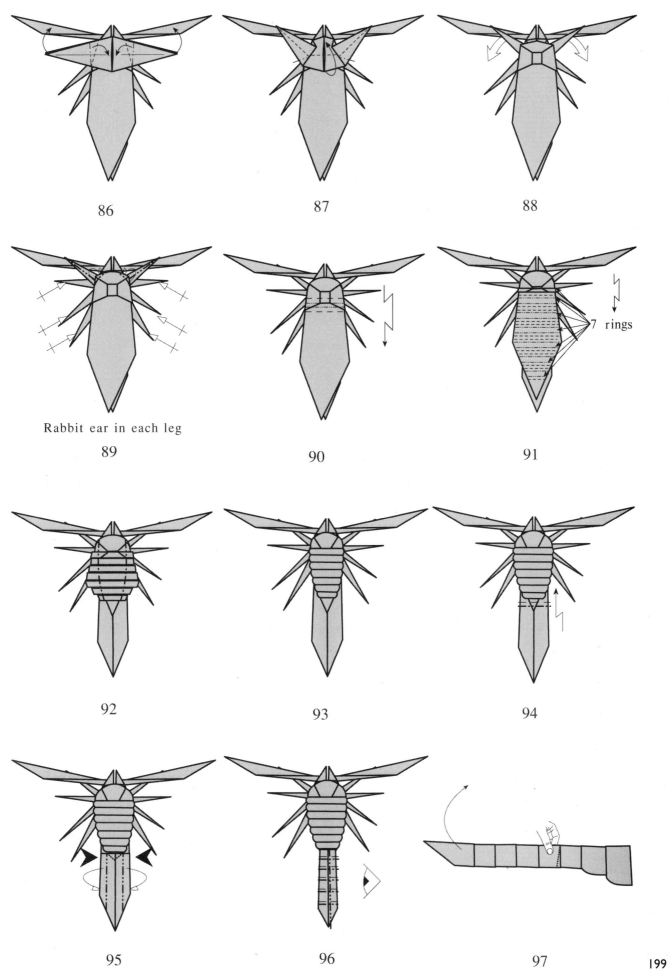

86

87

88

Rabbit ear in each leg

89

90

91

7 rings

92

93

94

95

96

97

199

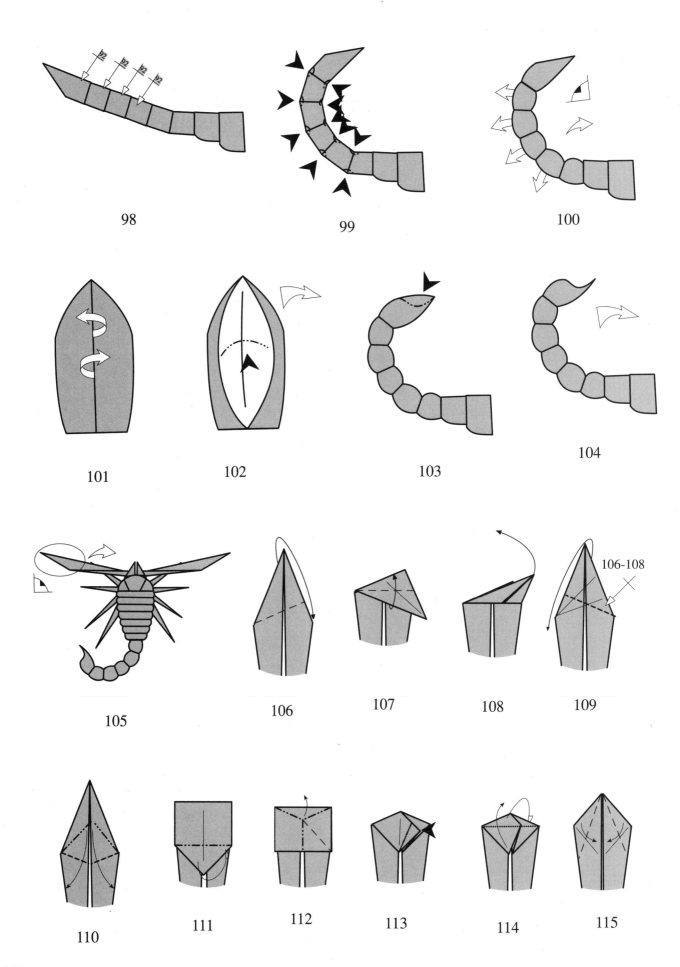

98

99

100

101

102

103

104

105

106

107

108

109

106-108

110

111

112

113

114

115

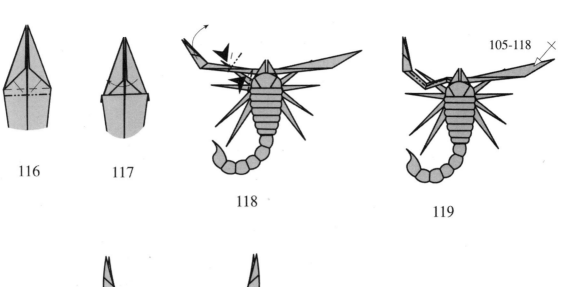

116

117

118

105-118

119

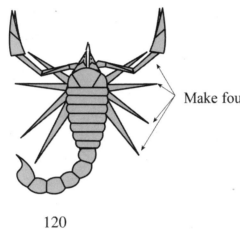

Make four segments in the legs

120

121

Stag Beetle
(*Cyclommatus imperator*)

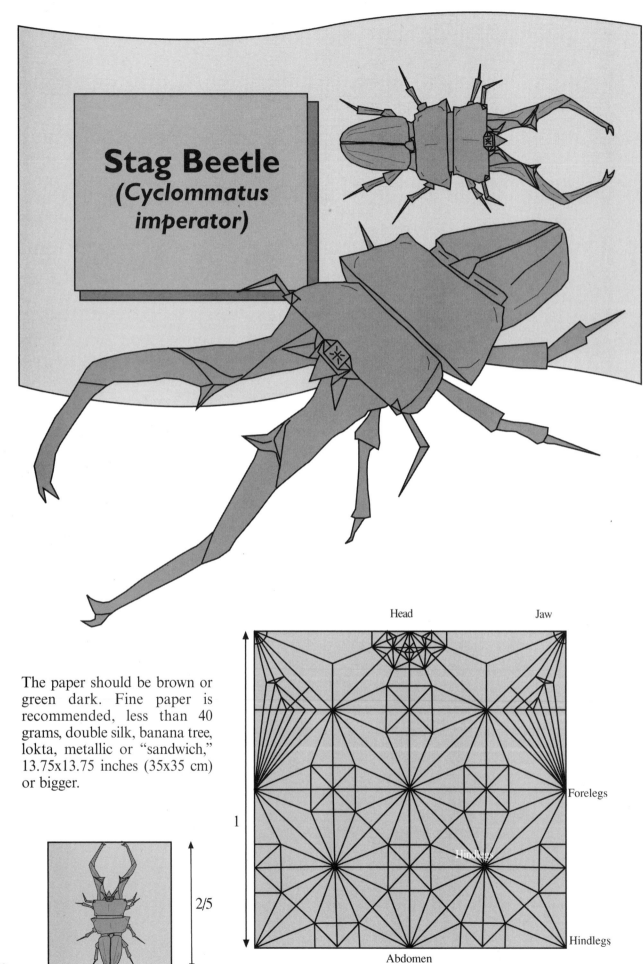

Head

Jaw

Forelegs

Hindlegs

1

Hindlegs

Abdomen

The paper should be brown or green dark. Fine paper is recommended, less than 40 grams, double silk, banana tree, lokta, metallic or "sandwich," 13.75x13.75 inches (35x35 cm) or bigger.

2/5

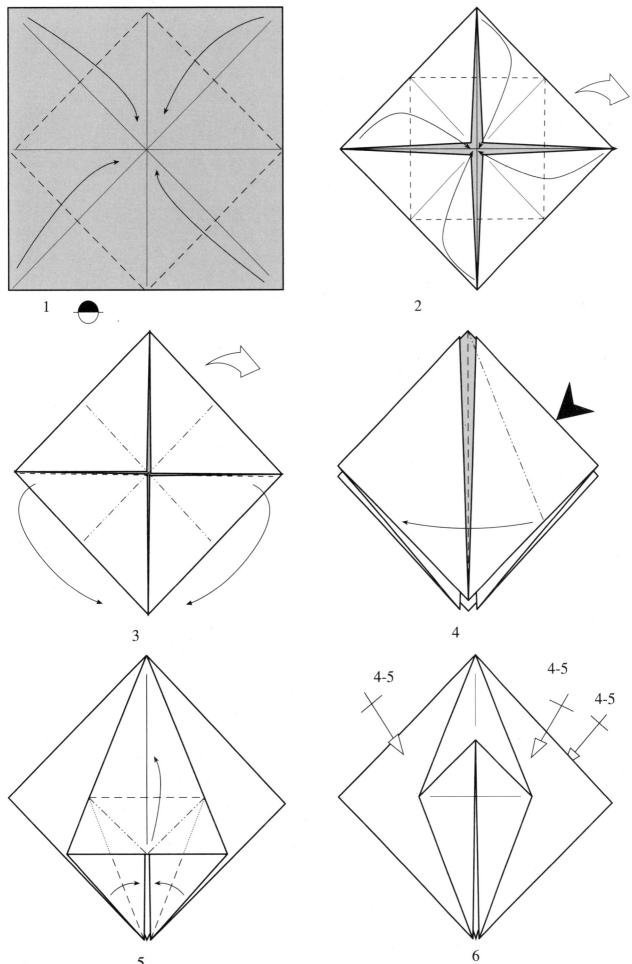

1

2

3

4

4-5

4-5

4-5

5

6

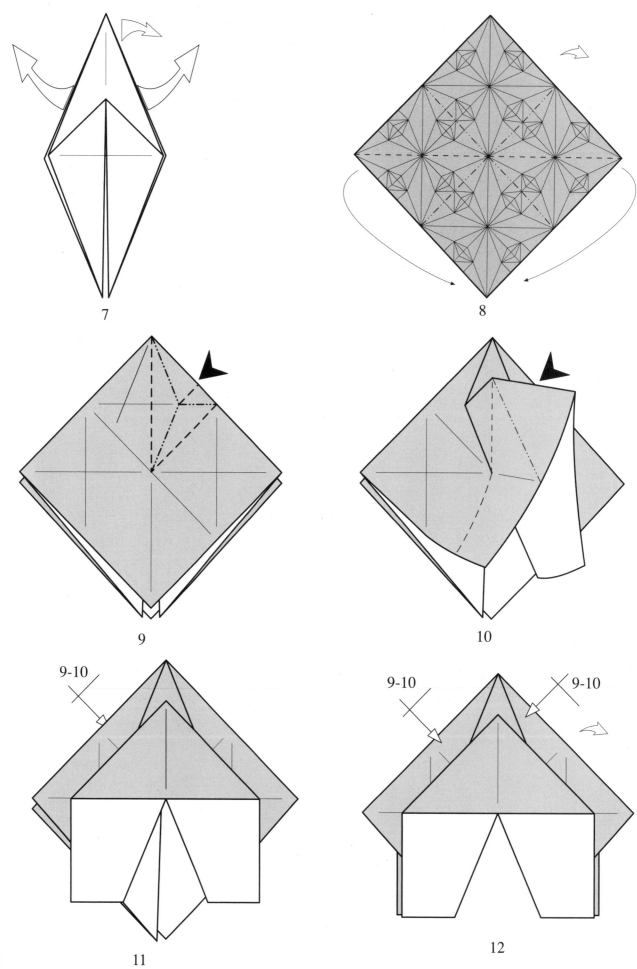

7

8

9

10

9-10

11

9-10   9-10

12

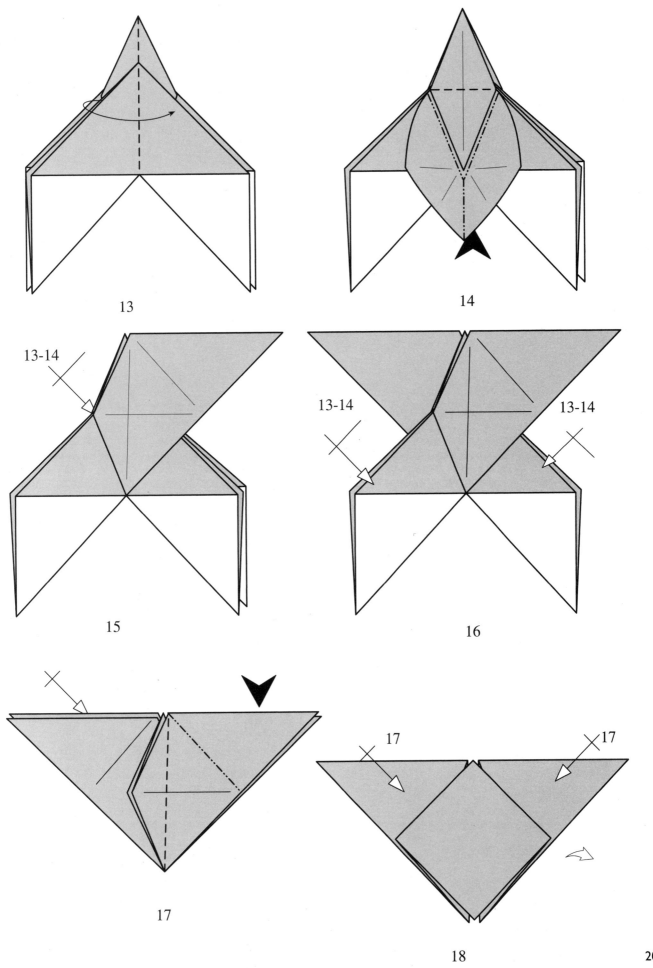

13

14

13-14

15

13-14   13-14

16

17

17   17

18

205

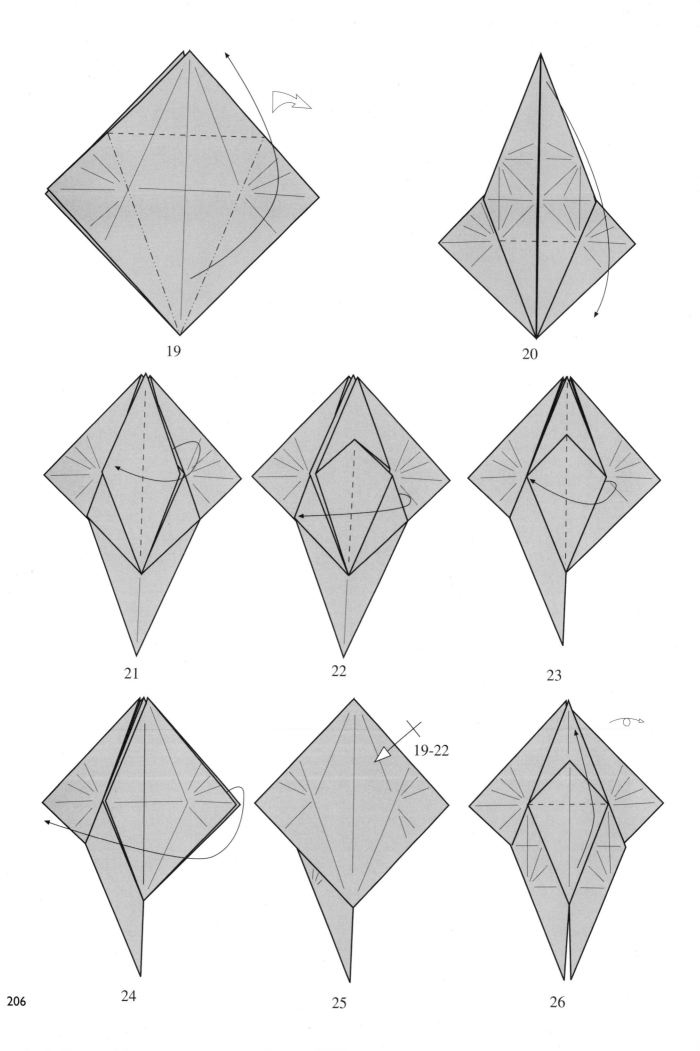

19

20

21

22

23

19-22

24

25

26

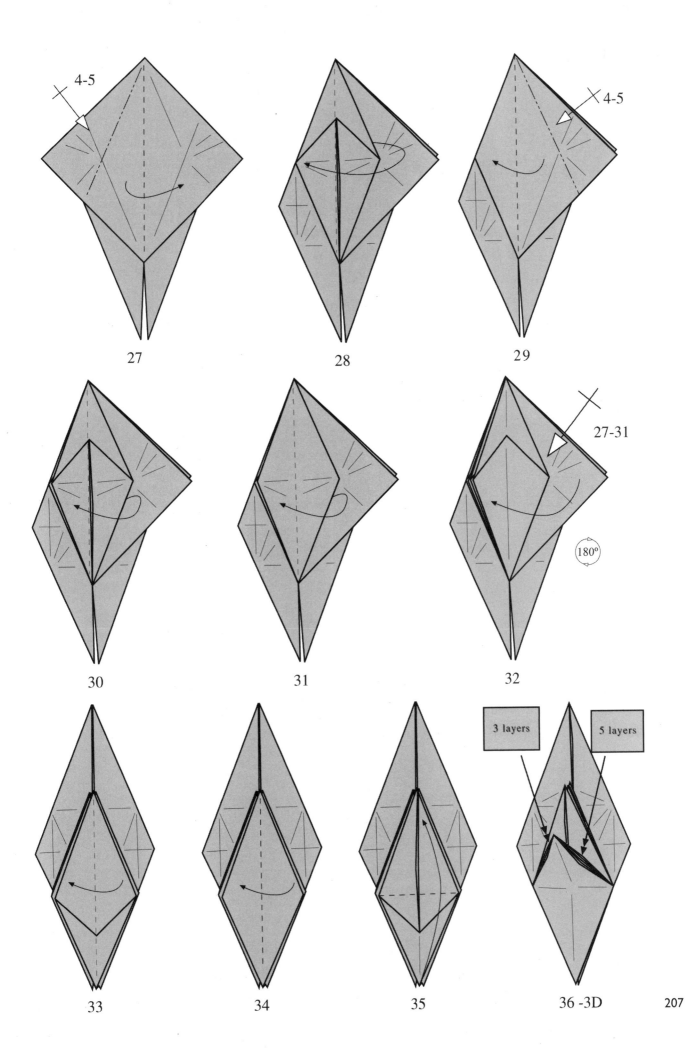

27

28

29

30

31

32

180°

33

34

35

3 layers

5 layers

36 -3D

207

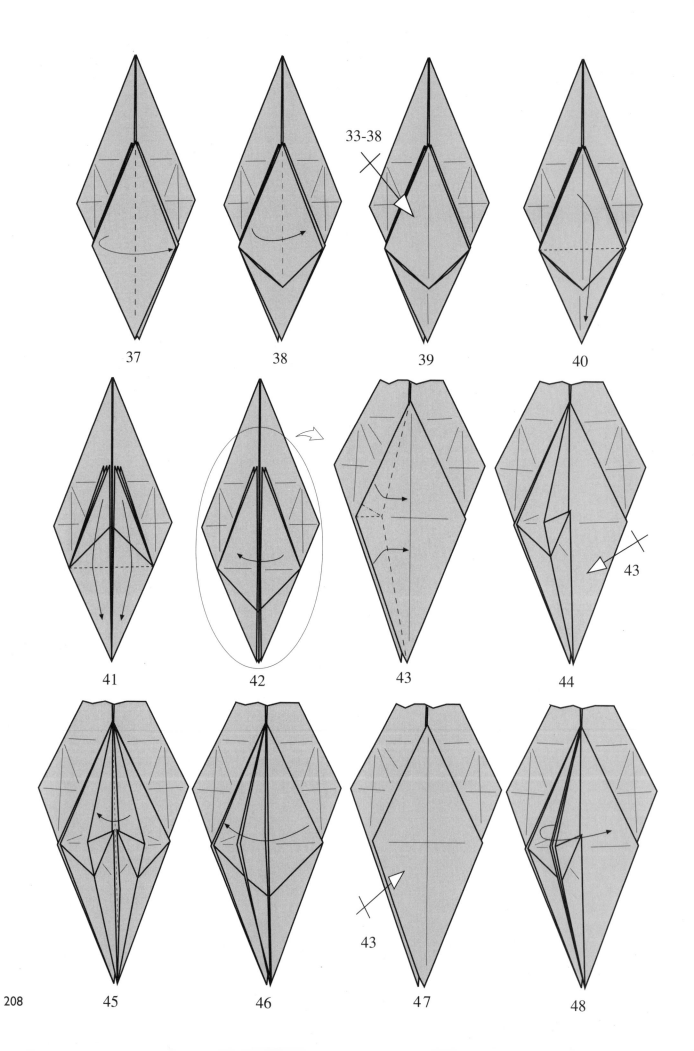

37

38

33-38

39

40

41

42

43

44

45

46

43

47

48

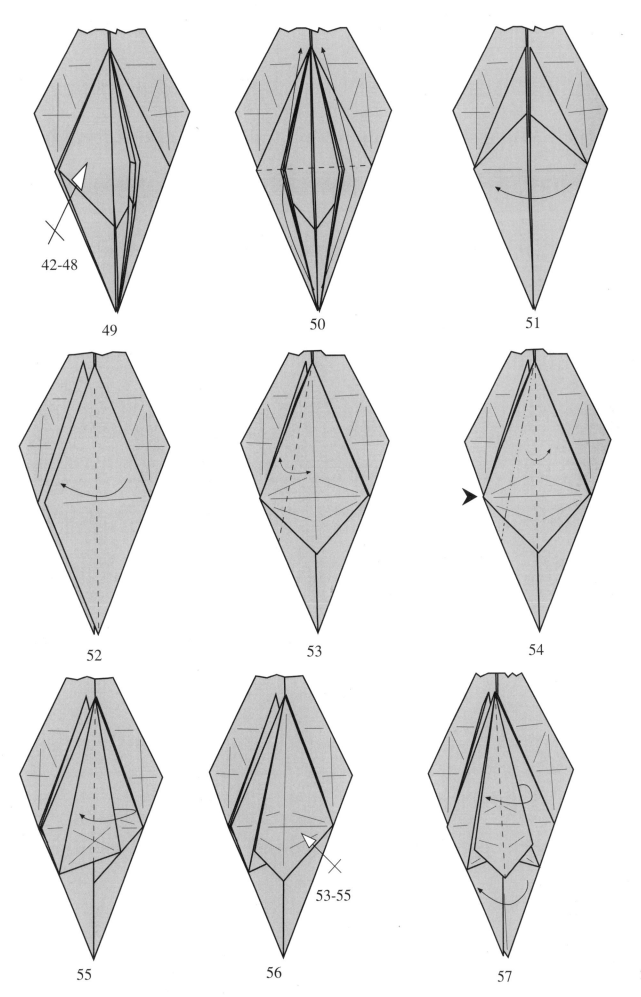

42-48

49

50

51

52

53

54

55

56

53-55

57

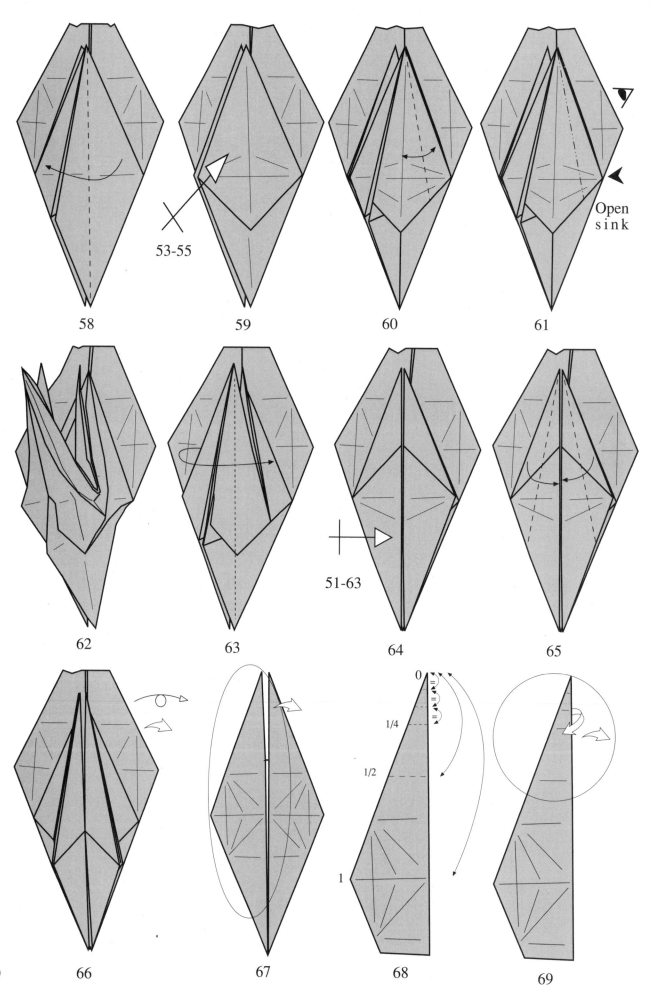

58

59

53-55

60

61

Open
sink

62

63

64

51-63

65

66

67

0
1/4
1/2
1

68

69

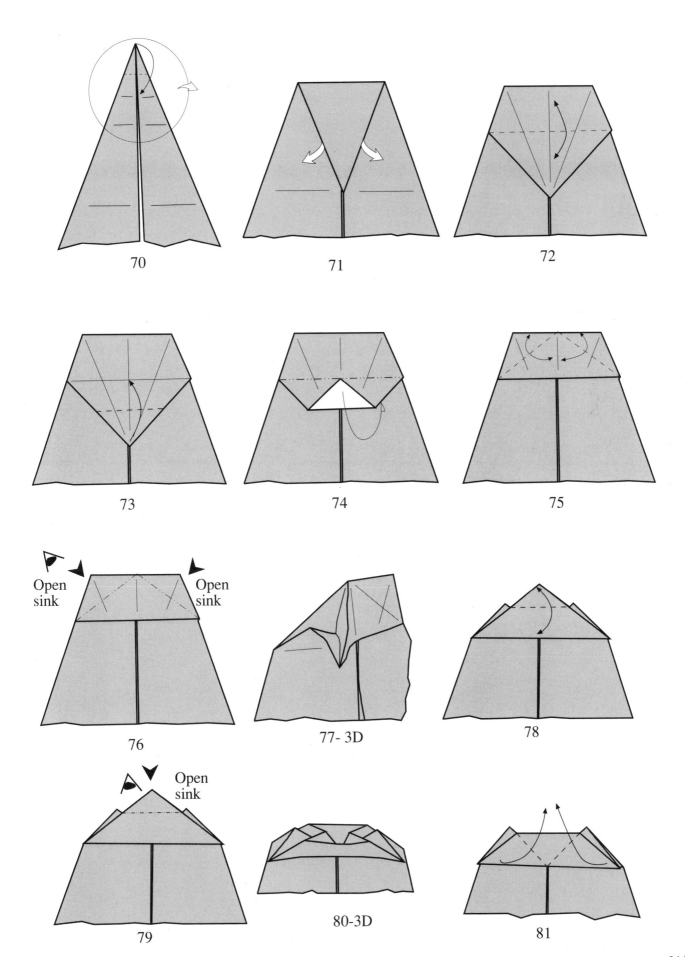

70

71

72

73

74

75

Open
sink

Open
sink

76

77- 3D

78

Open
sink

79

80-3D

81

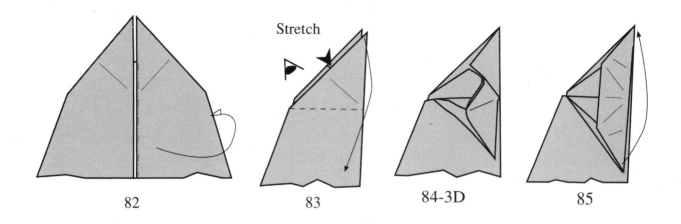

82

Stretch

83

84-3D

85

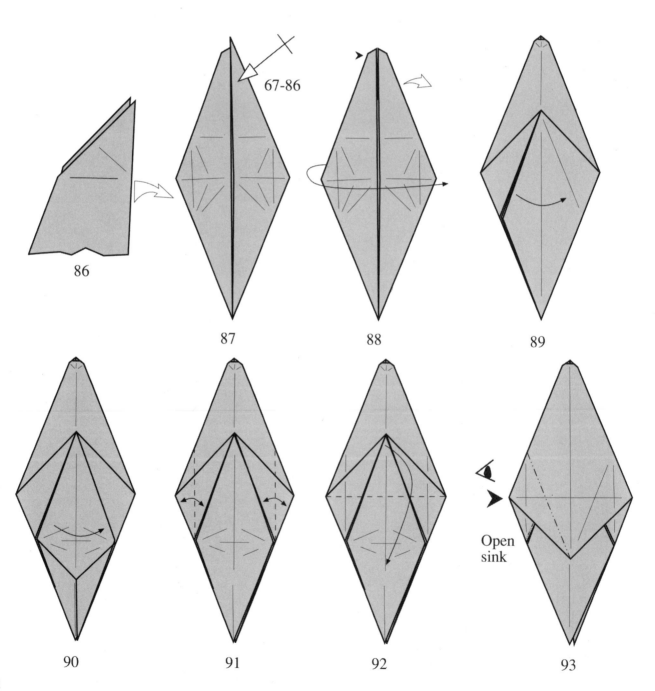

86

67-86

87

88

89

90

91

92

Open
sink

93

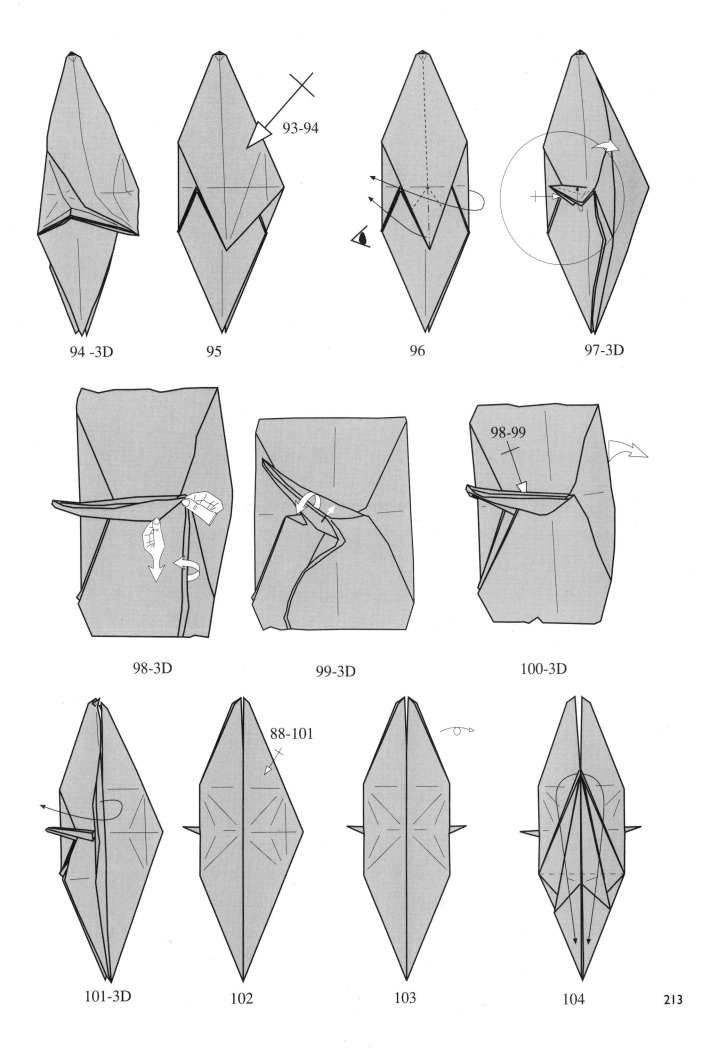

94 -3D

95

93-94

96

97-3D

98-3D

99-3D

98-99

100-3D

101-3D

102

88-101

103

104

213

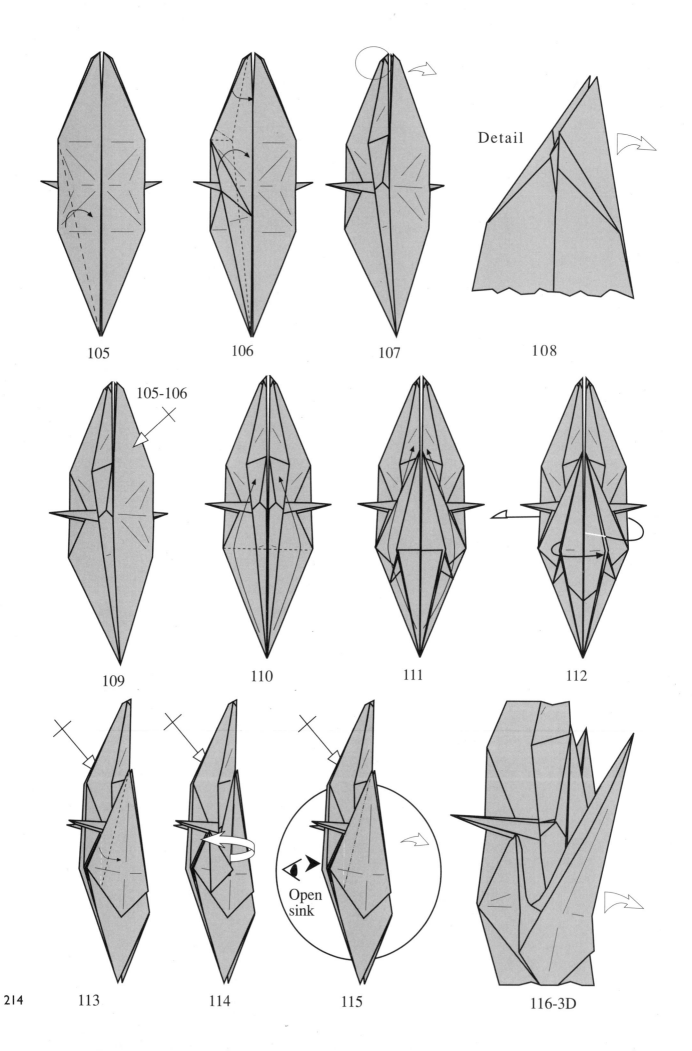

105

106

107

Detail

108

105-106

109

110

111

112

113

114

Open
sink

115

116-3D

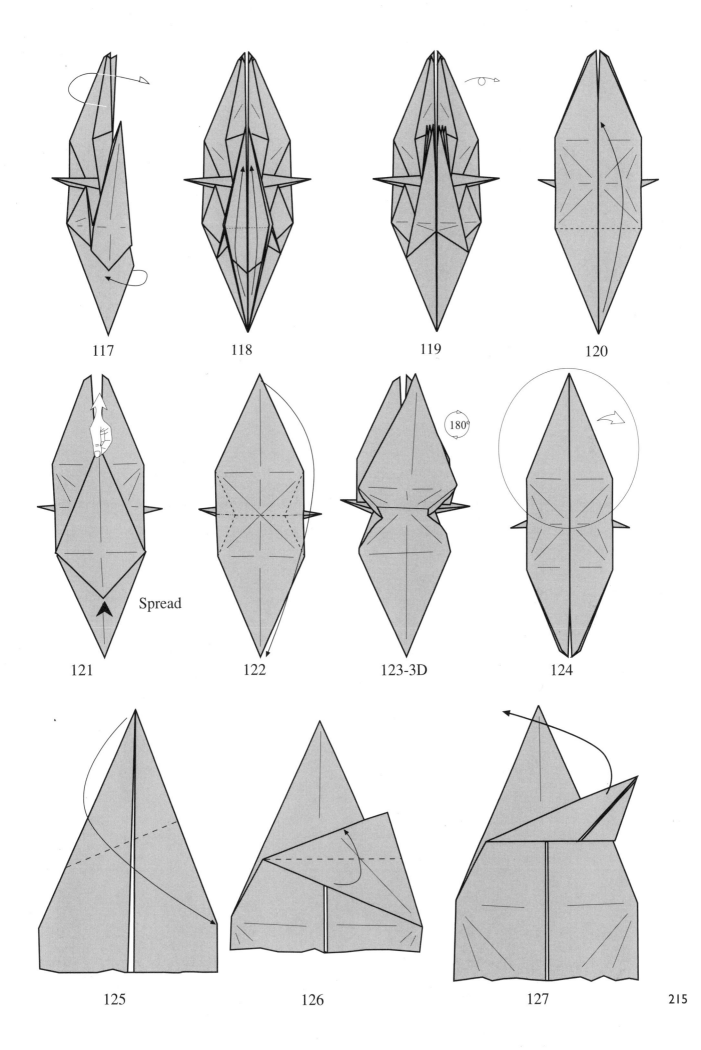

117

118

119

120

121

Spread

122

123-3D

180°

124

125

126

127

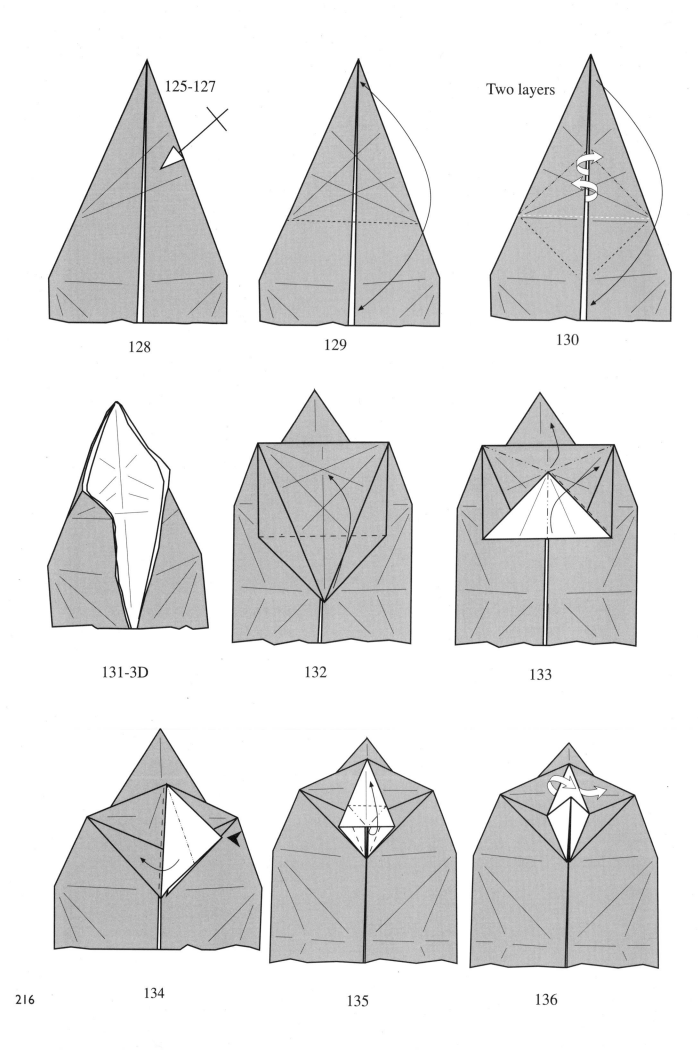

125-127

128

129

Two layers

130

131-3D

132

133

134

135

136

216

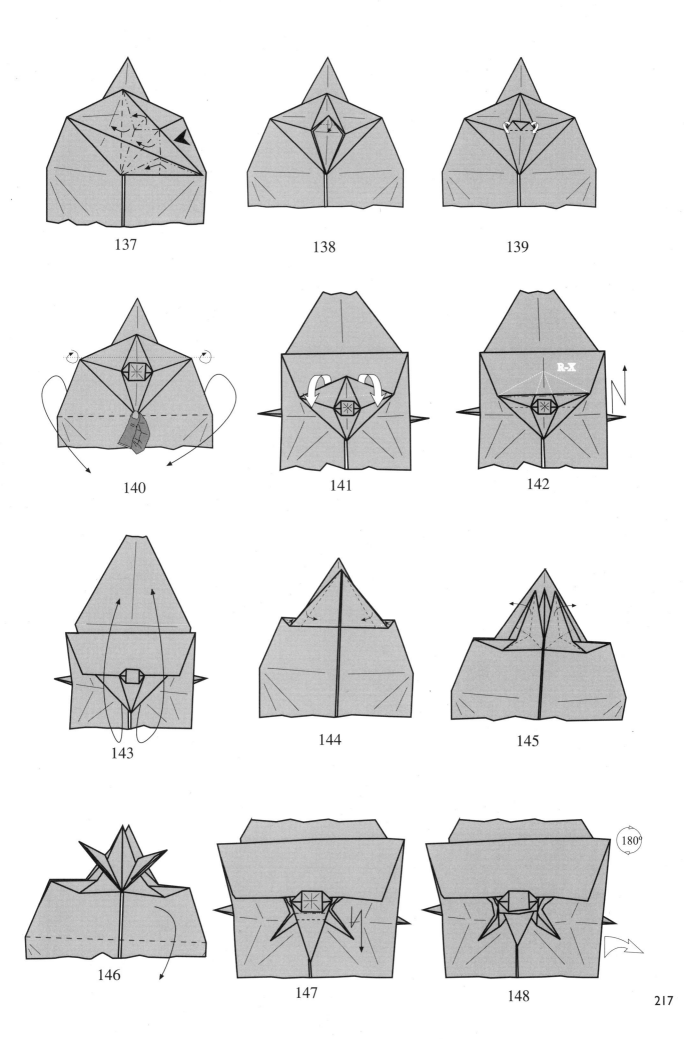

137

138

139

140

141

142

143

144

145

146

147

148

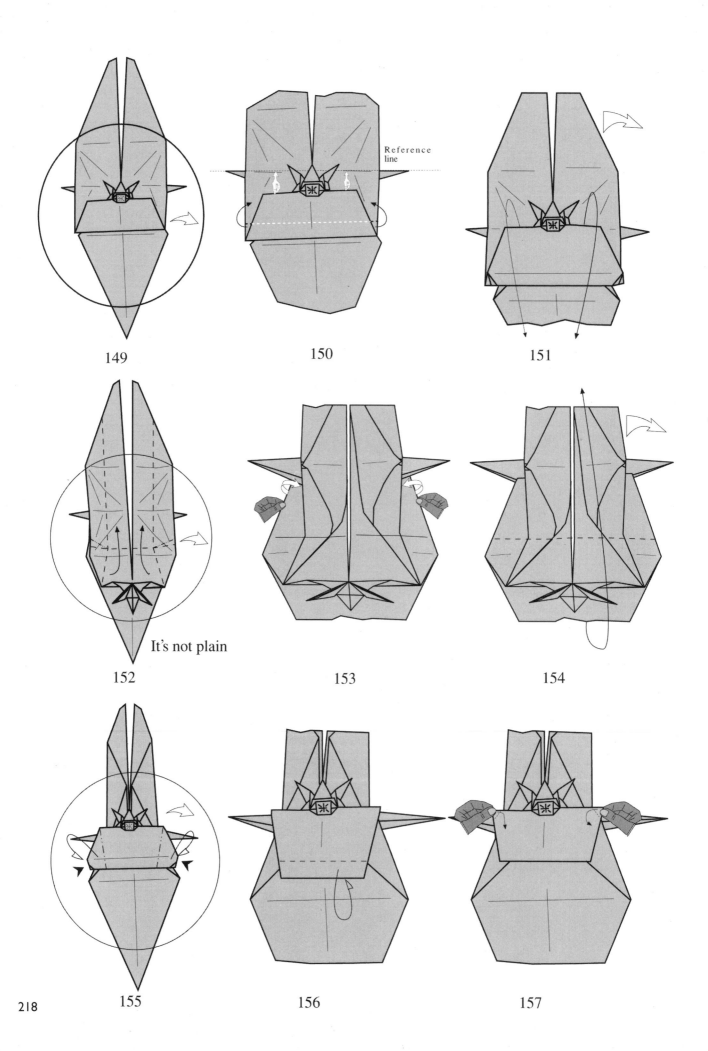

149

150

Reference line

151

152

It's not plain

153

154

155

156

157

218

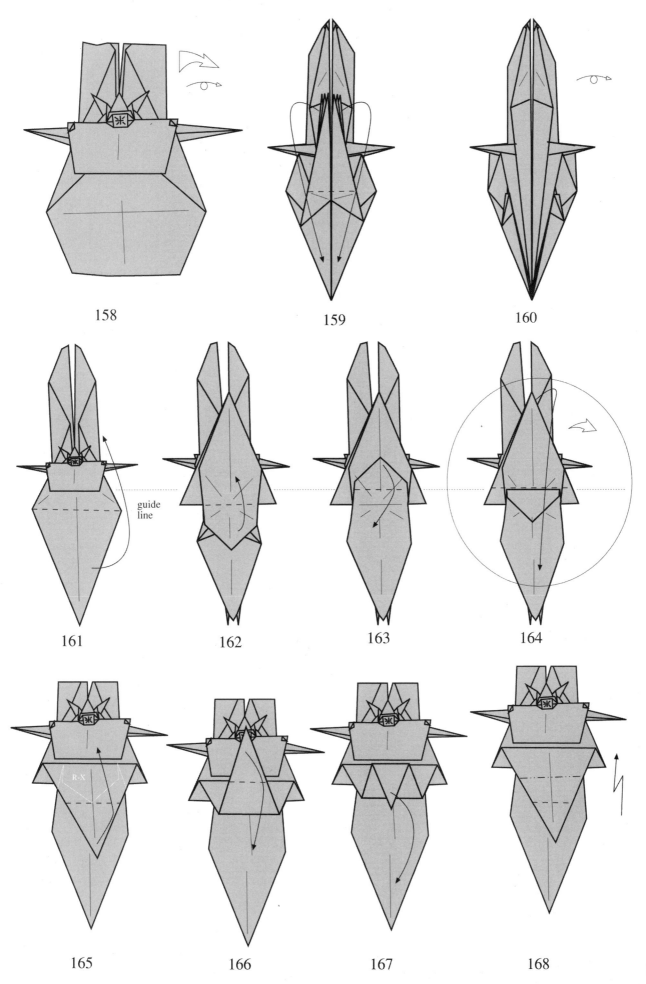

158

159

160

161

guide
line

162

163

164

165

R-X

166

167

168

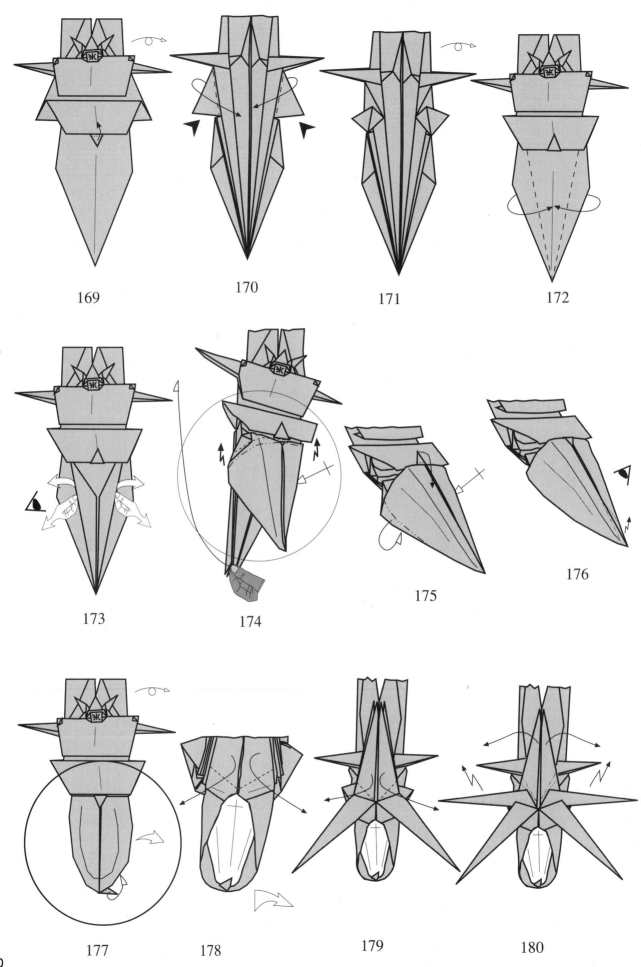

169

170

171

172

173

174

175

176

177

178

179

180

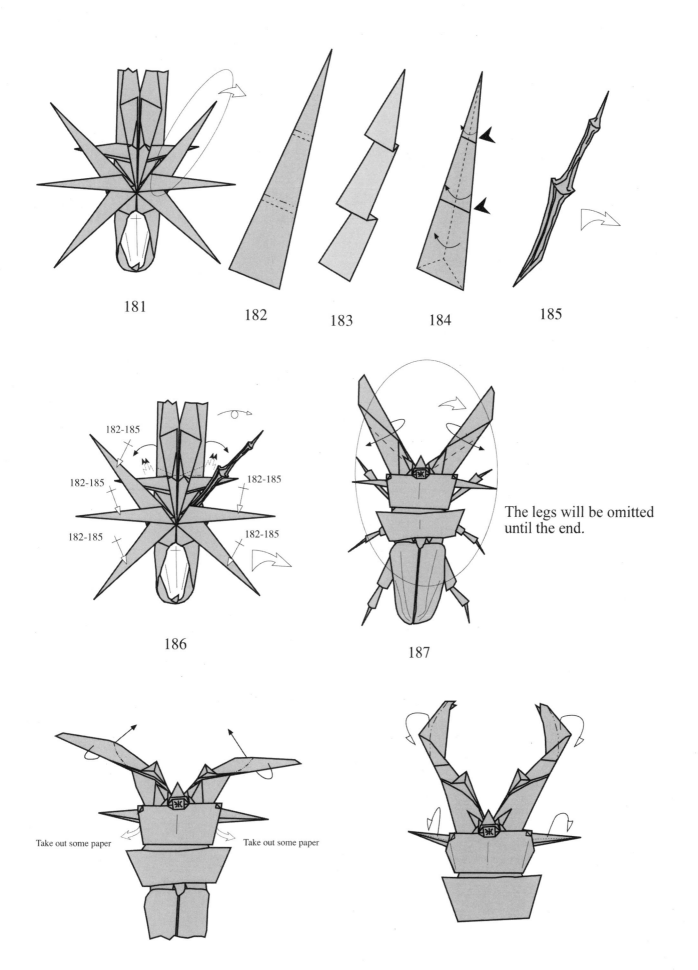

181

182

183

184

185

186

187

The legs will be omitted until the end.

188

Take out some paper   Take out some paper

189

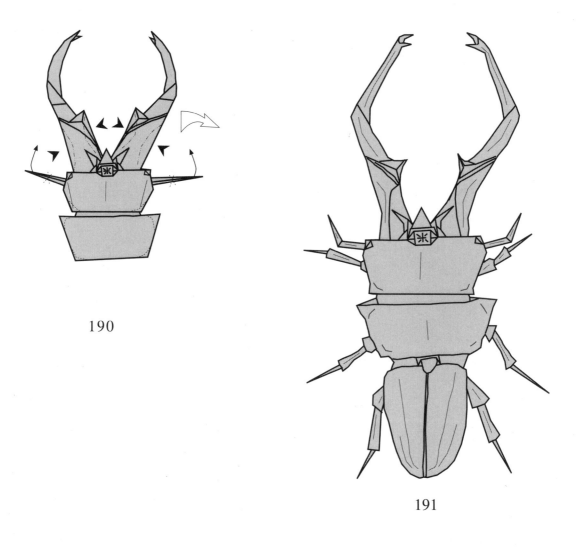

190

191

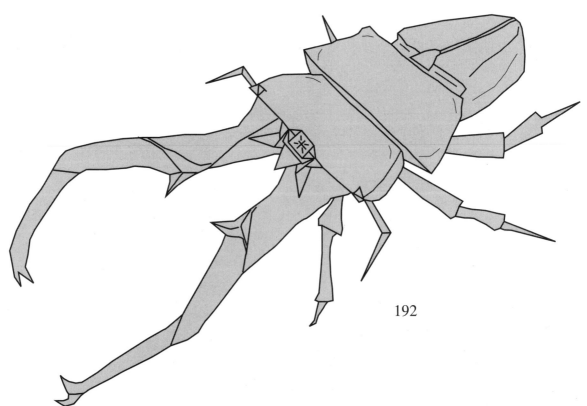

192

European Stag Beetle
(Lucanus cervus)

The paper should be dark brown and black. Fine paper is recommended, less than 40 grams, double silk, banana tree, lokta, metallic or "sandwich," 13.75x13.75 inches (35x35 cm) or bigger.

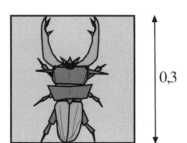

0,3

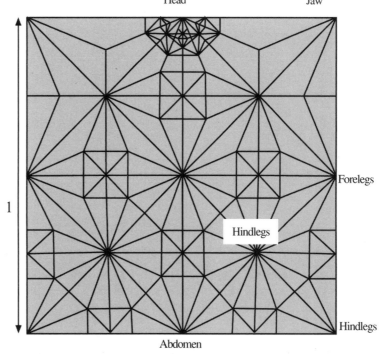

Head   Jaw

1

Forelegs

Hindlegs

Hindlegs

Abdomen

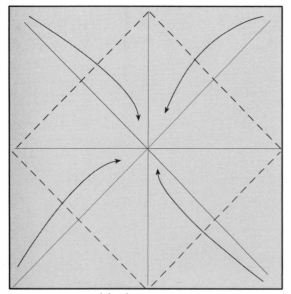

1 ⬤ black
   dark brown

steps 2 until 65 of Cyclommatus imperator ——→

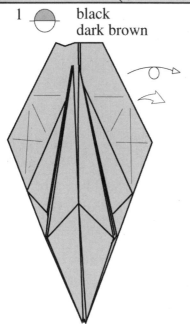

step 66 of Cyclommatus imperator

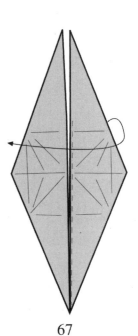

67

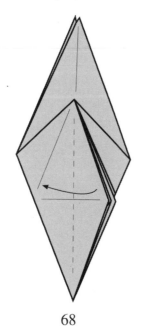

68

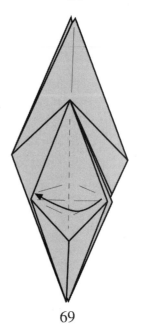

69

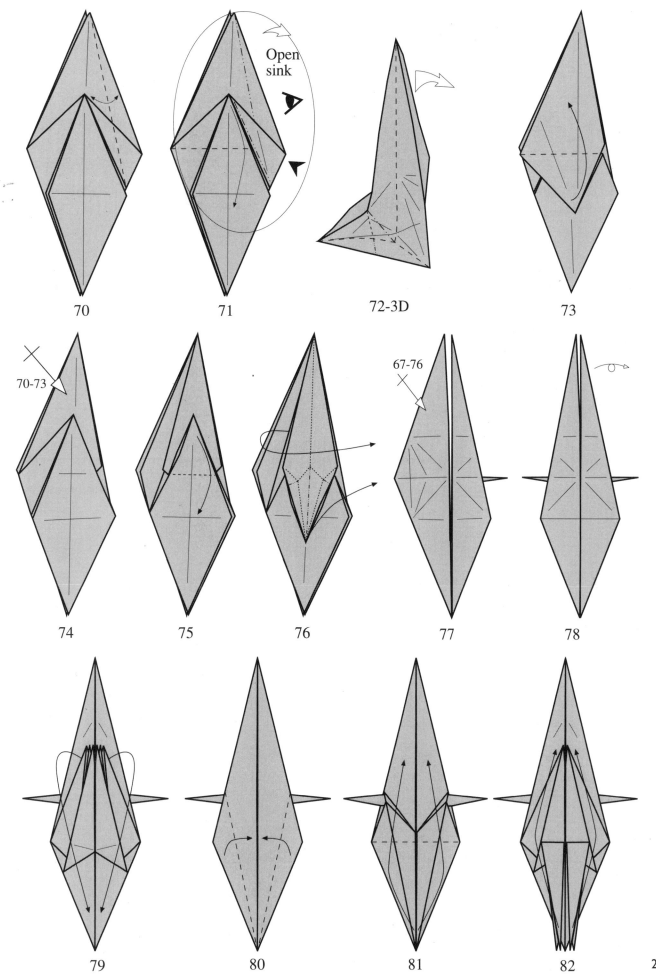

Open sink

70

71

72-3D

73

70-73

74

75

76

67-76

77

78

79

80

81

82

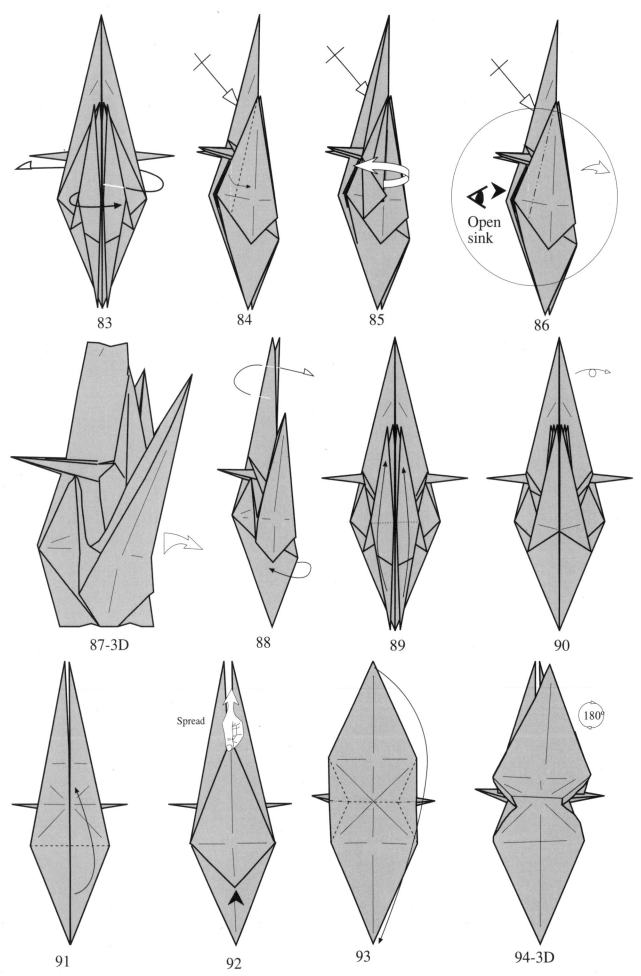

Open sink

83

84

85

86

87-3D

88

89

90

Spread

91

92

93

180°

94-3D

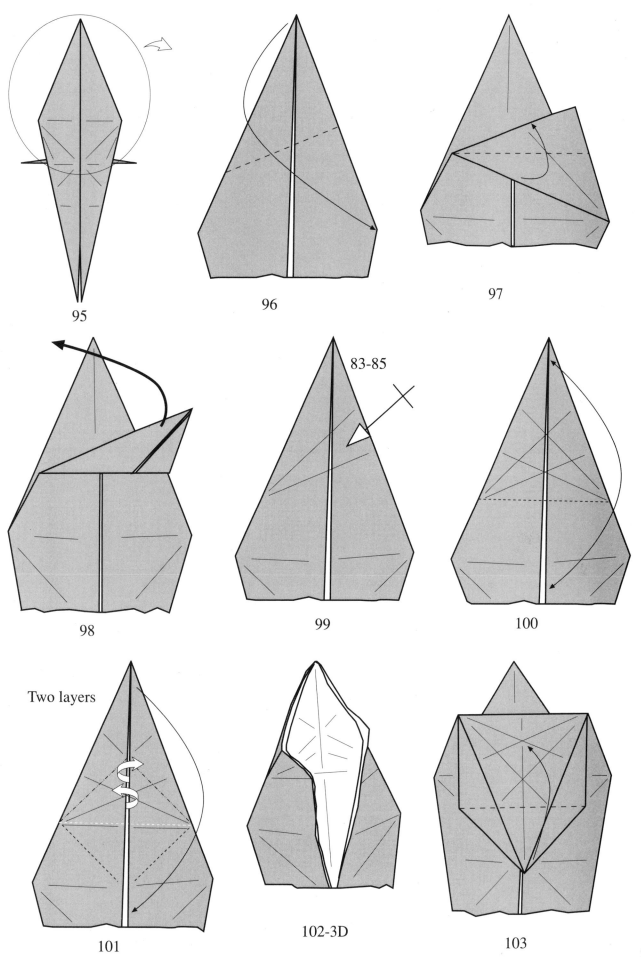

95

96

97

98

99

83-85

100

Two layers

101

102-3D

103

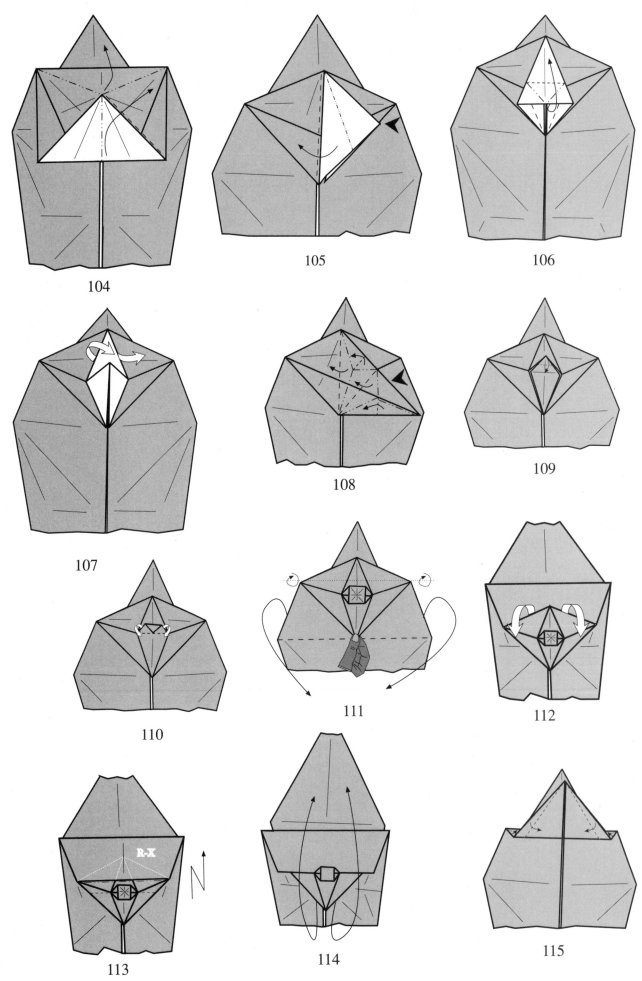

104

105

106

107

108

109

110

111

112

113

R-X

N

114

115

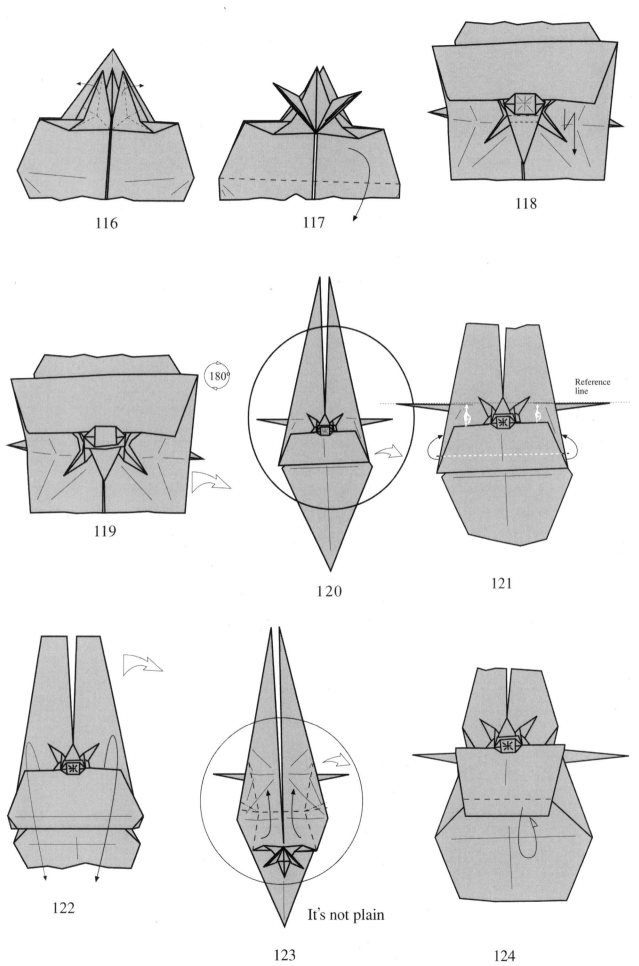

116

117

118

119

180°

120

121

Reference line

122

123

It's not plain

124

229

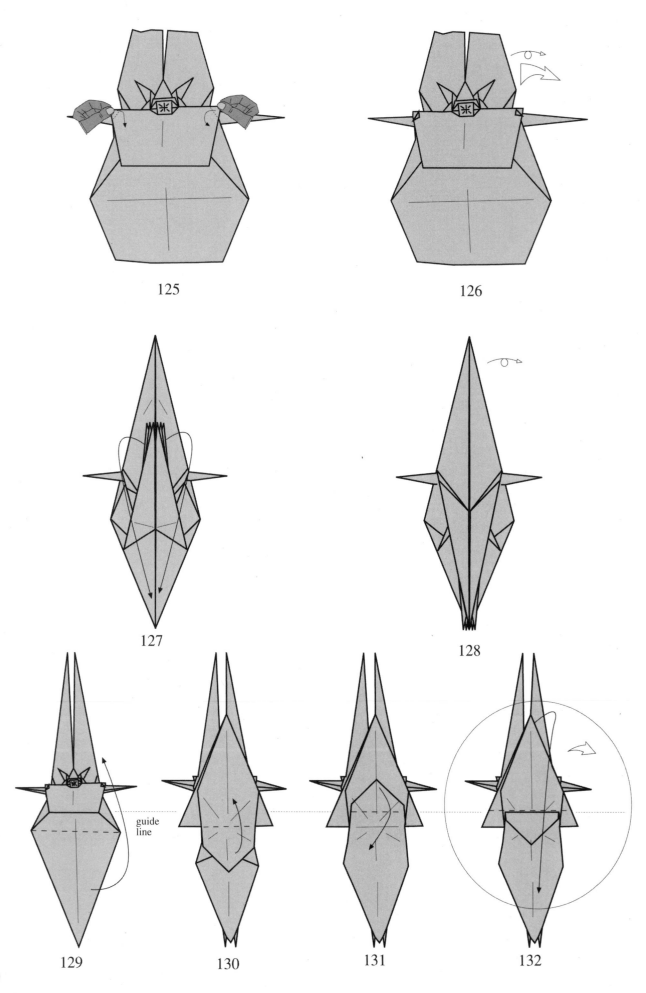

125

126

127

128

guide
line

129

130

131

132

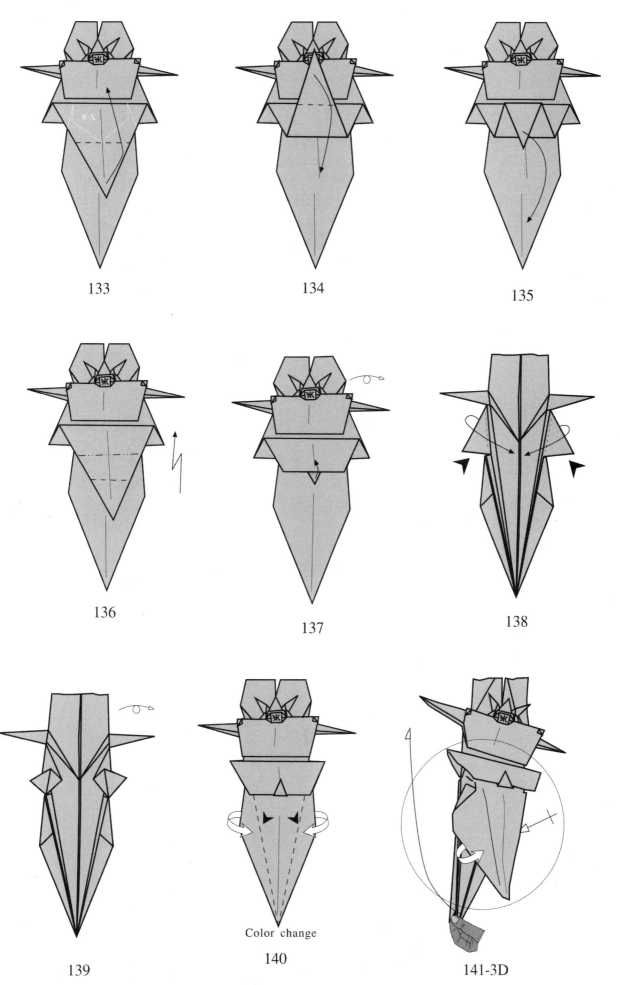

133

134

135

136

137

138

139

140

Color change

141-3D

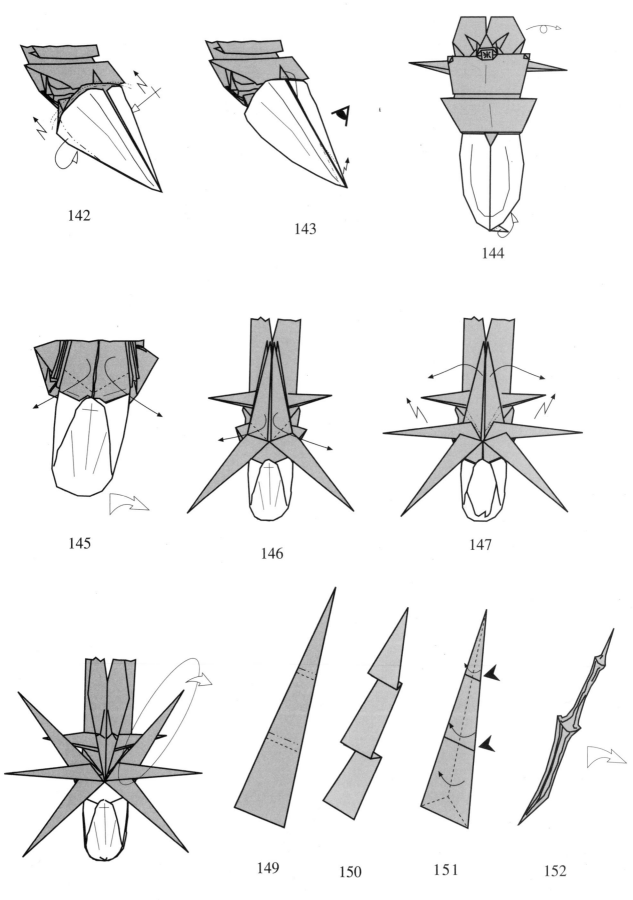

142

143

144

145

146

147

148

149

150

151

152

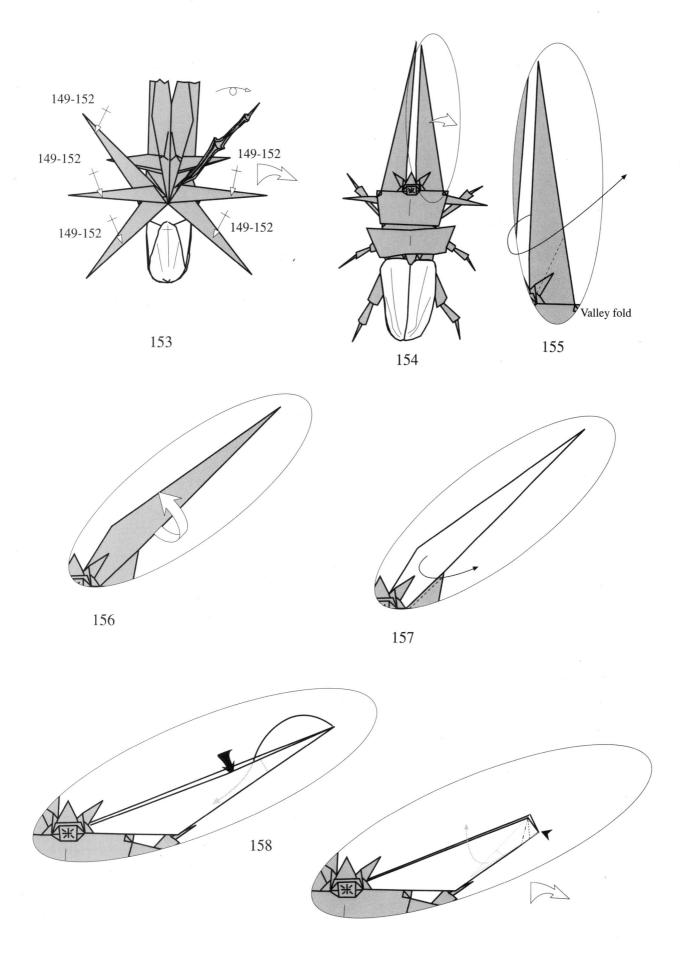

149-152

149-152

149-152

149-152

149-152

153

154

Valley fold

155

156

157

158

159

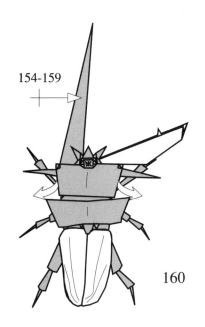

154-159

160

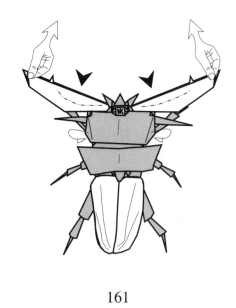

161

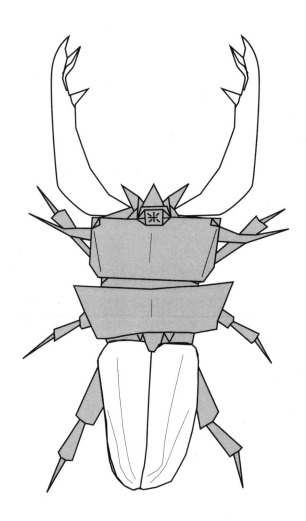

162

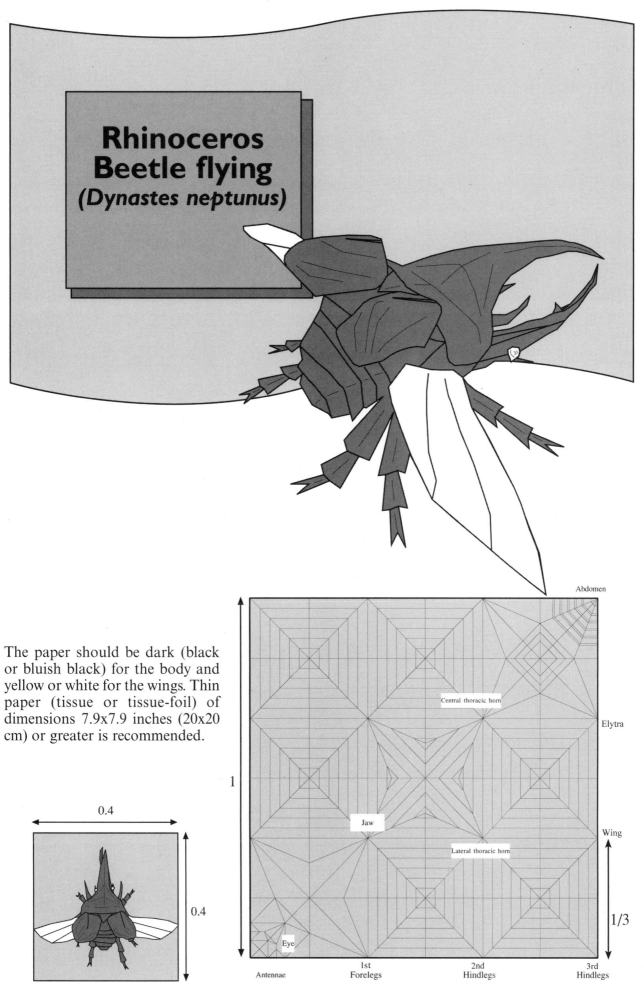

Rhinoceros Beetle flying
(Dynastes neptunus)

The paper should be dark (black or bluish black) for the body and yellow or white for the wings. Thin paper (tissue or tissue-foil) of dimensions 7.9x7.9 inches (20x20 cm) or greater is recommended.

0.4

0.4

Abdomen

Central thoracic horn

Elytra

1

Jaw

Lateral thoracic horn

Wing

Eye

1/3

Antennae

1st Forelegs

2nd Hindlegs

3rd Hindlegs

235

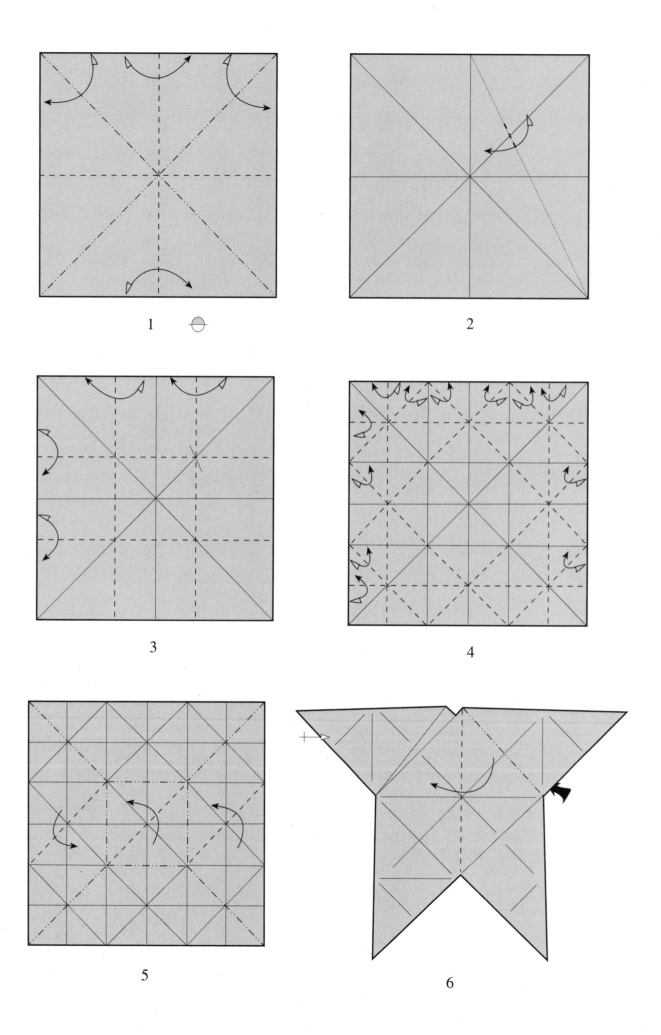

1

2

3

4

5

6

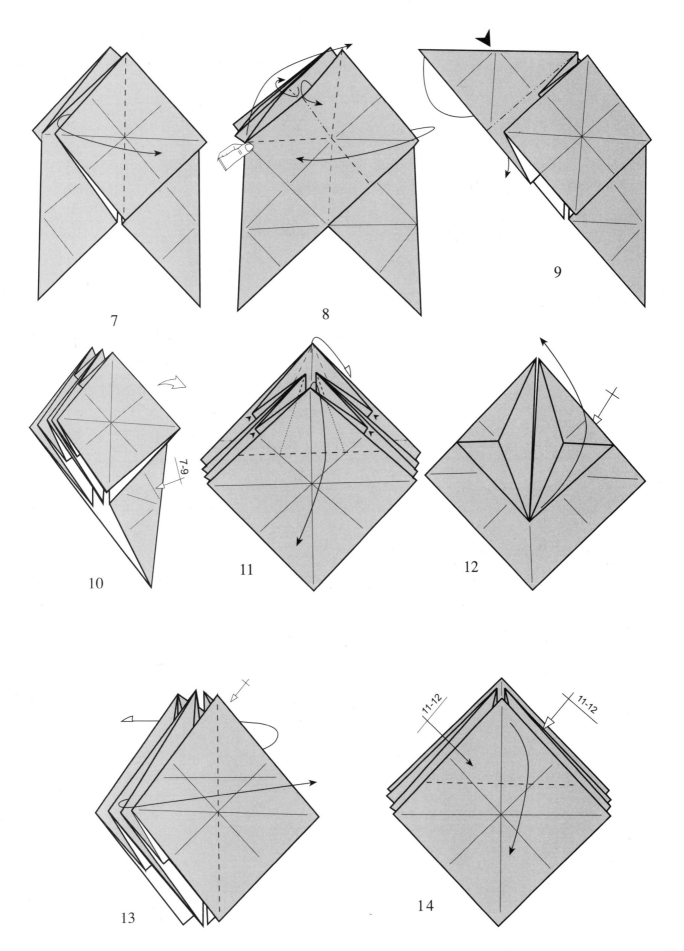

7

8

9

10

11

12

13

14

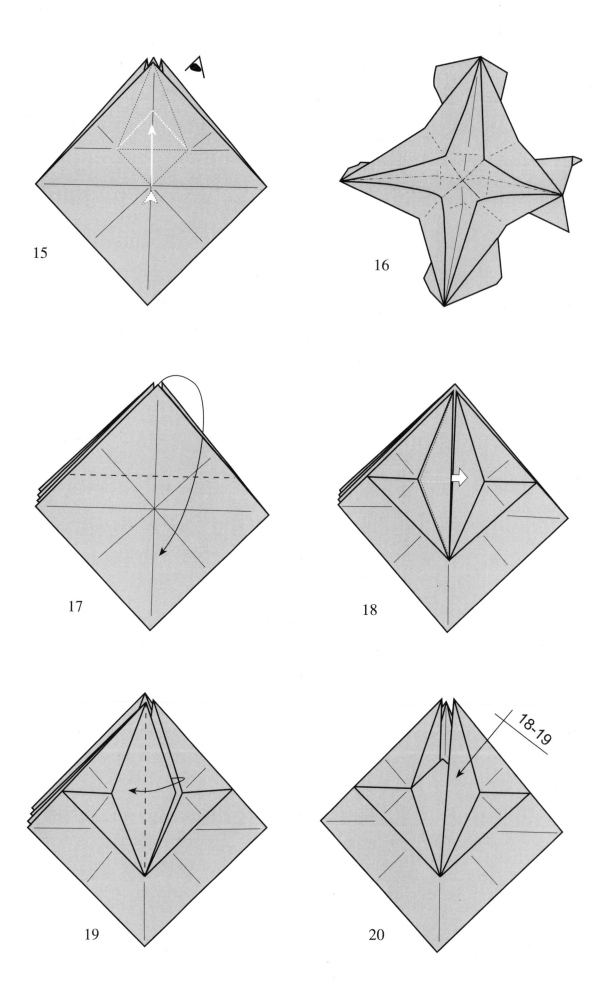

15

16

17

18

19

20

18-19

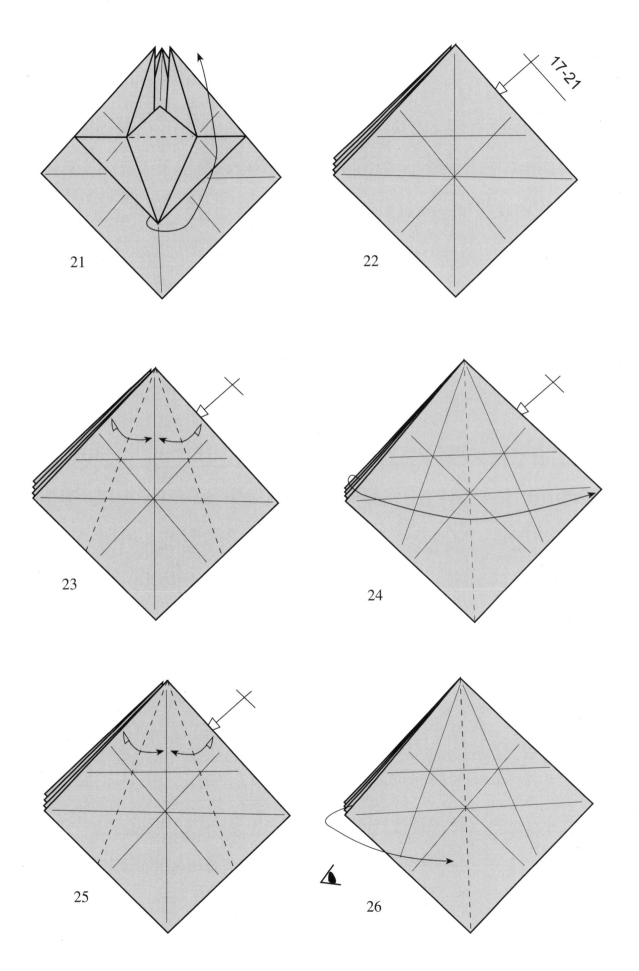

21

22
17-21

23

24

25

26

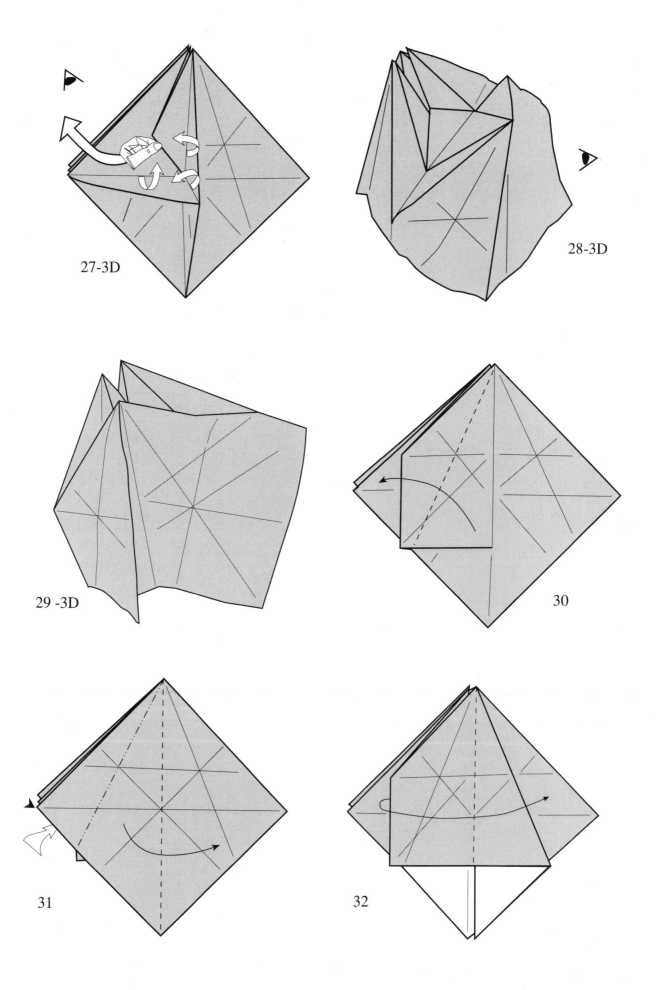

27-3D

28-3D

29 -3D

30

31

32

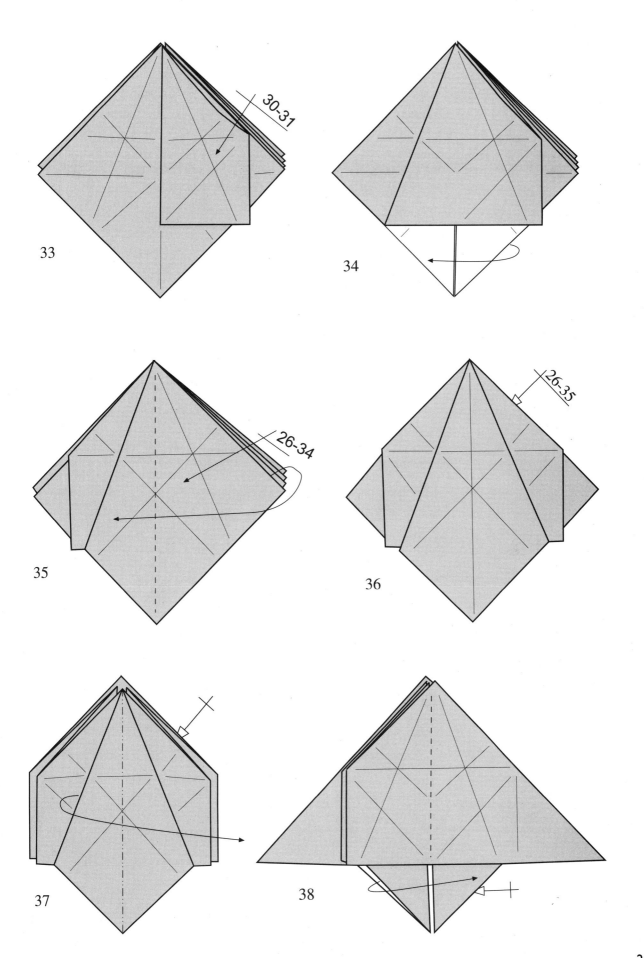

33

34

35

36

37

38

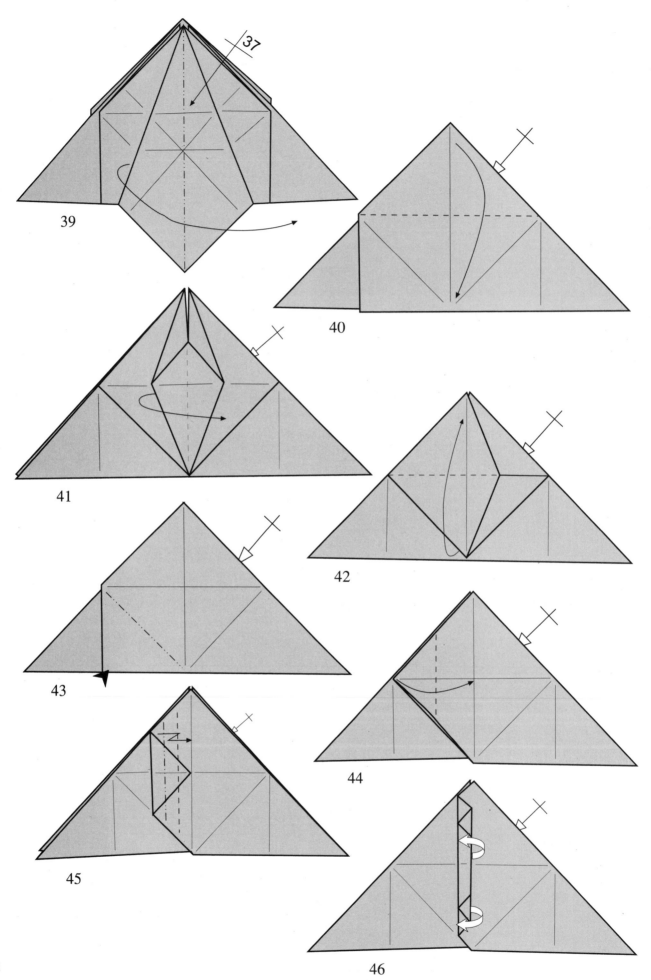

39

37

40

41

42

43

44

45

46

242

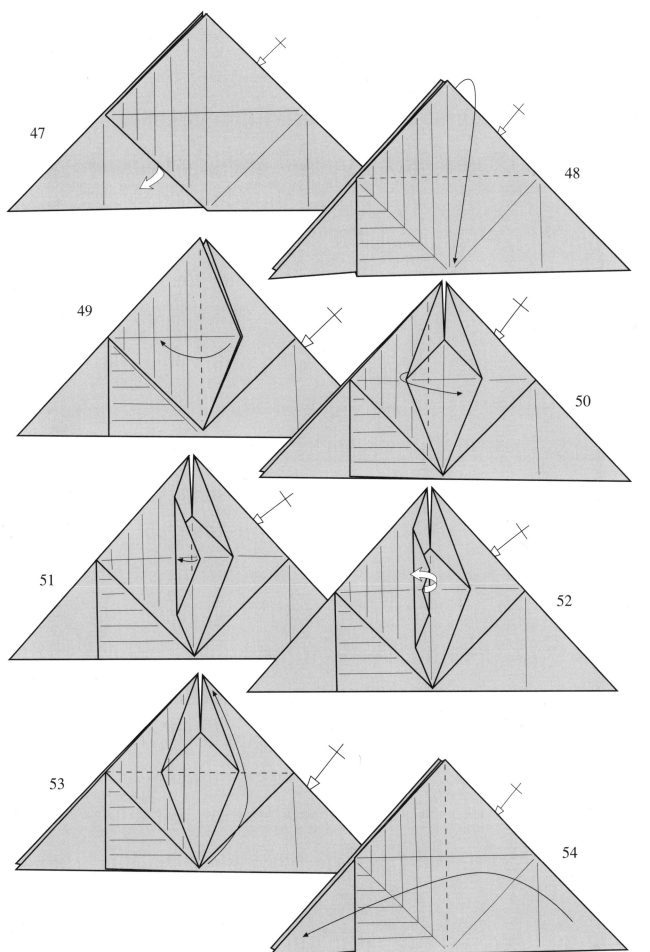

47

48

49

50

51

52

53

54

243

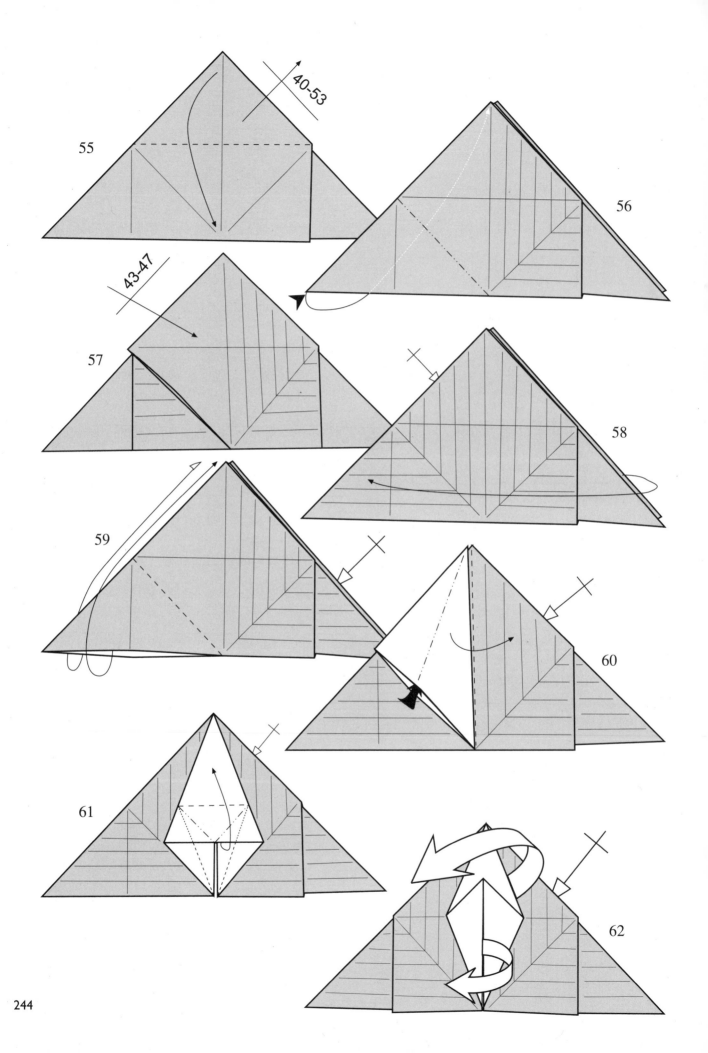

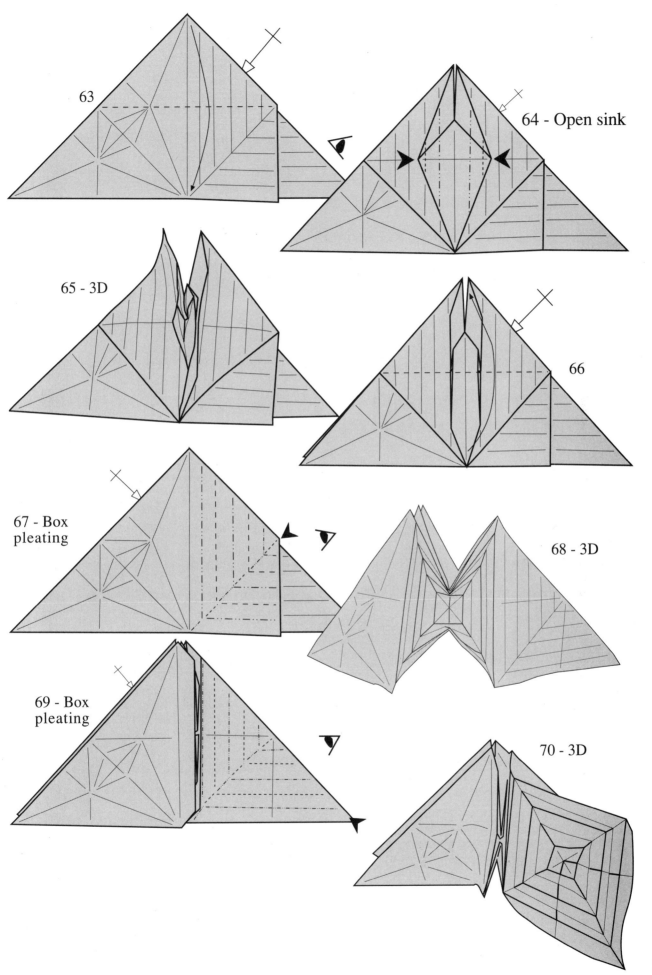

63

64 - Open sink

65 - 3D

66

67 - Box pleating

68 - 3D

69 - Box pleating

70 - 3D

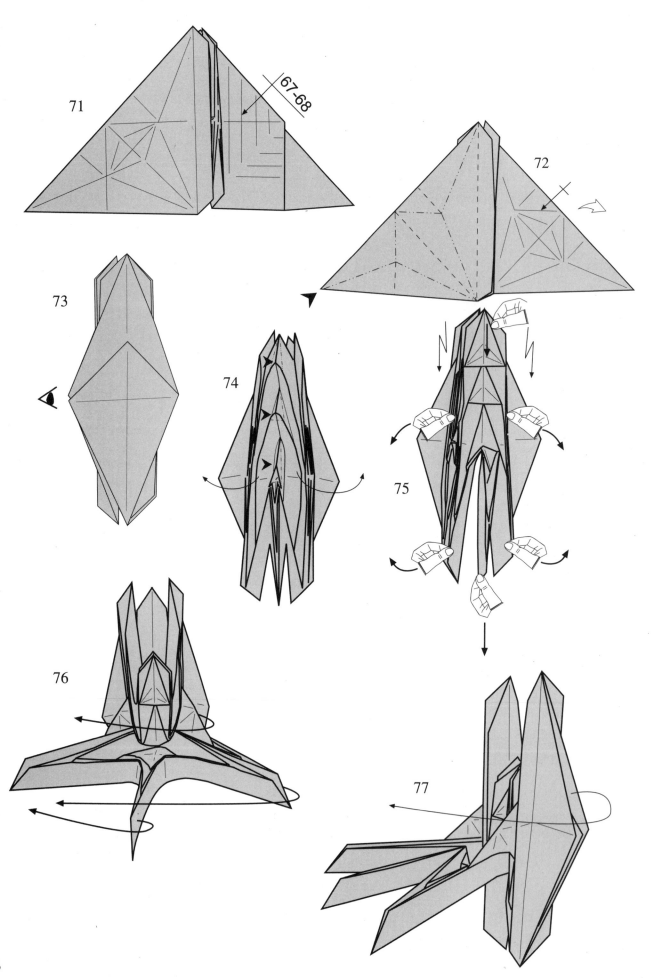

71

67-68

72

73

74

75

76

77

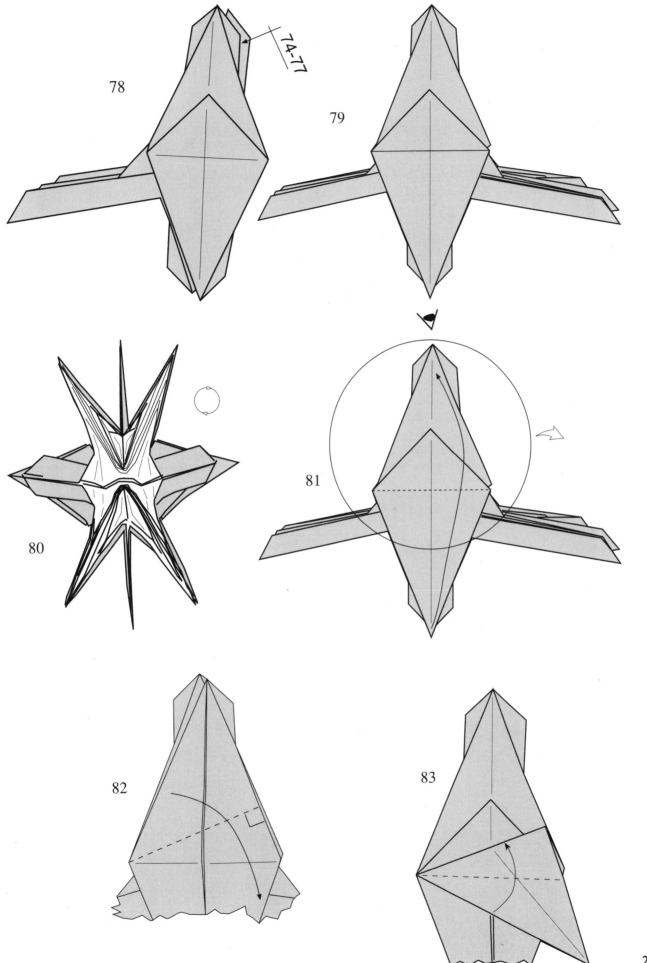

78

79

74-77

80

81

82

83

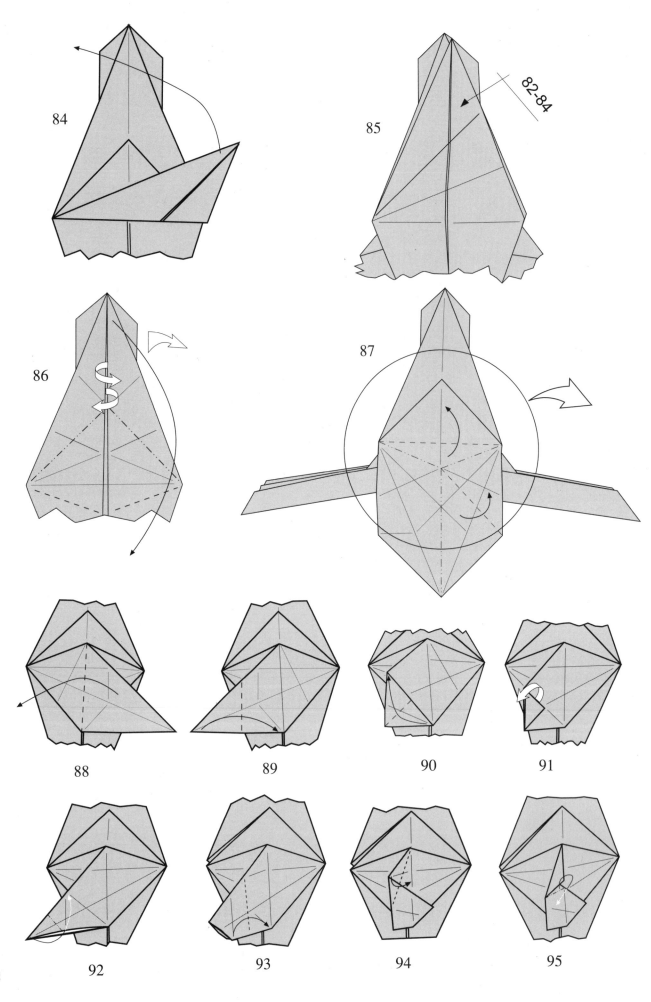

84

85   82-84

86

87

88   89   90   91

92   93   94   95

248

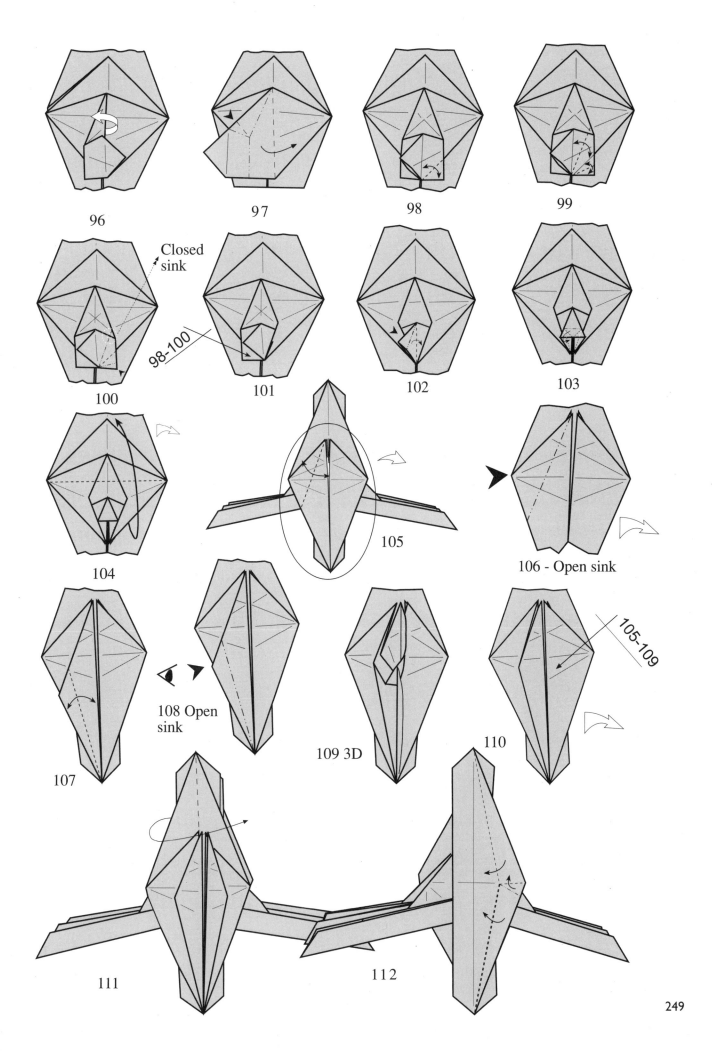

96

97

98

99

Closed sink

98-100

100

101

102

103

104

105

106 - Open sink

107

108 Open sink

109 3D

105-109

110

111

112

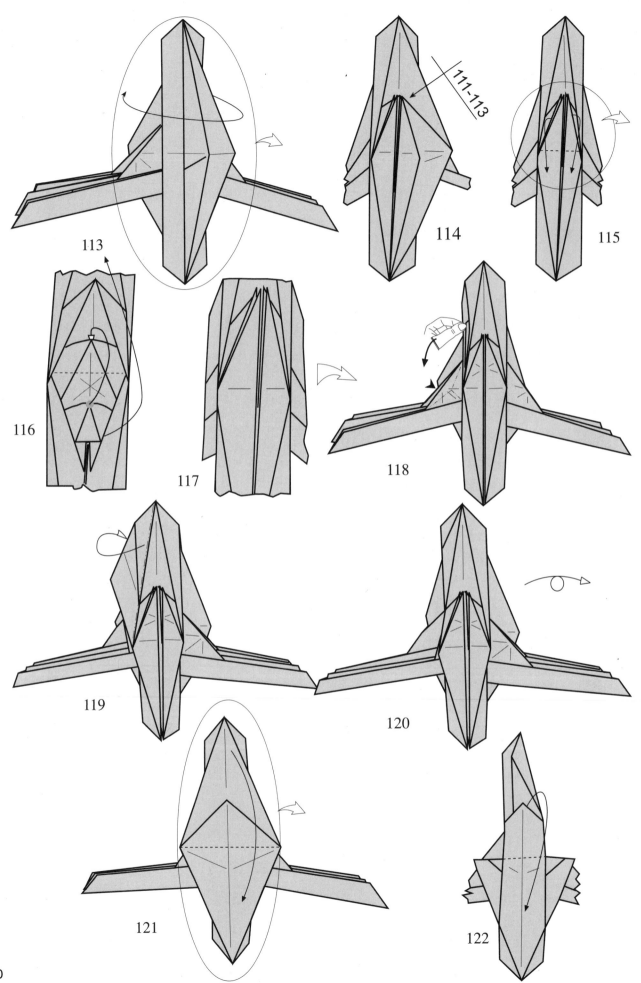

113

111-113

114

115

116

117

118

119

120

121

122

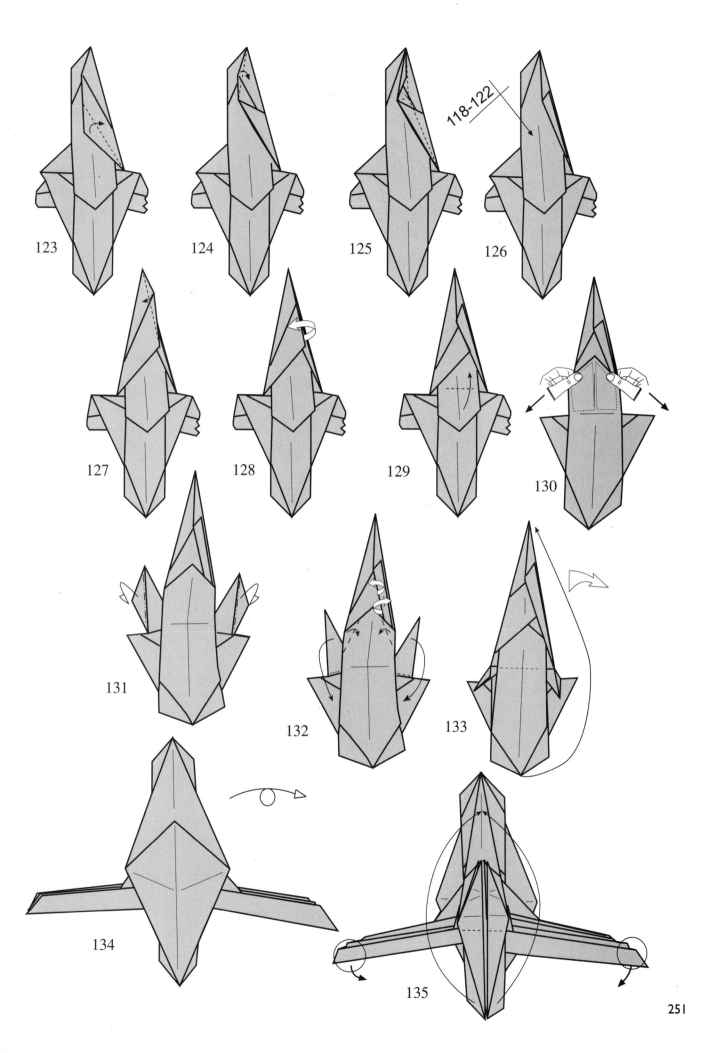

123

124

125

126

118-122

127

128

129

130

131

132

133

134

135

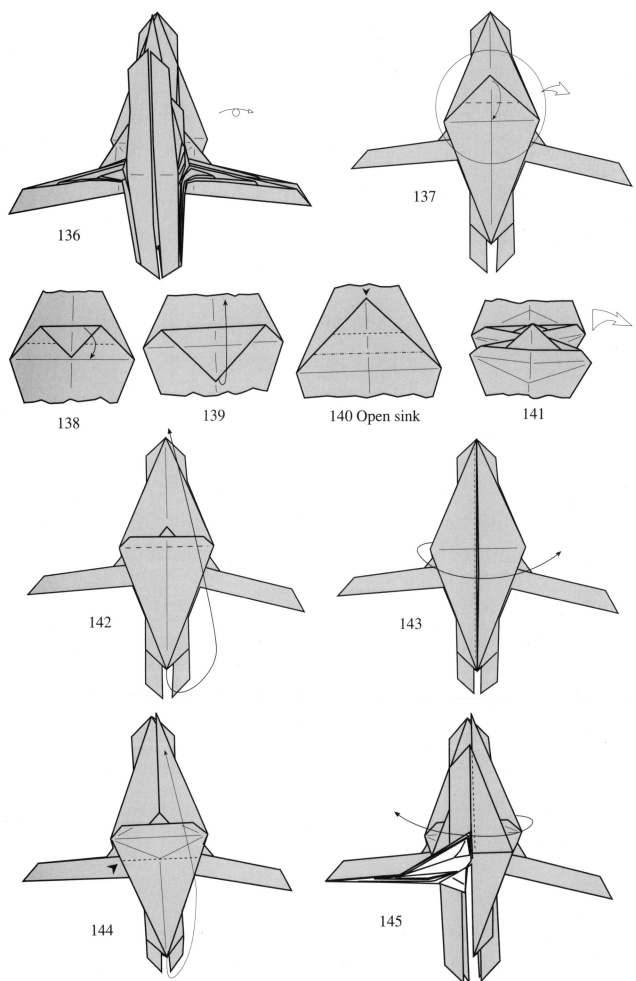

136

137

138

139

140 Open sink

141

142

143

144

145

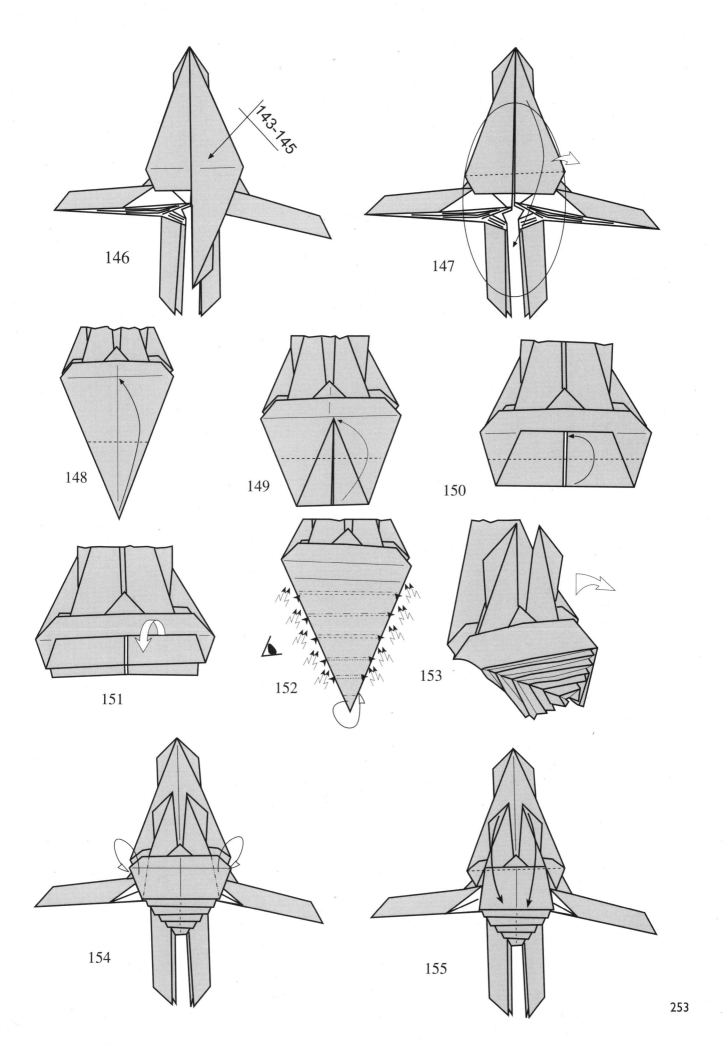

146

147

148

149

150

151

152

153

154

155

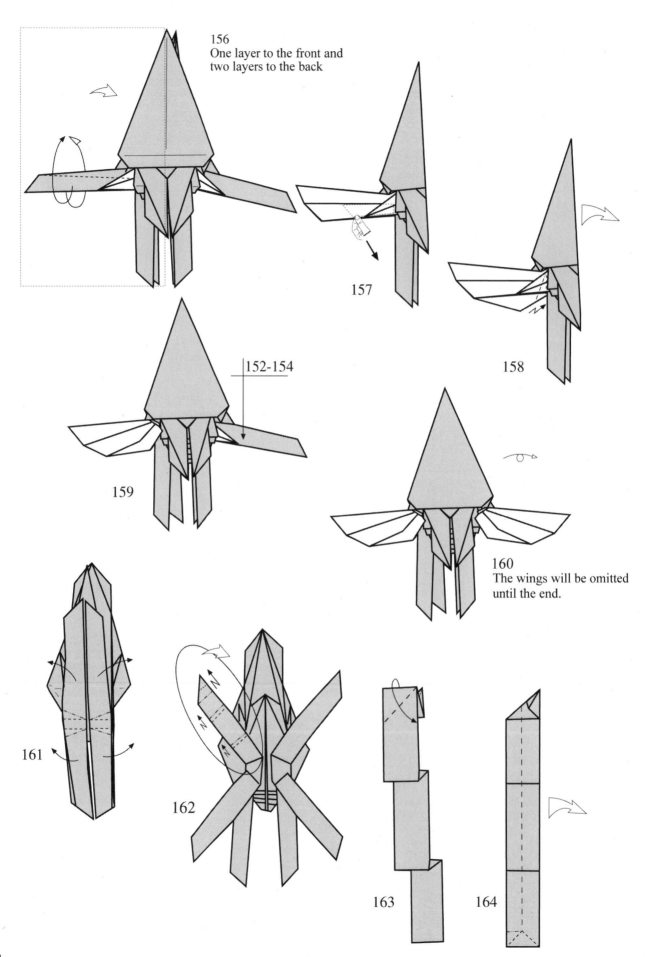

156
One layer to the front and
two layers to the back

157

158

152-154

159

160
The wings will be omitted
until the end.

161

162

163

164

254

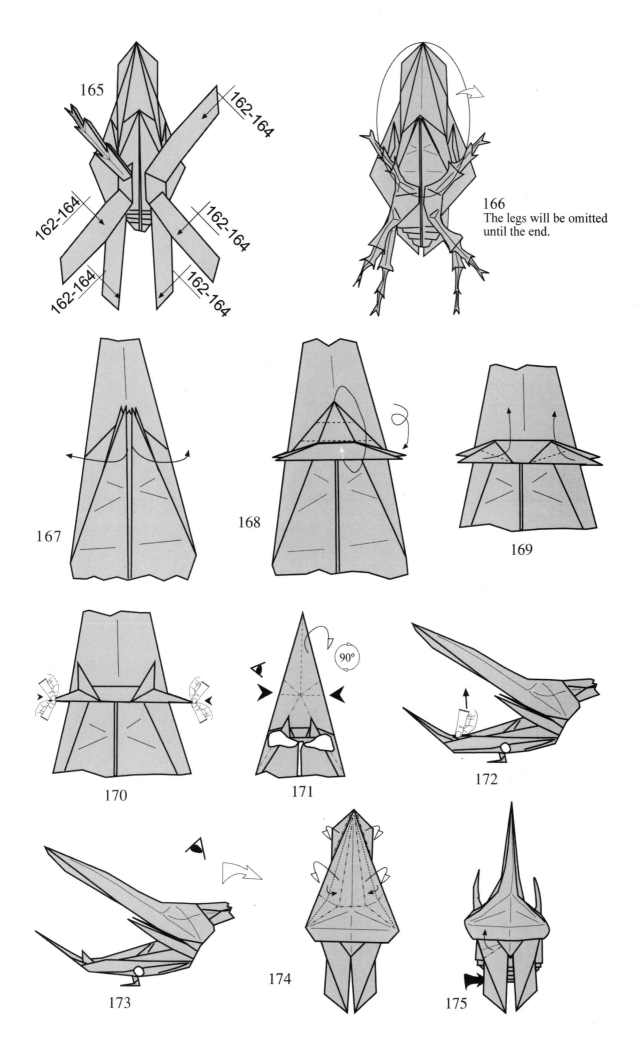

165

162-164

162-164

162-164

162-164

162-164

166
The legs will be omitted
until the end.

167

168

169

170

171

90°

172

173

174

175

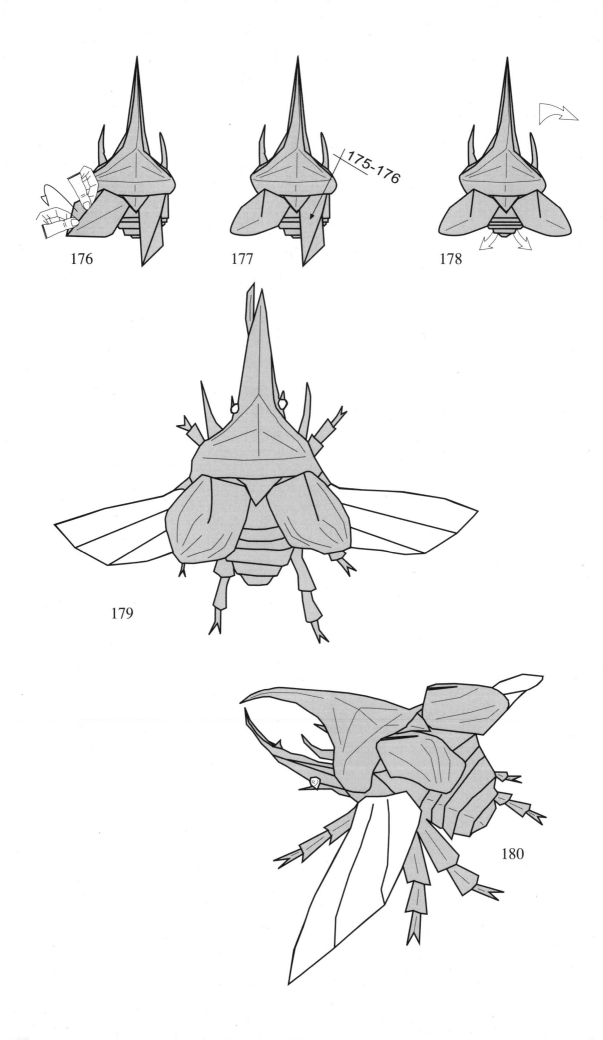

176

177

175-176

178

179

180

Swan swimming

Macaw

Dugong

Narwhal

Sea Lion

Black Widow

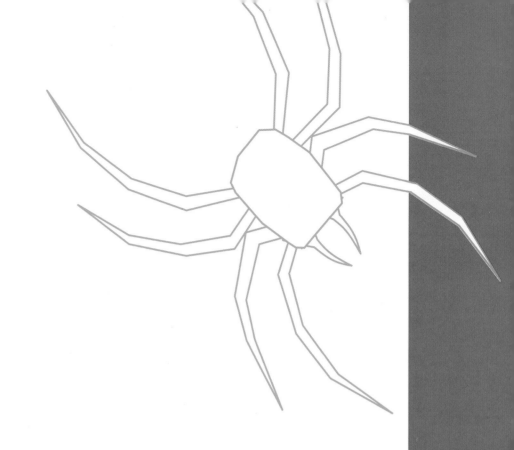

Harvestman *(Phalangium)*

Crocodile

Star

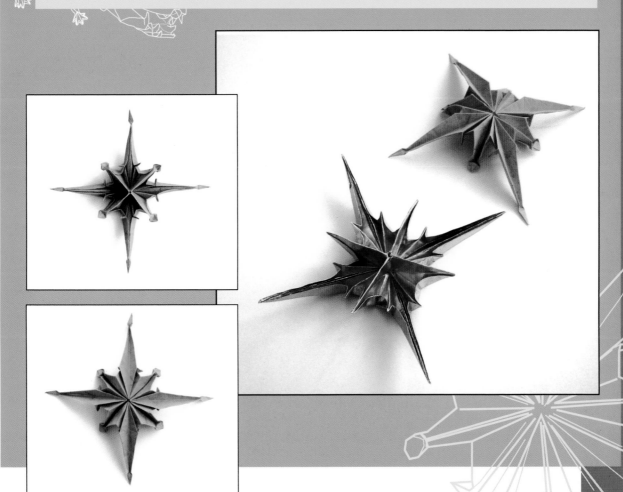

Swan

Walking Stick

Leaf Mantis

Stick Insect

Black Ant

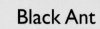

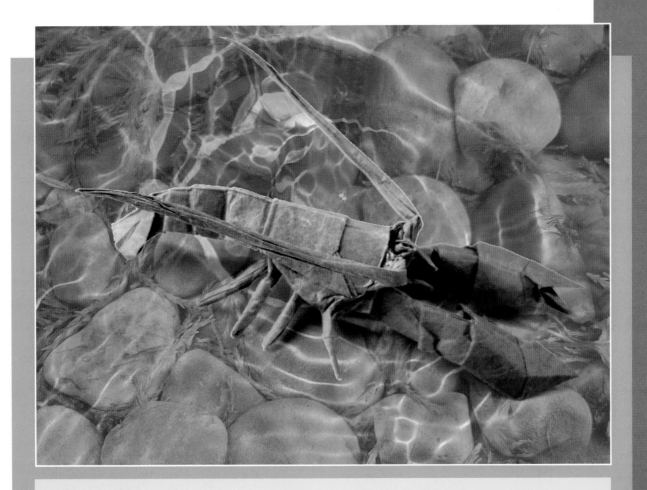

Crayfish

Pseudoscorpion

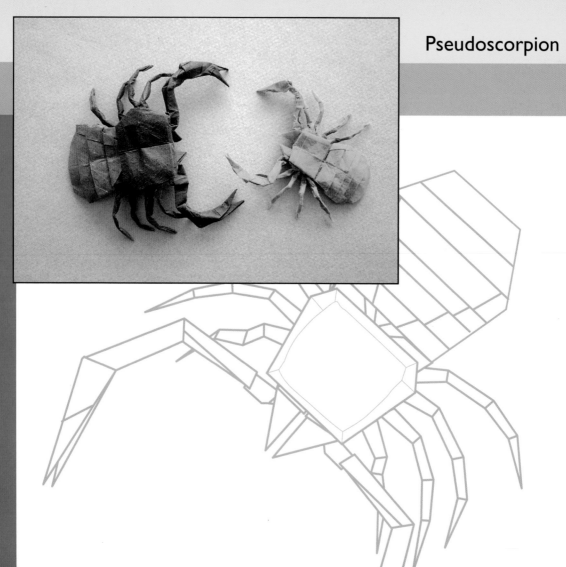

Scorpion *(Buthus)*

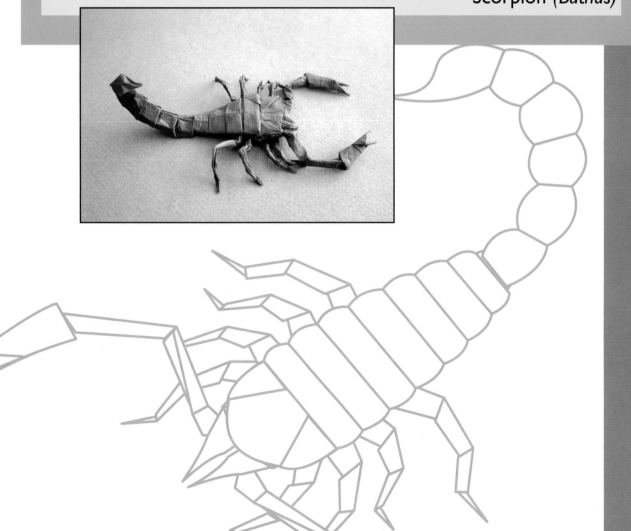

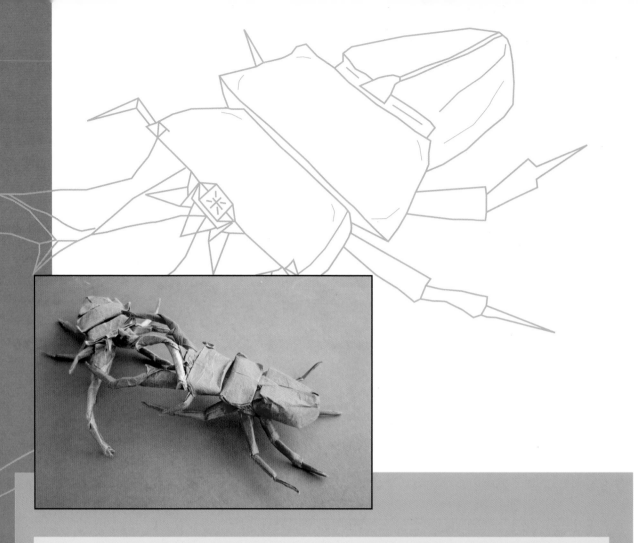

Stag Beetle *(Cyclommatus imperator)*

European Stag Beetle
(Lucanus cervus)

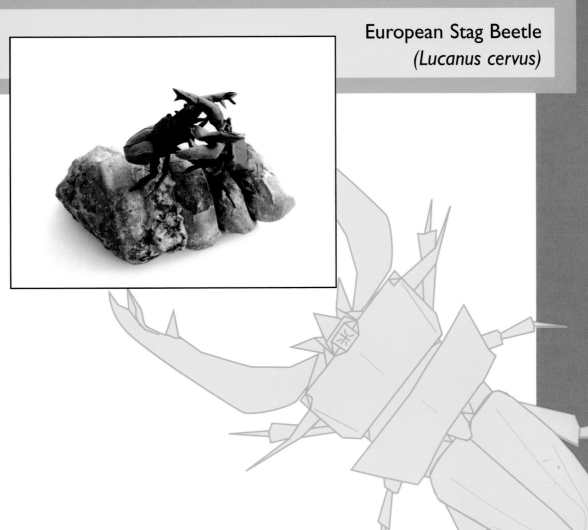

Rhinoceros Beetle flying *(Dynastes neptunus)*